CW01497188

THE BOYS IN THE B-17

T/Sgt James Lee Hutchinson, Eds

WW II Eighth Air Force B-17 Radio Operator/Gunner
Author Of "Through These Eyes" And" Bombs Away!"

authorHOUSE®

AuthorHouse™
1663 Liberty Drive
Bloomington, IN 47403
www.authorhouse.com
Phone: 1-800-839-8640

First published by AuthorHouse   11/17/2011

ISBN: 978-1-4670-6049-3 (sc)
ISBN: 978-1-4670-7022-5 (e)

Library of Congress Control Number: 2011919146

Printed in the United States of America

Dedicated to Norma June Hutchinson, MS
On our sixty fourth anniversary!

About the Author

Hutch says, "Today, at age 86, I concentrate on family, writing and golf, I often reflect on the many twists and turns in my life and people who helped me along the way. One of the disadvantages of old age is it's too late to thank them! I thank God for seeing that my travel through time was steered and protected by family and friends who helped push me up and over the hill. I hope my short stories give readers a glimpse of history as I lived it as a teenager in World War II.

At the age of nineteen, I had a front row seat on a B-17 bomber for the greatest air war in history. Aircrews in the B-17 and B-24 Eighth Air Force heavy bombers had one duty. We delivered bombs to destroy Germany's industries and military targets. Our job was to and wipe out Hitler's ability to wage war. U.S. fighters protected our bombers from the Luftwaffe fighters who tried to shoot us down. German anti-aircraft gunners filled the sky with exploding shells 88mm shells (flak) over the target to stop the planes from delivering tons of bombs that brought death and destruction. Violent death and wounds were facts of life for the boys on the aircrews of heavy bombers. I often wondered if I would ever see my twentieth birthday."

Hutch grew up in the hills of southern Indiana during the pre-war depression in a boyhood much the same as many of the sixteen million boys in service during World War II. He was drafted out of high school his senior year. His books contain short stories of a boyhood in the pre-war depression and combat duty in the Mighty Eighth. Other airmen also share amazing stories of their combat experiences. Holocaust stories tell why WWII was necessary. The author is co-host of a high school Indiana History Project to interview veterans and tape their stories to air on local educational channels. He speaks to school classes: "I introduce myself as a WW II veteran and a member of a fading generation with stories their great-grandfather might tell. Children should be told of the sacrifices of airmen who served in the largest air war armada in history."

Earning three Indiana University degrees (BS MS EDS) he served 37 years as elementary teacher, principal and Asst. Superintendent. February 18, 2008, he was honored for his book and service by Senate Joint Resolution Fifty before the Senate and House of the Indiana General Assembly. He is an ordained Presbyterian elder, Rotary Paul Harris Award winner and Masonic Lodge member (50 years.)

"I write to honor the men (boys) of the Eighth Air Force; those who died in the deadly skies and those who survived. My stories tell what we did and why it had to be done!"

-Hutch

Contents

CHAPTER ONE

HUTCH'S DVD INTERVIEW

This video interview, "Hutch, a WW II Airman," was directed by Rob Ramsey of the Smithville Phone Company after I wrote my first book, "Through These Eyes." Rob, a Brit who is now a U.S. citizen, was very interested in the history of the Eighth Air Force. I think he and his crew did an excellent job of weaving my stories into historic film footage of WW II bombing missions. I refer it to classes or audiences whenever I present a program, because it gives a very real picture of my teenage combat memories of life and death in the flak-filled skies over Germany!

Our B-17 Bomber formations flew at 25,000 feet and we were on oxygen. We wore heavy clothing over electric suits, gloves and boots for protection from 40 degrees below zero temperatures. The film from 66 years ago presents a realistic view of the airmen and planes of the Mighty Eighth in World War II.

The interview is divided into eight sections as listed below. I sold it as a DVD for a while before telling readers where they could find it on the computer. I hope you enjoy my interview and the WW II film. Tell your friends how to find it on The Smithville Phone website at;

http://video.smithville.net/?p=17 Wings over Europe
http://video.smithville.net/?p=738 Battle in the Sky
http://video.smithville.net/?p=730 In Enemy Hands
http://video.smithville.net/?p=732 Prisoner of War
http://video.smithville.net/?p=733 Touring London
http://video.smithville.net/?p=734 Mid air Collision
http://video.smithville.net/?p=736 Food Drop Missions
http://video.smithville.net/?p=737 The First Jet

"Through These Eyes" "Bombs Away" and "Boys in the B-17" are available online at Amazon, Kindle, Barnes & Noble and/or all bookstores. Autographed copies may be ordered at 812-275-4208 or emailjames_ hutchinson_693@comcast.net

THE BOYS ON THE B-17 COMBAT CREWS

The average age of the boys on a bomber crew was twenty-two and teenagers made up fifty percent of a B-17 Flying Fortress combat crew. They were too young to vote, but not too young to fight! Eighteen years olds enlisted or were drafted into service and quickly trained. Boys could complete basic training, gunnery school and aircrew training and be flying combat missions in less than eight months; they were eighteen year olds. Training for flight engineers, armorers and radio operators took three months longer, and like me, were nineteen when they went into combat. Pilots, navigators and bombardiers were older, but a large majority of the losses for the Eighth Air Force in WW II were teenagers! Records show 26,000 young men died, 22,000 thousand wounded and 28, 000 Prisoners of War.

World War II was an all out battle for survival. Axis powers had captured much of the world and had the military power to conquer the rest of the free world. Allied countries hurried to build up their armed forces. The United States developed the Selective Service System and every man between the ages of 18 - 35 was required to register be for military service. Ten million of the sixteen million men in the U.S. armed forces between 1940 and 1946 were draftees. I was one of the millions of teenagers 'caught in the draft!' I received my draft notice immediately after my eighteenth birthday and in my senior year of High School, but I was a "buck private" in the U.S. Army and on a bus to Ft. Benjamin Harrison in Indianapolis three weeks before the fall semester started! Sixteen months later I was a radio operator-gunner on the Lt. Bill Templeton bomb crew. We were aboard the Queen Mary in the middle of the North Atlantic and headed for combat! We arrived at the 490th Bomb Group Airbase in Eye, England on November 14, 1944.

LEST WE FORGET!

Today, schools often fail to stress the importance of World War II, revisionists try to minimize its importance and radical factions claim the Holocaust never happened. My books and television interviews of veterans are designed to present combat stories from diaries and oral history by fellow WW II veterans.

Young warriors of World War II left their homes and marched or climbed into tanks, planes and ships to face deadly combat, knowing the odds of survival were against them. They fought although they still remembered the faces or voices of buddies recently killed in battle. They served on land, sea and in the air to save our nation while civilians at home rallied to make ammunition, tanks, planes and a war machine to support them. Almost a half million Americans died in that terrible war against tyranny, thousands came home with debilitating wounds and seventy four thousand were listed as MIA (missing in action). Veterans came home to help build the greatest industrial nation in the world.

World War II veterans are rapidly fading into history. Time has reduced the sixteen million to less than three million and we are dying at the rate of 1,000 or so a day. The present generation should know of the sacrifices we made for the freedom they enjoy. Soon, this generation will no longer be able to hear firsthand stories of life in the Greatest Generation from those who lived it! Our victory over the Axis powers saved our nation and built it into a world power. Contrary to what many believe today, freedom is not free! Schools should be required to teach the causes and history of World War II. Our country needs informed citizens; education is the foundation of freedom.

The WW II generation survived the poverty of the greatest depression our country has ever seen and fought a war that saved our country. They were a generation who believed in capitalism, hard work and Christianity. They made the United States a leader in the free world.

My goal is to tell some of their stories before they fade away into history like so many other Americans who worked to make our country great. Great battles such as D-Day, Battle of Midway, Iwo Jima, Battle of the Bulge, the Ramagan Bridge and bombing missions saved the world. Sad to say, those decisive victories are unknown to 80 percent of today's generation. Newspapers and television tend not to recognize D-Day, V-E Day in Europe and even V- J Day, when Japan surrendered and World War II ended.

"Ignorance and Apathy are the greatest dangers to Freedom!" -Hutch

WINGS OF EAGLES
(A Tribute To WW II Airmen)

Lord, hold them in Thy mighty hand
Above the oceans and the land.
Like wings of eagles mounting high,
Along the pathways of the sky.

Immortal is the name they bear;
And high the honor that they share.
Until a thousand years have rolled
Their deeds of valor shall be told.

In the dark of night and light of day
God speed and bless them on their way,
And homeward safely guide each one
With glory gained and duty done.

Anonymous

SETTING THE SCENE

World War I was fought in Europe. It was a bloody war against Germany and its allies. It was a battle in the trenches; soldiers charged across "no man's land" to battle the enemy in hand-to-hand combat. Men and animals died from wounds and sickness. Primitive planes and tanks played minor roles in our victory. The League of Nations was formed to assure peace for future generations, but war had left all countries in debt and a few years later a worldwide depression was the primary cause of World War II, the war to end all wars.

World War II was a war of tanks, planes and warships that involved most every country in the world. Millions of civilians as well as military died. Cities and entire countries suffered horrible destruction. Only Sweden and Switzerland remained neutral. Peace after the first world war lasted less than fourteen years. Germany and Japan withdrew from the League of Nations in 1933 and Japan, under Emperor Hirohito, began ravaging China. Adolph Hitler in Germany and Benito Mussolini of Italy, first elected by the people, became dictators with unlimited power. They solved their unemployment problem by building huge military forces and factories to produce arms. Next they invaded neighboring countries.

In 1938 at age thirteen, I remember our gang sitting in Saturday movie matinees watching the Movietone News and laughing at the "goose stepping" German soldiers as they marched into Austria. Next, in 1939, Hitler "annexed" half of Czechoslovakia.

The leaders of England and France tried appeasement and went to Munich in 1938 to discuss peace. Hitler promised to behave, but continued building his armed forces. He invaded Poland a year later on September 1, 1939 and conquered it in ten days. Italy attacked their neighbors and invaded African nations. Meanwhile, England and France declared war on Germany because of Poland. The Soviet Union, then an ally of Germany, was attacking Finland. April, 1940 Germany invaded Holland, Belgium, Denmark and Norway. A month later France was attacked by both

Germany and Italy. Hitler's army marched into Paris after only forty-one days.

Suddenly, England was the last country blocking the complete Nazi control of Eastern Europe. Hitler coveted Great Britain, that free land just a few miles across the English Channel and he was determined to isolate and conquer it. Nazi submarine 'wolf packs' roamed the seas and sunk more than forty-five ships in the Atlantic and the North Sea.

September of 1940 Germany began the Battle of Britain from airfields in occupied France. In the next eleven months, through July, 1941, Luftwaffe bombers dropped thousands of tons of bombs on London and major cities. The British stood fast and Hitler made his first big mistake; he decided to postpone his plan of invading England and turned to attack Russia, his former ally. The United States was in the middle of a depression with very weak armed forces so they continued to watch and wait. Our government sympathized and sent supplies and lend-lease money to aid England while ignoring Japan's attacks on China.

REMEMBER PEARL HARBOR

Sunday, December 7, 1941 the Japanese made a sneak attack on Pearl Harbor while their envoys were in Washington discussing peace. The attack was truly, as President Roosevelt said, "a day of infamy." It ended all thoughts of isolation and propelled us into World War II. The leaders of the United States learned a basic fact that today's leaders should remember:

"Never trust a potential enemy who says he means to destroy you!"

Six Japanese aircraft carriers launched 353 planes (167 carried bombs or torpedoes) to attack the U.S. Navy base at Pearl Harbor. The Jap bombers sank four battleships, damaged fifteen other and destroyed 188 aircraft. The approximate military casualty list was 2,400 dead and 12,000 wounded. Japanese planes proved the success of aerial bombing.

The Japanese were very pleased with the partial destruction of our Pacific fleet. However, one general remarked, "I fear we have awakened a sleeping giant!" He was right! The people of the United States rallied to build an "arsenal of democracy" capable of defending our freedom and winning the war.

The day after Pearl Harbor, Congress declared war on the Axis Powers of Japan, Germany and Italy. Millions of men and women enlisted and millions more were drafted for service; all males from ages 18-36 were subject to the draft (Selective Service Act.) Few men were deferred and there were often two or more brothers from one family in the service. Our nation prepared for war and "Remember Pearl Harbor" became our battle cry as thousands of teenagers joined or were drafted to build our armed forces. They were too young to drink or vote, but not too young to fight for their country. Sixteen million American men and women served in uniform during WW II, almost half million died and thousands more came home with life-altering wounds. Today, there are twenty-four American Cemeteries on foreign soil.

A few years ago our Secretary of State, General Colin Powell, was attending an important conference in Europe. One participant asked him if sending our troops to Iraq was another example of United States empire building.

The General's response says it all:

> *"Over the years, the United States has sent many of its Finest*
> *young men and women into great peril to fight for freedom*
> *beyond our borders. The only amount of land we have asked for*
> *in return, is enough to bury those that did not return."*

The bombing of Pearl Harbor was a shock to our country because we were in the middle of a depression and unprepared for war. Men went to war and women went to work in shops and factories to build war materials. Everyone had a victory garden in the summer. Enemy submarines prowled the seas, sinking supply ships and causing severe shortages. Rationing stamps were issued for food and materials needed for the war effort! Civilians sacrificed through rationing of domestic products like sugar and meat, gasoline, tires and other hard- to-get items. Parents watched loved ones march off to war. No one protested the draft (selective service) because they knew our country was in danger of being conquered. Newspapers and radio programs warned of the need to conserve and ration food and materials. President Franklin D. Roosevelt reminded the nation *"The only thing we have to fear is fear itself."* The nation's unemployment rate went down from twenty-four percent to two percent as able-bodied men went to war and women replaced them in our factories. In the next three years our industries produced tanks, ships and planes to fight and win a war in both Europe and the Pacific. It was "Praise the Lord and Pass the Ammunition" time. (another rallying song.)

New factories and shipyards were constructed to build fighters, bombers and ships to defend our freedom. Fighters and heavy bombers like the

B-17 Flying Fortress and the B-24 Liberator rolled off the assembly lines at hastily built factories and those converted to produce war machines. More than 24,000 heavy bombers were built. Today, less than ten are still flying and they are relics of history, replaced by jet planes. The men who flew or maintained them are also passing away, taking their stories with them. Perhaps my books and television interviews will help preserve stories of their sacrifices for Freedom!

THE MIGHTY EIGHTH

The United States had watched and waited as the Axis powers of Germany and Italy and Japan continued their rampage. Our country was suffering through the Great Depression and was not prepared for war. In 1930, a small group of army officers, lead by General Billy Mitchell argued long and hard for a strong Air Force with heavy bombers. Their advice was ignored and General Mitchell was demoted. A few years later, President Roosevelt noticed the build-up of Germany's air force and asked congress to authorize the production of 50,000 military planes!

Army Air Corps General Henry "Hap" Arnold stated, "The number one job of an air force is bombardment. We must have the long range which can hit the enemy before he hits us --- the best defense is attack!" General Billy Mitchell's predictions had come true. Although he had passed away, his work helped save our country. He was exonerated, posthumously, and restored to the rank of Major General by President Roosevelt. The United States Air Force was not formed as a separate branch of the military until September 18, 1947. Today, General 'Billy' Mitchell is honored as the father of the U. S. Air Force, because he fought so long against popular opinion to prove the importance of airpower to win wars. Early in WW II, sixteen B-25 Billy Mitchell twin motor medium bombers took off from aircraft carriers to carry out the famous Doolittle Raid on Tokyo and avenge Pearl Harbor. That B-25 bomber mission was a great morale builder for United States citizens.

The Army Air Corps expanded precision bombing training. Confident bombardiers on the four motored B-17 and B-24 heavy bombers claimed they could drop a bomb in a pickle barrel. The United States set up a massive educational program to train the men (boys) who would serve as pilots, mechanics or aircrews on the new planes. Air Corps units were organized for the Army, Navy and Marines. The Eighth Army Air Corps was activated January 28, 1942 in Savannah, Georgia and the first B-17 Flying Fortresses landed in England July 1, 1942. Thirty- two B-17E bombers arrived by the end of the month providing the 97th Bomb Group had four squadrons (340, 341, 342 and 414.) Our country mobilized for war and new planes rolled off the assembly lines and new airmen were trained and were sent overseas to join the air war. Eventually, there were forty-three U.S. heavy bomber airfields crowded into the East Anglia farmlands, many only five or ten miles apart. Southeast England also hosted US fighter and Royal Air Force (RAF) fields. The sky over the United Kingdom was filled with aircraft by the summer of 1943!

The stories in this book tell the experiences of the men (boys) who served in the U.S. Army's Eighth Air Force during World War II. The Eighth Army Air Corps was formed with three major units: Bomber Command, Fighter Command and Ground Forces.

The Eighth under the leadership of General Ira Eaker and later, General Jimmy Doolittle, grew into the largest air armada in history; the 'Mighty Eighth!' By mid 1944, it had 200,000 members and could send out more than 2,000 four engine bombers and 1,000 fighters on a single mission against Third Reich targets. Heavy bombers of the 43 Bomb Groups in

England flew 6,866 daylight bombing missions against Nazi occupied targets in Europe from May, 1942 until the Nazi surrender May 8, 1945.

Heavy bomber airfields were stocked with fifty B-24 or B-17 heavy bombers and 2,500 men in airmen and ground crews to service or repair planes. An article in the March, 1945, Eighth AF Newsletter, Army Talks, said:

> *"For every heavy bomber there are thirty men on the base who never fly. Some service and maintain planes, others handle the bombs, bombsights, radar, machine guns, ammo, flying equipment or parachutes. Some are drivers and others man the Mess Halls. There are men who have little contact with the planes or flying, but are essential to the base and the success of missions."*

In many towns, G.I.s outnumbered local citizens by a large margin because most young Englishmen were in the armed forces. British author Roger Freeman reported a popular British historian saying about American GIs, "The trouble with the Yanks is, they're overpaid, oversexed and over here." Sometimes they added overfed and overbearing. Some locals resented the fact that GIs were paid three or four times better than British servicemen." U.S. soldiers showered the local girls with presents from the base PX and about 60,000 romances ended in marriage during the war years. Problems were sure to arise because of the millions of Americans in Great Britain prior to D-Day. However, the British welcomed the Americans who had come to their rescue when their backs were to the wall. Almost 350,000Airman served in the Eighth by the end of the war.

Post-war reports stated that the heavy bombers dropped almost 700,000 tons of bombs and the Fighter Command had 566 aces and 11,200 victories in aerial combat. German leaders said that the bombing caused their defeat. However the impressive record of strategic bombing was achieved at a very high cost! The Mighty Eighth lost 6,866 heavy bombers, 3,695 fighters and suffered almost half of all losses of the WW II Air Forces. Medals awarded to Eighth airmen included: Medal of Honor (17), Distinguished Flying Cross (220) and Air Medal (442,000.)

Airmen casualties were 47,483 out of 115, 332, which included 26,000 dead! One of the highest losses of any U.S. combat command! Almost three fourths of the graves in the American cemetery at Cambridge, England are Eighth Air Force airmen.

Bombers lost B-17 (4754), B-24 (2,112)

Fighters lost: P- 47 (1,043), P- 38 (451), P-51 (2,201)

A Royal Air Force Compliment:*"The US Eighth Fighter and Bomber Commands in late 1943and 1944 performed the impossible. They did what we, in the Royal Air Force, had told them they cold never do – what we, with our equipment, could never have done. What's more, the Luftwaffe generals – and indeed, the colonels who were actively mixing it in combat with the Fortresses and Liberators – had advised Hitler and Goering that it couldn't be done."*

Laddie Lucas, Royal Air Force, World War II

THE 490TH BOMB GROUP

Men or the 490th Bomb Group trained in B-24 bombers at Mountain Home Idaho and flew those Liberators on the southern route from Brazil to West Africa and on to England. They landed in England on April 28th. The 490th group was assigned to Station 134, a newly constructed airbase at station 134 in Eye, Suffolk, England. The group became a part of the 93rd Combat wing of the Third Division of the Eighth Air Force. The 490th had four squadrons; 848, 849, 850 and 851. The new airfield and its many Nissen huts for housing and storage were squeezed in among the small communities of Eye, Brome and Yaxley. The men promptly nicknamed their new base, "The Bromedome." Mechanics erected tents or built small shacks near the hanger, to be; on the flight-line and closer to their work. The crew chiefs, their mechanics and the many support personnel were a vital part of any airbase. They were the guys who patched the flak holes and repaired the damage to keep the bombers in the air. The 490th flew its first mission May31, 1944 and the last April 20, 1945. It completed forty-one missions as a B-24 unit before being switched to the B-17 Flying Fortress. The last B-24 mission was flown August 6, 1944. Three weeks were devoted to transition training of crews in the B-17 Flying Fortress before going back to work. The group commander, Col. Frank P. Bostrom, had previous experience flying the B-17 in combat. Pilot and co-pilots were checked out in take-offs and landings, before practicing assembling into the combat box formations Mechanics, armorers, bomb-loaders, turret specialists and other maintenance units were also trained on the new plane. August 27th and 30th the 490th flew the first missions as a B-17 group.

June 7, 1944, the day after D-Day, Germans fighters pulled a sneak attack on bomber bases in England. Luftwaffe fighters crossed the channel and were waiting to catch Allied bombers returning from missions as they landed. Radio messages quickly alerted returning 490th bombers not to land, but scatter to other bases. Enemy fighters shot down several bombers, but luckily no planes were lost from our group.

Bomb Groups, usually flew in formations of thirty six bombers, but that varied due to number of available aircraft and crews. By the end of the war, the 490th Bomb Group had flown 158 missions, (5,060 sorties) and dropped 13,600 tons of bombs, nine tons of chaff, and gunners had fired over 450,000 rounds of 50 caliber ammunition. The missions from September, 1944 through April, 1945 were to some of Germany's most heavily protected targets. Total losses totaled 47 bombers and 180 men in accidents and combat, which was the lowest of any heavy bomb group. After the truce, between May 1st and 15th, the Bomb Group flew five "food-drop" missions to Holland and a 'repatriation' flight to Linz, Austria to take French prisoners (slaves) home.

Like all bomb groups in the Eighth Air Force, the men of 490th Bomb Group endured flak, fighter attacks, mid-air collisions and crash landings to help win victory in Europe.

Today ---The 490th Bomb Group Association of surviving airmen and family members keeps the memory of the group and the Eighth Air Force alive with a quarterly newsletter and annual reunions. One of the crowning achievements of our Association occurred during our annual reunion in Washington, D C in September of 2006. My family and I were proud to witness a solemn ceremony in Arlington National Cemetery. Four leaders of our Association: George Picard, Les Reekers, Rich Stratton and Bob Barraclough, placed a wreath at the Tomb of the Unkown Soldiers in honor of 490th Bomb Group members who died in combat and those who have since passed away.

"Taps" had a special meaning that afternoon as the mournful sound of the bugle drifted over the 330,000 white tombstones in the rolling hills of Arlington National Cemetery!"

490TH BOMB GROUP AWARDS AND DECORATIONS

345 Distinguished Flying Cross with 10 Oak Leaf clusters
37 Bronze Stars
1910 Air Medals with 5339 Oak Leaf clusters
60 Purple Hearts (approximate figures)
8 Croix de Guerres

BATTLE STARS FOR:

Air Offensive, Europe, Normandy, Northern France
Rhineland, Ardennes and Central Europe

My time with the 490th Bomb Group at Eye airbase was from November, 1944 until we boarded our war-weary planes on July 8, 1945 for our last mission. The mission we all were eager to fly; the Northern route across the North Atlantic. It was OPERATION HOME RUN! We were taking our planes back home to use in the Pacific war!

> *"I salute all members of the Eighth Air Force, and especially those who perished ------I'm so thankful that my eighteen combat missions were with the men (boys) of the 490th Bomb Group at Eye, England"*

Hutch

MISSION ALERT

Mission alert, we're scheduled to fly
another day of combat; perhaps to die.
Early to bed for a restless night
we'll get the call before dawn's light.

Breakfast, briefing and out to our plane,
we pray to survive combat again.
Loaded bombers soar into the sky
hundreds on both sides are going to die.

Eighth Air Force aircrews in WW II
faced flak-filled skies and fighters too.
I'll always remember the B-17 boys;
the deadly missions and the terrible noise.

Sixty- six years have come and passed
since I heard "mission alert" last.
Victory was won at a terrible cost.
Today, I salute the boys we lost.

World War II airmen share my tears as
our ranks grow thin with the passing years.
Many know nothing of those days of glory
and so I write to tell our story.

James Lee Hutchinson, 2011

The morning of December 7, 1941 the US Navy fleet at Pearl Harbor, Hawaii was attacked by 350 bombers from six Japanese aircraft carriers This sneak attack sank or disabled many ships, killed 2,450 and launched our nation into World War II. Theater of operations for the Eighth Air Force in England and the Fifteenth Air Force in Africa and Italy

CHAPTER TWO

DRAFTED

My Uncle Sam sent me a "present" for my 18th birthday, June 12, 1943. It was an invitation from the local draft board to serve my country in the armed forces. The war had been going on for a year and a half and the situation was serious. Compulsory military service was mandatory if the United States was to survive. Therefore all males, eighteen and over were required to register for military service. I was classified One A, which literally meant "ready to go" as soon as I turned eighteen. It was the same "Greetings" letter sent to millions of men drafted to save our country from the Axis powers!

> *"Greetings: Having submitted yourself to a local board composed of your neighbors for the purpose of determining your availability for training and service in the land or naval forces of the United States, you are hereby notified that you have now been selected for training and service therein. Your friends and neighbors ask you to serve your country. Report for induction August 4, 1943"*

Well, I hated to turn down my friends and neighbors, but I had just finished the first half of my senior year at Bedford High. I only needed six hours to earn my diploma when I received my 'invitation' from Uncle Sam. I appealed to the three board members of the local Selective Service (draft board) for a delay until I could complete the fall semester and earn my High School diploma. They denied my request and the chairman of the board said, "Son, we are taking everybody." and I said, "But you guys are still here!" I guess that's how I ended up on the bus!

August 4th rolled around quickly and I reported to ride the bus to Louisville for induction. I had the choice of Army, Navy or Marines. I chose the Army, was sworn in and given three weeks "to settle my affairs" before reporting for duty. Well, I wasn't having any affairs, but it was nice to have time to get used to the idea of leaving home. Parents around town with sons in the service were beginning to give the "evil eye" because I was still home. Mom insisted on a family picture, before I left, just in case! (I treasure that faded old photo of a depression family in1943.) Three weeks later, I said goodbye to Mom and Dad, my little sister and brother and packed a paper bag for the long journey planned by my friends and neighbors.

Get On The Bus!

Fifteen of us boarded a Greyhound bus and headed for Indianapolis and Ft. Benjamin Harrison. We waved back to relatives and loved ones as we pulled out of the bus depot. My family and hometown had never looked so good and I knew it would be a long time before I came home again. Sadly, some came home with life-changing wounds and others some died in combat! A bronze plaque on the courthouse lawn lists the names of 123 young Lawrence County heroes who died defending our country.

We pulled out of town on the 25th of August and for a final twist of irony, on the way out, we drove past the drug store of the chairman of the Draft Board! My class of 1944 at Bedford High School started on the 5th of September, but by then I was deep in the heart of Texas. Two years later in May, while I was still in England, my mother was invited to the High School graduation to receive my diploma. I didn't feel any smarter, but Mom was extremely happy. I completed twenty missions (two Chowhound missions to Holland) before I was twenty, the war in Europe was over and the 490th Bomb Group was preparing to fly the Northern route back to the states. Japan had not yet surrendered and we were scheduled for the war in the Pacific --- but, I finally had that diploma from Bedford High School.

You're in the Army Now!

We were in the Army and headed for war. Only God knew what the future held. Some guys had enlisted, but most of us had received our Selective Service (draft) notices shortly after turning eighteen, although a few guys were leaving behind a wife and children. It was nice to be wanted, but this was overdoing it!

The Greyhound bus carried us up Highway 37 over the hills and dales of Southern Indiana to the Fort Benjamin Harrison reception center in Indianapolis. A loud- mouthed Corporal welcomed us to Ft. Ben that afternoon. He yelled out all his instructions as if we were hard of hearing as he took us through the necessary paper work to sign in and pick up our "dog tags.'" Those two small aluminum tags on a chain were stamped with our name, serial number, religion and blood type.

The Corporal said, "Men, these are your identification tags, never take them off .You are to wear them around your neck twenty four hours a day. There are two tags because if you are wounded or dead, they can take one for records. Your serial number will identify you as long as you are in service."

Next, he marched us to the Supply Room for shoes and an armload of clothing, everything from the dress uniform to underwear and socks was greenish olive drab. Then we marched back to a long street lined with huge two story barracks. They all looked alike, but were numbered. The Corporal led us to number 25 and we followed him up the stairs to our new home, a huge room filled with bunk beds. He told us to pick out a bunk, throw our small items in the foot locker (a small wooden chest,) hang up our new uniforms and put on our fatigues. Then, as if we hadn't already figured it out, our new master said:

"Boys, you're in the Army now! Fatigues are your new work uniforms you can send your "civvies" home or toss them in the trash. Mess (supper) is at 0500, now fall out on the street in front of the barracks to march to the Mess Hall. You'll have free time after Mess." We marched down the company street the gigantic Mess Hall, got in line, picked up a metal tray and passed down the serving line. The servers slopped ladles of food into each section of the tray and we were directed to empty tables. It was my first introduction to Army food. It tasted good and I was glad there was so much of it.

A bugle call blasted us out of our bunks at five the next morning and at six we made another trip to the Mess Hall. They kept our little Lawrence County group together for the next few days for processing and classification. A march to the barber shop for a GI haircut was one of the first items on the list! That barber sheared me right down to the scalp for my first GI haircut. The GI hair-do was required for all soldiers, not only for cleanliness but to make life difficult for head lice! The barber chair was surrounded by a large pile of hair when we ex-civilians left his shop.

Psychological tests, physical exams and shots were next on the list, so we were marched over to get in line for the medics. They were really busy and we cooled our heels for over a half hour. It was our first introduction to the Army expression, "Hurry up and wait." The Psychiatrist asked several easy questions like, "Do you like girls?" The obvious answer was "sure, do you know any?" I stifled the urge to say it, because I had already figured out that the Army didn't like comedians! I just kept my mouth shut and moved on to the physical exams, which were not very hard and I knew they just wanted to see what they had to work with in basic training. We already knew they were taking anyone who had a pulse and could walk; we were already in the Army!

The final line was for the dreaded shots we had been warned about! We had been told about the big syringe with a long square needle, used on a very tender, private spot in the groin area! Thank heaven it was just a joke on new recruits. However, I got nervous when the big bruiser in line ahead of me fainted before he got his first shot! They picked him up and got him to a cot while I inched along expecting the worst when I stepped up for my turn. The three shots didn't hurt much and I rolled down my sleeve and stepped out into the sunshine. I saw the other guys watching me as if they expected something. Then it hit me, I felt a sudden jolt in the shoulder like someone had slugged me! The tetanus shot had taken effect! I rubbed my arm and joined the group to watch the other guys as they felt the 'jolt' of the famous tetanus shot.

We finished indoctrination in four days. We were Buck Privates in the infantry and would soon be shipped out for basic training, meanwhile they found all kinds of work for us. We were up at daylight (0500) for breakfast and then assigned to a work detail for the day. One day two of us were assigned to mopping the barracks stairway with a bucket of soapy water and a toothbrush! I still don't know what we did to tee off the Corporal, maybe we were talking in line. It was a boring job, but at least we got to stay out of the hot August sun all day. On other days our group white-washed trees, hauled dirt and laid sod on the parade ground. Heck, we were in the landscaping business, but we got one break because we were never put on KP (kitchen police) or Latrine (toilet) duty.

One morning the Corporal told us about a chance to apply for the Air Cadet Program. The details were posted on the bulletin board. The Army Air Corps needed pilots, bombardiers and navigators and they were taking guys who could pass a physical and a color-blind test. Right then and there I decided I needed a career change. It seemed too good to be true, but I guess they really needed airmen. I never stopped to wonder why. I took the test because by that time, I knew that I would rather fly than walk into battle. This was a way to leave the infantry and fly into combat as an officer and gentleman. There is a cardinal Army rule, "never volunteer," but I broke it and volunteered to fly!

I was classified as a VFT (Volunteer Flight Trainee) the rest of my time in the service. In less than a week, a large group of Hoosier soldiers were on a troop train, headed to Air Corps basic training at Amarillo Air Base.

The three day troop train ride from Ft. Harrison to Amarillo, Texas was no picnic in the heat of late August. We had day coaches all the way and the farther south we traveled, the hotter we got. Air conditioning was unheard of and every available passenger car in the U.S. was in use. One guy swore he once rode in a car so old that there was a sign over the window saying, "Please don't shoot buffalo while train is moving."

Open windows gave us a breeze that helped, but often smoke from the coal fired locomotive drifted in with the hot air. I had several trips on a troop train, but never had a Pullman car with bunks. We slept in our seats or on the pile of duffle bags in the rear of the coach. The train had a dining car for the first leg of our journey. The food wasn't that great and the waiters thought we should leave a tip! Heck, everyone was broke; we had not yet received our first month's twenty-one dollar pay.

The best event on my first train ride happened on our second day when our troop train pulled into the station in downtown Texarkana, Texas. We were marched off the train into a large restaurant, complete with red and white checkered table cloths, silverware and pitchers of iced tea! The waitresses in starched blue and white uniforms really added to the experience. Maybe it was the relief of getting off the train for a while, maybe it was the girls, but that was one of the best meals I ever had in the Army. It was a memorable welcome to the great state of Texas!

We climbed back into those hot day coaches and headed out across the Texas plains and before we knew it, we were deep in the heart of Texas and training like mad! The air war was growing, losses were heavy and a lot of air crews were needed to replace those who had been shot down or the "Lucky Bastards" who had completed their missions. I found out that the Air Corps had been recruiting men from every branch of the army. I met guys from tank and engineer outfits and then it dawned on me why those tests at Ft. Benjamin Harrison had been so easy!

Note --- I visited Texarkana a few years ago. The station was closed and abandoned and most of the stores had closed or moved out to the Shopping Mall. Time marches on and the railroads of WW II have gone the way of the buffalo herds!

Basic Training – Amarillo, Texas

Amarillo Air Base was one of those windy, dusty air bases, sometimes referred to as the "armpits of the west." We were assigned to a tarpaper barracks anchored to the ground by cables at each corner. It was bunk beds again and my bunk-mate was Bill Irk from East Chicago. On the evening of our third day, our drill instructor, Corporal Joe Gannon, marched us down to a 'barber shop' in an empty barracks. We had received a GI haircut just three weeks before at Ft. Ben, but the 'Non-com's (non-commissioned officers) had set up a makeshift shop for their own fundraiser. We were charged 50 cents for another GI haircut. Most of us had only a few dollars, but we contributed to their fundraiser. We figured we had been clipped twice by those guys! One of our buddies was so broke he wrote a letter home on toilet paper to ask for money! The thirteen weeks of basic training in the heat and dust storms in the panhandle of West Texas were designed the make us soldiers and toughen us for the Air Corps. We were awake before the rooster crowed, dressed and fell out for formation at 6:00 am. The desert air was so cold that we wore our field jackets to march to the Mess Hall. However, we shucked them fast when the sun came up, it was blistering hot. Week days were filled with lots of drills, exercises and inspections. Our barracks formation marched to classes and the Mess Hall. We often marched double-time and sang to build our lungs for flying because we were volunteer Air Cadets in training.

My Lucky Ring ---The end of August was payday and Corporal Gannon marched us down to an empty barracks where an officer sat at a small table and handing out our first payroll. The grand sum of twenty-one dollars! We got a twelve hour pass into Amarillo at the same time. Twenty-one dollars a month seemed like a lot of money to an eighteen year old kid from southern Indiana. I wasn't in town very long that Saturday before a sterling silver Air Cadet ring in the window of a downtown jewelry store caught my eye. I bought it for about eleven dollars, sent some money home and was broke the rest of the month. However, the ring was a good investment. I wore my "lucky" air cadet ring through all my twenty missions. See my photo as a 19 year old, taken by our Bomb Group photographer after I finished my 12th mission. We had just earned our second Air Medal! The ring is on my left hand. Today, when signing books, I show it and say:

"I know God got me through combat safely, but maybe the lucky ring helped" Hutch

Washed Out! --- Cleanliness was stressed in barracks inspections and drilling on the dusty parade ground was extremely hot. The minute Cpl. Gannon shouted, 'dismissed,' we headed for the latrine and the cool showers. We solved both problems by stepping into the shower fully dressed! It was a great way to cool off and wash our clothes at the same time! Our fatigues and boots were half dry by the time we reached the barracks. We changed into our other set of fatigues and boots, knowing the wet ones would be dry the next morning! Evenings were free time for letter writing, polishing brass and boots or resting. A trip to the PX (Post Exchange) for a coke was always a treat. The PX was a combination malt shop, store and a place to relax for a while. It was mostly empty during the day, but there was always a big crowd in the evening when we had free time.

We took all kinds of physical, mental and ability tests to stay qualified for the Air Cadet program. However, the bubble burst at the end of the eighth week. Drill Sgt. Sakakini gave us the sad news; most of us had been "washed out" of the cadet program. Only three guys out of the forty in our barracks were selected to continue. They were older and had some college training. I wasn't too surprised, because I had secretly doubted that a green teenager without a high school diploma would make the grade. Heck, I couldn't even drive a car.

Just like that, the rest of us VFT's suddenly became aerial gunners! I guess we should have read the fine print. The sad news simply reinforced the age old rule of <u>never volunteer</u>!

We had been washed out as Air Cadets, but nobody wanted to go back to the infantry. We were VFTs and destined to serve in the Air Corps! Technical Schools were the next option for us and we began the testing to qualify for training as mechanics, armorers or radio operators before going to aerial gunnery school. Boys who didn't qualify for a technical school went to ground crews or directly to gunnery school, combat crew training and overseas.

Luckily, I was one of several who qualified for radio operator school and in late November we said goodbye to hot, dusty Texas and boarded a troop train to spend the winter in the sub-zero temperatures at Radio Technical School in Sioux Falls, South Dakota. Several of those guys I knew in basic training were wounded, killed or had finished their missions before I completed radio school, gunnery school and combat crew training.

RADIO SCHOOL IN SIOUX FALLS

It was another long train ride and the most excitement was from a bunch of southern boys who had never seen snow! They got their fill of it that winter when our camp got the usual 150 inches of snow that winter. We moved in two days before Thanksgiving. Our new address was Squadron 809, barracks 421. Our Sioux Falls barracks were one story un-insulated buildings designed for warmer climates and were heated by three large pot bellied-stoves. One man had to miss class each day for "barracks guard duty." He was truly the "keeper of the flame." His main duty was to keep the home fires burning, haul out the ashes and bring in the coal from the bins on the alley out back. He also kept the gallon buckets on each stove top (our humidifiers) filled with water. The stoves were included in inspection and had to be clean at all times. Worse still, our company latrine was also out back and 50 yards down the alley.

The radio school ran two shifts a day and our class drew the midnight shift from 3:00 to 11:00 pm. During the next six months, we studied radio mechanics and Morse code. There were frequent proficiency tests on our knowledge of radios and speed of sending and receiving Morse code (we had to make twenty words per minute to graduate). We practiced in 'mock-ups' of a plane's radio room to give us the location of equipment and the feel of being a radio operator on a real bomber.

Classes were seldom cancelled because of snow or frigid weather; in dark afternoons we marched to class in sub-zero temperatures wearing gas masks to protect our face! Coming back to the barracks after was an even colder march. Luckily, our barracks was only a half mile from the classroom buildings. However, long johns, four- buckle boots knit caps and heavy winter overcoats were the order of the day! That rule was strictly enforced to avoid flu and pneumonia cases. Army buses ran a regular schedule to town with specific drop-off and pick-up stops. It was so cold that many guys caught the flu and spent time in the base hospital. (I spent four days, but managed to stay in my class.) Guards checked to see that we were properly dressed for zero weather before we were allowed to board the bus. Those not wearing their 'long johns, boots and overcoat' were not allowed to leave the base.

Our sergeants were a lot like the Post Office, they delivered us to class regardless of the weather. Most of our radio instructors were combat veterans who knew the skills needed by a good bomb crew radio operator. They all had the same goal; the Air Corps needed radiomen overseas and they were determined to provide them! One of my instructors, Jim Guthrie, was from my home town. Sixty three years later, I met another former instructor, Harold Plunkett. He had finished 55 missions as a B-17 ball turret gunner and radio operator in Africa and Italy early in the war. Harold's combat diary is included in my second book, Bombs Away!

MESS HALL BLUES

The Mess Hall was not my favorite place that winter. It was always crowded at noon and the food was not the best. The 'chow line' often extended out into the bitter cold with a long wait to get inside. Eventually we got into the warm hall, grabbed a compartmentalized metal tray, and they dished food in it as we moved down the chow line. I didn't like some of the food, but the servers slopped it on my tray as we moved along. To make matters worse, there was a big sign over the exit which said:

"You Must Eat All the Food on Your Tray!"

There was only one way to avoid eating all that food and foil the Mess Sergeant's plan and escape the steamy Mess Hall. We wrapped leftover food in a napkin, crammed it into our fatigue pockets, turned in an empty tray and strolled out the door! But, I outsmarted myself by skipping meals and eating too many Hershey bar and milkshake lunches at the PX. As a result, I spent four days in the base hospital with the flu. Of course, I blamed it all on the Mess Hall food!

THE SAGA OF DIRTY HARRY

Saturday morning barracks inspection was the highlight of our week, because it was a weekly test we had to pass to earn a few hours in town. If one guy's bunk area failed, we all failed.Our passes were cancelled and no one left the base. This rule promoted devout cooperation from everyone and anyone who messed-up faced big trouble!

The officers at the Sioux Falls Radio Technical School were really serious about neatness and cleanliness. They had "barracks inspection" down to a fine art! I mean they were after us every week! We realized this fact the very first week after our class (809) moved into barracks 421, because we failed our first inspection, took off our dress uniforms and spent our weekend at the base PX. Joe, one of the 'older guys' (age 24) in the class, called a barracks meeting as soon as we returned from the Mess Hall on Monday afternoon. It was perfect timing because we marched to class at 3:00 pm. Joe said, "Boys there are forty of us in this barracks and

I know you all faced inspections in basic training, but this is a new deal. If we want to get Saturday passes, we've got to work together. Now, I want a pass worse than anybody, 'cause my wife's living in town! I'll volunteer to be barracks leader if you want me."

We all accepted Joe to lead us and he gave us a lot of advice during the week. He even held a mock inspection of a couple bunk areas to illustrate:

1. Neat and orderly footlocker open for viewing
2. All uniforms on clothing rack facing same direction
3. Shoes neatly polished, arranged under bunk
4. Blanket on bunk must be taut enough to bounce a dime
5. Soldier stands at attention at foot of bunk- lower bunk on the right; top bunk on the left
6. Concrete floor must be clean, dust the stoves and bunk area.

Saturday morning rolled around and we were nervous as cats, but ready. We were dressed in full uniform and ready to go to town. I could almost feel that pass in my hand! Joe posted a look-out to watch down the company street and warn us when the Inspection Team was near. The three man team entered the barracks, someone yelled "<u>Attention</u>**!**" and the show was on! So help me that 2nd Lieutenant was wearing white gloves to check for dust and sure enough, he bounced a dime on my bunk blanket. Thank heavens that coin bounced! The team moved quickly down the aisle and out the back door. We had our passes! We all chipped in and while Joe was in town, he bought a can of stove polish and a bag of sweeping compound for the concrete floor. Our barracks really shined that winter!

We failed inspection only one other time during the six months. Maybe we became over-confident, but we didn't pay enough attention to Private Harry D. and he caused us to fail. Harry had a single bunk down by the rear door. We assumed everybody was keeping up their bunk area ready for inspection. Saturday morning his bunk area failed inspection. The Lieutenant denied our passes; Harry's bunk area was dirty and had that 'certain air' of body odor.

The temperature was zero or below for several weeks that winter and our Latrine (restroom) was a separate building used by four barracks. It was out our back door and about twenty yards down the alley. (sort of like my old outhouse at home.) A guy had to dry carefully and dress warmly when he showered or he could freeze on his way back to the barracks. Harry had skipped the showers too many times and his B.O. and smelly bunk had cost us a pass. We were doomed to spend another dull weekend at the base PX.

Dirty Harry paid dearly for his sins that Saturday afternoon. He was the special guest at our barracks GI Bath Party. We nabbed him when he came back from the Mess Hall and dragged him cussing and fighting down the alley to the Latrine. Joe told him to strip to his shorts. He refused, so we threw him into a shower and washed him down with a big bar of yellow soap and scrub brushes! Harry fought like a wildcat, but the "barracks committee" gave him a 'G.I. bath' to remember. We all got soaked in the process, but we got the job done before we turned him loose with a stern warning to clean up his bunk area. Harry sulked all week, but he got the message and his bunk area was sparkling clean at the next barracks inspection. We all caught the bus to town that Saturday afternoon and we even invited "no longer Dirty Harry" to come along!

"Harry had learned his first lesson about working as a bomber crew member!"

GUNNERY SCHOOL – YUMA

Spring came to Sioux Falls on schedule. Our class graduated in April, with a yearbook and a certificate to prove we were Radio Operators. This was about the same time the snowdrifts were beginning to melt and the base was thawing out. Our class had spent the winter in mountains of snow and a lot of zero weather in the frozen north. We boarded a troop train looking forward to gunnery school and a warm climate. However, by the time the train passed through Phoenix, we were suffering from the sizzling heat of the hot Arizona desert. It suddenly dawned on us that the Army had done it to us again! It was summer and we had been transferred from one weather extreme to the other. Yuma temperatures hovered above

100 degrees the entire summer and we had to wear silver painted helmet liners to prevent sunstroke. I mean a guy could get sunburned in an hour and tans were a dime a dozen. There were some air conditioned buildings with offices and classrooms, but none in the barracks. Our cooling system was simply adding moisture to the air with overhead pipes dripping water into gutters hanging under them. It was better than being out in the sun, but not much!

They moved us quickly through gunnery school. We were needed overseas, but there were several tasks to master before we earned our gunners' wings. The fun part of this school was skeet shooting time on the gunnery range. They took us there early in the morning to beat the heat. The range was an oval track with several small sheds for launching the clay pigeons. Some of the guys had never fired a twelve gauge shotgun; they ended up with a black and blue shoulder. We took turns shooting or loading and firing the clay disks from a shed. Our first lessons were on the ground and we had to lead (aim ahead) of the clay pigeon to hit it. Later we fired from the back of a moving pick-up truck as it sped around the oval track past the clay pigeon shacks. Now, since we were moving, we had to aim behind the target to hit it, just like firing from a bomber!

Aircraft recognition classes were in an air conditioned building and scheduled after we came in from the heat of the firing range. No one knew were we would be sent, so we learned to recognize a U.S., British, German and Japanese fighters. Like radio school, most instructors were men who had completed their tour of duty. They were dedicated teachers who had survived the horrors of combat and wanted the same for us! Instructors stressed the fact that a gunner's job was to quickly recognize and shoot down enemy aircraft --- not our escort fighters. The process was simple, they flashed a plane's photo on the screen for an instant and we wrote down the name. It was much like 'counting the dots' when you visit your optometrist. We had to pass tests on the German Messerscmhit ME-109, Fockwolf-190, our P-51 Mustang, P-47 Thunderbolt, the British Spitfire and Hurricane, and the Japanese Zero. Nobody had trouble recognizing the twin-boomed P-38, but we had to know them all, Quick recognition could mean the difference between life and death on bombing missions when every bomber's gunners were searching the sky for "bandits."

Our third task was completely mastering our weapon, the .50 caliber M2 Browning machine gun. We spent many hours in class taking it apart and putting the dozens of finely machined pieces back together properly. Instructors created malfunction problems for us to solve and correct. A non-working gun was a definite no- no during a fighter attack!

Our final test too graduate was to take the machinegun apart and put it back together while <u>blindfolded</u>. I still have 'The Proper Head-spacing' booklet issued to every gunner. Headspace was that 16th of an inch space between the barrel and recoil plate and was critical to the correct firing of the automatic .50 caliber machine gun. Aerial gunners carried a thin tapered gage with two ends labeled, 'go or no go' to check the headspace of each gun before or on a mission.

MY FIRST B-17 RIDE

My first flight on a B-17 Flying Fortress was during the last few weeks of gunnery school. Aerial gunnery from a B-17 was the last phase of training. This was what we had been waiting for and on a hot September morning our group of eight climbed in the waist door of an old B-17. It roared down the runway, lifted off and soared out over the desert. We were airborne for our first flight and aerial gunnery lesson.

Once in the air, we were allowed to roam all through the bomber until we reached the 'firing range.' I spent a lot of time in the radio operator seat checking out the equipment. We were a 'Gung Ho" bunch, eager to learn as much as we could about our future battle stations. We had no idea of which heavy bomber we would someday ride into combat, it would most likely be a B-17 Flying Fortress or the B-24 Liberator. However, the B-25 and B-26 two motor medium bombers looked pretty good, too.

Our first session was a using the left waist gun to fire 'live' ammunition at targets on the ground. The waist gun was fed six inch shells from a metal ammo belt hanging from an overhead canister. We took turns firing as the bomber made flights along the range to help us get used to firing the jarring .50 caliber gun. We flew two more days firing at ground targets. On Friday, the Sergeant asked for volunteers for a trip in the desert Saturday morning. The scuttlebutt was that a plane had crashed and we could get some souvenirs. Three of our guys agreed to go, but I passed up that opportunity (never volunteer.) Those guys spent their day off erecting new air-to-ground targets in the desert sun!

Our final training was firing air-to-air. The target was a long cloth sleeve on a very long cable towed by a B-17 flying ahead of us. The ammo belt had sections of shells painted eight different colors. The instructor assigned each guy a color. He said he could later check the sleeve to see how many hits were made by each man. We spent a week in air-to-air target practice. The chattering machine gun, swagging ammo belts and brass shell casings spewing onto the floor added a new dimension to our training.

We were not issued parachutes for these short low-level flights. A pilot, co-pilot and our instructor were the only regular crew members and it was OK for us to explore the bomber. Walking the eight inch cat-walk from the radio room through the bomb bay to the top turret and pilot area was tricky, but everybody wanted to ride in the plexi-glass nose or stand in the top turret. The big thrill was to walk through the bomb bay on the narrow catwalk. When the bomb bay doors were open, you could see the desert scenery rushing by several thousand feet below. It was especially exciting since we had no parachute!

On our last flight, a guy lost his cap and it fell down on the closed bomb-bay doors. He quickly climbed down on the doors, jammed the cap on his head and pulled himself back up on the cat-walk. Later, he nearly passed out when we learned that B-17 bomb-bay doors were designed to open automatically at 100 hundred pounds. It was a built-in safety measure in case a bomb got loose from its rack and fell on the doors. Our 160 pound buddy had escaped death that day and we all agreed that the kid had really lived up to his nick-name; "Lucky!"

"They say what you don't know can't hurt you:
but Lucky disagreed with that statement!"

COMBAT CREW TRAINING - SIOUX CITY

We had definitely earned our silver gunner's wings and Corporal's stripes at Yuma Airbase. We were a happy group of sun-tanned 'non-com's (non-commissioned officers) when we boarded the troop train for the Lincoln Nebraska Airbase to be assigned to a combat crew training airbase. The waiting was finally over and I got my wish. I and was assigned to combat crew training on a B-17 Flying Fortress at the Sioux City Airbase! So, I was going back north to Iowa, not too far from Sioux Falls. This would be my final stateside duty before going overseas and I was really anxious to meet my pilot and crew members to train for aerial combat. I was destined to know these men (boys) and the Flying Fortress very well!

Our ten man crew came together for the first time in September of 1944 at Sioux City, Iowa. We met on a crisp autumn day. Each man was the product of an efficient technical training program. During WW II, our government created the largest "educational system" that ever existed. For example, the Army Air Corps had to take inexperienced young men and teenagers from farms, small towns and urban areas and train them for specific skills needed to win an aerial war. It created technical schools that eventually trained: 193,000 Pilots -----50,000 Bombardiers ----- 50,000 Navigators and 297,000 Gunners to serve in all areas of the war. I had endured the hot dusty basic training in Amarillo, radio school in frozen Sioux Falls, and the desert heat of gunnery school in Yuma. Now, I was ready for fall in Sioux City, Iowa. However, I suspected that the coming winter overseas in combat would be very hot! These were the guys I would fly with or maybe die with on deadly bombing missions. I was now part of an aircrew and I was hoping that they all got high marks in their training, but of course everyone was thinking the same thing about me! We would all be tested over the next few months. Each man had to prove he was competent at his position and to be accepted by our pilot, Lt. Bill Templeton. We all had one thing in common; we were glad that we were training on a B-17 Flying Fortress. The Lt. Templeton crew members were:

Pilot	Lt. William D. Templeton	CN
Co-pilot	Lt. Dale F. Rector	IA
Navigator	Lt. Bruno P. Conterato	IL
Bombardier	F/ O Walter L. Benedict	MI
Flight Engineer	Ewing G. Roddy	PA
Radio Operator	James Lee Hutchinson	IN
Armorer	Bert B. Allinder	OK
Waist gunner	Orville L. Robinson	NY
Ball turret	Wilbur L. Lesh	MO
Tail gunner	Ralph E. Moore	OH

We were truly an All-American crew; no one came from the same state. We six enlisted men were housed in a barracks with other crews. We soon became buddies and looked forward to flying and learning more about each other's crew position on the plane. Orville was the oldest (26) and Ralph the youngest (18); Wilbur, Rod, Bert and I were also teenagers. The officers were in their early twenties. Our crew was together most of the day, although each man took refresher classes for his special job. We enlisted men spent a lot of evenings at the base Post Exchange. The PX was a great place for cokes and other beverages. It also stocked a lot of drugstore items from toothpaste to shoe polish.

I didn't realize how important the PX could be until we got overseas to Eye and they handed me a ration card for PX supplies. In England the base PX was only open two days a week, the clerk would check my card on every visit: Eight per week was the limit on cokes, candy bars gum etc. Every two to four weeks I could buy things like razor blades, toothpaste or fruit juice. I got a taste of what the folks at home were experiencing with ration stamps for meat, sugar, tires and gasoline etc.

Our crew bonded easily and we enlisted men usually went into town together on weekend passes. I hated the fact that we still had weekly barracks inspection. One Friday, we had to clean the barracks latrine and we used a razor blade to scrape stain out of the six stools. Boy, we really wanted that weekend pass! Sioux City residents were very kind to us they knew we were headed for combat. One of our downtown hangouts was the Town Pump, a bar down an alley and in a basement. The Pump was a favorite with non-coms (non-commissioned officers.) We were well qualified because we were all Corporals and on the low end of the army pay scale. Promotions wouldn't happen until we were overseas. Once we were in combat, I went from Corporal to Tech Sergeant in three months. Our officer's pay allowed them to visit the town's higher class 'watering holes' in the ritzier section of town. We all knew we had to become a good bomber crew, very soon our lives would depend on how well we operated our plane in combat. We didn't know where we would be sent overseas, but we all knew the high percentages against surviving combat missions.

Our four officers lived in Officers Quarters and had an Officers' Club on base for meals and recreation. Enlisted men had bunks in the big two story barracks and dined in the Mess Hall. We felt no resentment toward our officers, because we knew they had trained and earned their silver wings at a higher level. We would depend on them to get us safely through our training and combat missions. We met each morning at the plane to complete our flight training. The Army believed that enlisted men and officers were different and should be separated. However, it didn't take long for our officers to realize that their future safety would depend on the abilities of every man on the crew. Lt. Bill Templeton made sure that our crew was integrated. There was no saluting and we all worked well together. We knew the pilot was the boss and we were on the low end of the totem pole! The officers often visited our barracks and occasionally treated us to a night in town. We were a team preparing for combat in the very near future!

The B-17 was a beautiful plane, graceful in the air and tough as nails. Our instructors and combat reports assured us the Fort could take a lot of punishment and bring you home. There were countless photos of badly damaged bombers returning to base on a wing and a prayer.

We were late for the war and newsreels at the movies were full of stories on the Eighth Air Force in England and the role of the B-17 in the strategic bombing of German targets. We all hoped that our crew was headed for the Eighth Air Corps. Our crew's battle stations were in specific areas of the plane; the bomb bay was in the center of the bomber, the cockpit in front of it was the command center and seated our pilot Bill Templeton and

Co-pilot, Dale Rector. The flight engineer and top turret gunner, Ewing Roddy, had a seat behind the co-pilot. The navigator, Bruno Conterato, and the bombardier, Walt Benedict had small desks down in the plexi-glass nose. My radio operator's desk was over the left wing, just behind the bomb bay. The two waist gunners, Bert Allinder and Orville Robinson, could sit at their combat positions and search the sky for 'bandits.' The tail gunner crawled back behind the tail-wheel for his lonely seat and the ball turret gunner slid in under his guns into his "bubble" beneath the plane before we entered enemy territory. Each crewman tried to become familiar with other areas of the plane during training flights just in case he had to go there in an emergency. One night on a flight over Sioux City, our ball turret gunner, Wilbur Lesh talked me into taking a ride in his ball turret. I had a cramped and exciting view for miles while hanging under the plane in that 'fish bowl', but I never had the desire to do it again!

Most crew titles are self explanatory; Roddy, our Flight Engineer, was a gunner and trained mechanic. He monitored engine operation and fuel consumption while in flight. His seat behind the cockpit was just a step away from his battle station, the all-important top turret. Once we made lead crew, I was on the radio from take-off to landing and responsible for reception of messages from the base and any necessary transmissions back to our base. In case of emergency, I could take the place of a waist gunner injured during a mission. My radio equipment could help us to safety in case the navigator was hit. I could break the 'radio silence' rule in case of an emergency. Pilots had voice radio and could communicate with planes in our group during flight, but maintained 'radio silence' to keep the frequency clear for emergencies. We had the same deal with the plane's intercom system. Our motto was, 'keep quiet and listen unless you have something important to say!' Bert Allinder, our armorer/waist gunner, was an expert on bombs, ammo, and machine guns. Orville Robinson, right waist gunner and the old man of the crew, (26) often gave good advice to us young enlisted men. Wilbur Lesh had the ball turret, and his twin guns would be very important to our protection. Tail-gunner, Ralph Moore, had to crawl back past the tail wheel to reach his place of business! His twin tail guns provided a 'stinger' for our bomber.

The thirteen .50 caliber machine guns on our B-17G were deadly weapons. In combat they would be belt-fed from ammo trays with six inch shells that fired two inch slugs at up to 2,000 mph and had a accurate range of up to 1,000 yards .Bert said a 50 caliber machine gun could fire 750 to 1,000 rounds per minute. A gunner could burn out a barrel if he held the trigger down longer than three minutes. A good gunner fired short bursts and every fifth shell was a "tracer" bullet to show the gunner his line of fire. The B-17 was the Flying Fortress.

We finished combat crew training in October of '44, and received a short furlough to visit home. Shortly after we returned to base, our class of ten crews was shipped out by train to Camp Kilmer, New Jersey where the gigantic Queen Mary, with three smoke stacks, was waiting in the New York harbor. The giant British Luxury liner had been converted into a troopship and could carry thousands of troops on each voyage.

November 4th was my Mother's birthday and the day we shouldered our duffle bags and marched up the gangplank. The band was playing the march, "Our Director,'" which was my Bedford High School song. Six days later we sailed up Scotland's Firth of Clyde (my Dad's name.) Talk about coincidences!

'Nobody knew me from Adam, but they sure were 'rubbing it in!'

STRATEGIC BOMBING

England's Royal Air Force fighters had repelled Germany's Luftwaffe bombers in the Battle of Britain in 1940 and Wellington, Halifax and Lancaster bombers had bombed German targets. They welcomed the United States entrance into the war. The Eighth Air Force set up the first of its airfields on RAF bases in February of 1942. It was the beginning of the great high altitude precision bombing crusade to destroy Germany's war machine. Later the United States built many airfields and eventually established forty three bases for heavy bombers. The Eighth Air Force daylight strategic bombing missions would last over three years and result in the highest casualty rate of any U.S. Army unit.

By the end of combat in May, 1945, the Mighty Eighth had flown 440 missions and dropped 697 tons of bombs. Casualties were high, more than 26,000 airmen were dead or missing; shot down to become prisoners of war and 28,000 more wounded. Approximately 4,700 heavy bombers and 2,400 fighters were lost in action, crashes or mid-air collisions. Early bombing missions had heavy losses because our fighters did not have the fuel range to escort bombers all way to the target and back. Air crew members were required to complete a twenty-five mission tour of duty (later raised to thirty-five.) The young airmen were lucky to make it through six missions. In fact, the Air Medal was awarded for every six missions completed. The Memphis Belle was the first bomber to complete twenty-five missions. The plane and crew were returned to the United States on a tour of major cities to sell War Bonds.

Only thirty percent of bomber crews safely completed their tour of duty before December 5, 1943. This was the date our bombers became protected by escort fighters with 'drop fuel tanks which could be jettisoned for combat. This improvement increased the range of fighters so they could escort bomber formations to the target and engage enemy fighters. Drop tanks enabled the Eighth Air Force B-24 Liberators and B-17 Flying Fortresses to carry out safer and more successful missions. The Mighty Eighth flew daytime missions while the Royal Air Force (RAF) flew the night shift. Germany was pounded by the around the clock bombing.

The top recruiting poster of World War II
Sixteen million men enlisted or were drafted
for Uncle Sam's military service!!!

Posters helped with recruiting and encouraged people to endure rationing and support young men fighting for freedom. Many enlisted and more than ten million of the sixteen million in U.S. Armed Forces in WW II were drafted into service to protect our country.

The Browning Machine Gun, caliber .50, is a highly efficient automatic weapon built to precision standards. The very fact that its machined parts are fitted to close limits makes proper assembly and adjustment doubly important. The most important adjustment to insure proper functioning, and to prevent damage to certain vital parts, is proper headspacing. This adjustment must be made each time the gun is reassembled or each time another barrel is inserted. The following pages describe and illustrate "PROPER HEADSPACING."

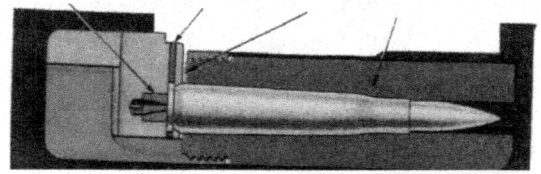

HEADSPACE SIGNIFICANCE

CREW POSITIONS ON THE B-17

FLYING FORTRESS

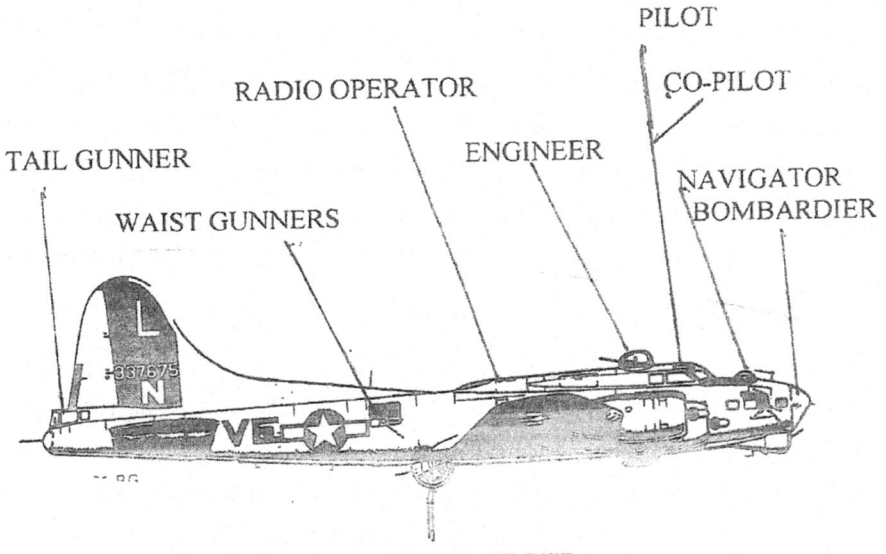

PILOT

RADIO OPERATOR

CO-PILOT

TAIL GUNNER

ENGINEER

NAVIGATOR

WAIST GUNNERS

BOMBARDIER

BALL TURRET GUNNER

Bomber formations flew at 25,000 feet. The ten man crew worked in cramped areas wearing oxygen masks and dressed for 50 below zero. They were connected only by the bomber's inter-com system.

CHAPTER THREE

EARLY MISSIONS

The first mission of the Mighty Eighth was carried out by the 97th Bomb Group on the first of August, 1942. Twenty-four bombers, with a fighter escort of British Spitfires, bombed the railroad yards at Rouen, France. Our fledgling air force had few bombers. They also had a limited range and the escort fighters had even less. Early missions went after German targets and submarine pens in occupied France. The German air force, (Luftwaffe) controlled the skies and often bombed English cities. RAF and Eighth bomber and fighter bases were also bombed by German planes based in France. Germany developed un-manned rockets shortly after D-Day. Giant dirigible shaped balloons, moored with 500 foot cables floated over were major British cities to stop low flying enemy planes. During air raids powerful searchlights broke the 'black-out rule' and probed the dark skies to spot the attackers or buzz bombs for anti-aircraft gunners.

British RAF (Royal Air Force) fighter and bombers carried the brunt of the operations until U.S. factories could produce more heavy bombers and fighters. In the spring of 1943, Eighth Air Force bombers joined the RAF to repay the favor by blasting German cities to lower their morale. However, our bombers were carried out those raids without the protection of a fighter escort. Allied fighters did not have the fuel capacity to go all the way to distant targets in Germany.

Luftwaffe fighters waited to attack our bombers as soon as our escort fighters reached their fuel limit and had to turn back to base. The bomber formations flew on and aircrew gunners were left alone to fight off their attackers. In those days, the bombers had to fight their way to the target, drop their bombs and fight back to where they could meet their escort fighters.

The Eighth Air Corps had received more bombers by August of 1943 and were strong enough to go after Hitler's munitions plants, ball-bearing factories and oil storage depots. The new bombing strategy was the same as the first; destroy Hitler's war machine. Many of the most important targets were in the Ruhr Valley industrial area of east central Germany. Cities like Munster, Dusseldorf, Essen etc. were so heavily protected that airmen called it 'Flak Alley' or 'Happy Valley.' However, there were important targets scattered all over Germany. Berlin, the ball-bearing factories at Schweinfurt and Regensburg's airplane industry were especially important and among the most heavily protected by flak and fighters.

FLAK - AN AIRMAN'S NIGHTMARE

A teenager flying combat missions quickly experienced the terror of flak. I was scared to death every time we had to fly into the deadly stuff over the target. I only did it eighteen times. I can't imagine the mental strain on airmen who flew twenty-five missions without fighter escort in the early days. By the time our crew arrived in the fall in 1944, we were required to complete thirty-five.

Exploding shells filled the sky with harmless looking puffs of black smoke that drifted away in the wind. But the anti-aircraft shell was like giant shotgun shell that exploded in black smoke and filled the sky with iron slugs. On the close ones, you saw a dirty red flash in the center of the smoke and a "whump" sound as it shook the plane and showered it with hot shrapnel slugs that sliced into the aluminum body of the bomber. Close flak could mean wounded crew members. A direct hit meant disaster. Aircrew members feared flak more the fighters. Gunners could see fighters and fire back at them, but flak was a deadly invisible enemy that struck without warning. Flak was designed to wound or kill, knock out engines, cause a fire or blow our bomber out of the sky! Anti-aircraft guns with radar gun-sights were responsible for the terrible loss of bombers and young men. Bombers could <u>not</u> take evasive action during the bomb-run. Once the formation left the "initial point," they had to fly directly into a barrage of flak with bomb-bay doors open. The bombardier took control of the plane with his bombsight and autopilot until he released the bombs. All we could do was hunker down and trust God, a steel helmet and 40 pound flak jacket to protect us as we flew into a sky blackened with exploding shells. It was a perfect time to have a chest-pack parachute hooked to your harness, there were cases when a plane exploded from a direct hit and sent airmen flying into space; <u>without parachutes!</u>

German defense batteries had three sizes of anti-aircraft guns and all reached a height of 30,000 feet or higher. The ten man crews on the 88 mm could fire over 15 rounds a minute and shells burst in a thirty foot radius. The 105 mm and 150 mm guns were slower, but fired bigger shells with larger bursts of flak. Shells had timed fuses set to explode at the height of the attacking bomber formations. Flak gunners had the option of two types of defense; they could lay a flak barrage over the target or use the more accurate tactic of tracking bombers on the bomb run. The 88mm anti-aircraft gun or Flugzeugabeweher-kanone was one of Germany's most effective weapons. The cannon was a triple threat, it had two types of shells. Shrapnel shells were used against troops and planes. Its armor-piercing shell could knock out a tank at 2000 yards.

Germany produced 18,000 various models of the 88 mm guns. Thousands were mounted in towers to protect important targets from Eighth Air Force daylight and RAF night raids bombing missions. However, many anti-aircraft guns were mobile; some were installed on trains and barges. Eighth Air Force Intelligence marked the locations of all reported enemy flak areas on bomb group briefing maps, but on one mission the 490th BG lost three planes when hit hard by unexpected flak from barges anchored in the Rhine river.

Nazi anti-aircraft gunners used two types of defense: lay down a "box- barrage" of flak over the target or use the more accurate tactic of tracking bombers on their long bomb run. Radar equipped anti-aircraft guns determined the altitude of our bomber formation and gunners set the shell fuses to explode at that altitude to fill the sky with metal slugs. A ten man crew could fire fifteen shells per minute! Names like Regensburg, Schweinfurt, Hamburg, Munster, and Augsburg were really bad news at mission "briefings" because crewman knew there could be heavy losses. Bomber crews would fly 200 to 450 miles into deadly fields of flak, drop their bombs and head for England!

Chaff (eight inch square aluminum coated strips of paper) was a bomber formation's defense against flak. Crew members in leading squadrons would feed bundles of chaff into a special chute in the radio room and fill the sky with fluttering aluminum strips to confuse the radar sights on the flak gun. Late in the war some planes carried "jammers" to mess up German radio signals and radar on flak guns.

Note – I still have a piece of chaff. S/Sgt. Wilbur Lesh, our former ball turret gunner, was a jammer operator when his plane was shot down over Czechoslovakia on the next to last 490th BG mission, April 19, 1945. He and ten others bailed out. One escaped, but nine were captured, interrogated and murdered by SS Troops. Their bodies were thrown into a mass grave. Germany surrendered eleven days later and the Czech people marked the grave. The bodies were later recovered and my buddy S/Sgt Wilbur Lesh now lies in the U.S. Ardennes Cemetery in Belgium. See Bombs Away! for the amazing stories of this deadly mission.

The Eighth Army Air Corps lost 26,000 men in bombing missions from 1942-45. Bombers returning from missions also carried back thousands of wounded airmen. Flak and fighters brought down or damaged hundreds of bombers on those deadly missions.

"If you ain't gittin' flak ---- you ain't over the target!

BOMBERS GOING ALONE!

British RAF (Royal Air Force) fighter and bombers carried the brunt of the bombing raids in the spring of 1943. Eighth Air Force bombers soon joined with the RAF to repay the favor by blasting German cities to lower their morale. Early in the war, our bombers were forced to carry out those raids without the protection of a fighter escort. Allied fighters did not have the fuel capacity to go all the way to distant targets in Germany. Eighth air corps bombers were heavily attacked by enemy fighters that quietly waited until our fighters had to turn for home. The bomber formations flew on and air crew gunners were left alone to face swarms of Luftwaffe fighters.

The Eighth Air Corps had received more bombers by August of 1943 and were thought strong enough to go after Hitler's munitions plants, ball-bearing factories and oil storage depots. The new bombing strategy was the same as the first; destroy Hitler's war machine. Many of the most important targets were in the Ruhr Valley industrial area of east central Germany. Cities like Munster, Dusseldorf, Essen etc. They were so heavily protected that airmen called it "Flak Alley" or "Happy Valley." There were important targets scattered all over Germany and Mighty Eighth daylight bombing and RAF night missions needed to destroy them all. Berlin, the ball-bearing factories at Schweinfurt and Regensburg's airplane factories were especially important and among the most heavily protected by flak and fighters. Dreaded targets brought fear to air crews because of high losses in planes and men. Losses were extremely high in those early days and thirty percent of our airmen never completed their first three months of duty planes. The reason was clear. Number one: Hundreds of anti-aircraft gun batteries guarded targets and filled the sky with flak. Number two: Eighth bombers did not have escort fighters with a fuel range to provide round trip protection to the target. German fighters simply waited to attack after our escort fighters turned back. Bomber formations flew alone to fight off swarms of Luftwaffe fighters. Air crew gunners fought their way to the target and back. During that period, the life expectancy of a combat airman was 8 to 12 missions, or about 50 percent! The Air Medal was awarded to airmen for every six missions completed. Purple Hearts were there for the wounded or dead. That was the medal nobody wanted!

August 17, 1943 Raids

Eighth Air Corps bombing missions in the early air war of 1942 through the spring of 1943 were mainly small numbers of bombers to German targets in occupied France. British and Eighth fighters could provide fighter protection for those short raids. Bomber strength grew as the Army trained more aircrews and workers in U.S. aircraft factories produced more planes. By the summer of '43, the Eighth could put up Bomber Groups of more than 300 heavy bombers. However, the German air force (Luftwaffe) had a large force of fighters to attack our bombers. We were losing many men and planes. Everyone knew the brutal fact; we needed long range fighters to escort our bombers to the target and back. Allied generals began plans for more intense bombing raids on Germany's factories, oil storage and transportation system to shorten the war. Luftwaffe planes and Panzer tanks would be useless without fuel. Allied leaders were willing to accept a ten percent loss of men and planes to destroy critical targets!

Leaders of the Eighth planned a two-pronged raid for August 17, 1943. It was to be a double mission to bomb two very important targets on the same day. Both targets were in Flak Alley and involved a large number of bombers in a regular mission and a 'shuttle mission' to Africa.

1. 230 planes would hit Schweinfurt ball-bearing factories and return to England.

2. 146 planes would hit the Messerschmidt ME- 109 airplane factories and near-by airfields at Regansburg and continue flying a "shuttle mission" (with extra fuel tanks) and land at 15th Air Force bases in North Africa.

The missions were designed to divide Luftwaffe fighters, who would be forced to defend targets against two separate bomber raids. However, several problems developed to ruin the original plan.

The Regansburg bombers, led by Col. Curtis Lemay, had to take off early in order to bomb the target and have enough daylight to fly on to North Africa. Meanwhile, the weather in the skies over England worsened and prevented an early take off for the Schweinfurt group. They were late in getting into the air to rendezvous with their formations and head for Germany. Thus, the plan failed from the start and bad weather ruined the plan of a two pronged attack. Hundreds of German fighters were able to attack the first group all the way to Regansburg, shoot down a dozen or so and turn back in time to join the attack on the second bomber stream headed for Schweinfurt.

Col. Lemay's shuttle group blasted their target and flew on over the Alps, some damaged planes landed in Switzerland, 5 ditched in the Mediterranean Sea. The group lost 24 bombers; only 115 made it to Africa. However, only 60 B-17s were air-worthy for the return shuttle mission. Those planes picked up a new bomb-load and bombed a German airfield in France on their return trip to England.

Col. Fred Castle was leader of the Schweinfurt mission. Their take-off was delayed by bad weather and as soon as the P-47 escort fighters had to turn back, the formations were savagely attacked by nearly 200 Luftwaffe fighters. Several B-17s went down before reaching the target. This group lost 36 planes (17 from the 100th BG) only 194 planes returned to their bases in England, but many of those were badly damaged and no longer air-worthy.

That same night, the Royal Air Force (RAF) sent bombers on massive raid on the Peenemunde Rocket Research base in Northern Germany. Their mission was to destroy the underground factories where German scientists were close to developing un-manned flying bombs and rockets (Operation Crossbow.) The raid was only a temporary success. Prisoners from a nearby concentration camp (Mittelbau-Dora) were forced to rebuild the underground factory and it soon resumed experimental work on flying bombs and rockets. During the war the Nazi regime used thousands of slaves to help build the V-2 factory and assemble the rockets. I was reported that at least 10,000 prisoners died from illness, beatings, accidents or starvation at Peenemunde.

NORTHERN ROUTE - 1943

Information in this section is from the Flight Log of Lt. Joel Punches, Navigator on the Lt. Robert "Tex" Taylor B-17 crew of the 385th Bomb Group at Great Ashfield, England. Joel served in the Eighth Air Corps from Sept. 5, 1943 to Feb. 21, 1944. I have edited or re-arranged the material to give readers a better understanding of his amazing experiences. I find this diary very interesting because it reveals the extreme dangers faced by bomber crews serving in the early Eighth Air Corps bombing missions without fighter escorts. The loss of men and planes was very heavy. Airmen faced overwhelming odds against coming home alive! My own combat time started almost a year later when we had our 'little friends,' the long range P-51 and P-47 fighters, to protect us from the Luftwaffe. Perhaps the flak was more intense, but we were escorted by fighters to and from the distant targets deep into Germany. The designers of the long range, heavily armed B-17 Flying Fortress and B-24 Liberator said they could protect themselves, but the German fighters had proven them wrong. We needed fighter pilots, those cowboys of the sky, who dueled with Luftwaffe fighters on dozens of bombing missions and hundreds of hours in combat!

Note ---After the war, General Eisenhower and other Allied commanders said the Allies could not have won the war without the Air Force heavy bombers. However, I would add --- we would never have won without our long range fighters!

"Tex" Taylor's Diary - 1943

Navigator, Lt. Robert "Tex" Taylor's diary ---Orders had come through, the B-17 bombers and crews were to leave our base at Grand Island, Nebraska and fly the northern route to England. It was September, 1943 and the Eighth Air Corps needed our help to destroy Hitler's war industries. We flew to Bangor, Maine to start the first leg of our journey to Goose Bay Labrador. The next day we were over the ocean again. We saw large convoys of ships and icebergs before we landed in Greenland. The next hop was to Iceland and we ran into bad weather. It was fall at home, but winter here in Iceland. The weather kept us grounded and we were forced to lay over a day. Some of us started to hike down to a fishing village along the cold blue sea, but we aborted that chilly walk. Iceland was a cold, windy and barren place full of boulders. Someone later said that Icelanders sided with the Germans, so it was probably a good thing we turned back. Next day the weather eased up, but we weren't cleared for take-off until noon, several hours later we landed safely at Prestwick, Scotland. We flew the northern route across the North Atlantic in about a week. Many planes and crews were lost while flying the Northern route.

We flew on to England where they took away our new plane. Our next trip was in a day coach on a small English train to temporary quarters and a training site for new arrivals, We were north of London and the classrooms were cold Quonset (Nissan) huts. We had five days of survival classes on about everything from ditching a plane to how to escape if shot down over enemy territory. In our free time, we learned that English beer (bitters) was really bitter, Nazi "buzz bombs" could hit anytime, and there were four girls for every guy at the local dances. English blackouts were strictly enforced because German bombing raids were a constant threat. One night, they hit an airport about ten miles north of us. We heard the explosions and flashes of the exploding bombs lit up the night.

Two weeks later we finished the training classes and were assigned to a Bomb Group a few miles farther north of London. We packed our bags, boarded army trucks and moved out to our combat base. We thought we were ready to take a bomber into combat, but we were wrong."

Note --- Mighty Eighth bombers were flying missions every day good weather was forecast over enemy targets. New aircrews were needed, but not until they were ready. Group commanders and squadron leaders wanted to make sure the 'replacements' were ready to fly in a combat formation. Nobody wanted a bunch of "greenhorns" flying close formation with them on a mission. Mid-air collisions were too frequent and too deadly! Therefore, new crews spent the next nine days in classes on the ground and in the air over England.

"It was great to get aboard a B-17 and back into the air. Ground instructors and those on the training flights made sure we knew what to expect on long high altitude missions. We were warned to double-check all equipment, guns, ammo and to be especially alert over enemy territory. Heavily oiled guns freeze up when its 40 below zero. Frostbite or worse and oxygen masks are dangers, too! Battling the sub-zero temperatures and oxygen loss (anoxia) was stressed. When an oxygen mask fails, the wearer does not know it. Ice crystals in the mask or flak damage to an oxygen tank can cause failure and death. The pilot should appoint someone to make periodic intercom checks on every position.

Our training did not keep us isolated from the realities of war. I suppose the same type of events were happening at our other forty two heavy bomber bases in England, but it did seem like our base was extremely active:

1. Loaded B-17 with 23,000 gallons of gas caught fire in the flight line and exploded killing a fireman and blowing the engines two blocks away.

2. Plane in the landing pattern ran out gas and crashed - no survivors.

3. Germans bombed the airbase east of us last night.

4. Gunner on the flight line accidently fired his .50 caliber machine gun and killed a ground crew mechanic.

5. One night an RAF plane on fire, spun and crashed near the base.

6. Our final exam: a simulated mission of all three squadrons (fifty planes) out over the North Sea was a practice mission, so none of the bombers had machine guns. The lead navigator took us out too far and we ended up about twenty miles from the Holland coast and a German airbase, (Schipol.) We turned tail and ran for home, but three ME-109 fighters hit the rear squadron and shot down two B-17's before anyone knew they were there. One bomber exploded and the other managed to ditch in the North Sea. We lost two bombers and twenty men. Those fighters could have shot down everyone our unarmed planes! Somebody should be court-martialed for that fiasco!
The deadly accident warnings came true all too soon!

Diary continues: First mission 9-28-43 Rheims, France --- A little more than three weeks after we left the good old USA we were flying the first of our twenty-five missions. We flew 130 miles into France to bomb an airbase with an escort of P-47 fighters --- had some flak on the way in, but could not drop our bombs because of the overcast. Saw ten ME- 110 fighters on the way home but they did not attack. We dropped our bombs in the English Channel and were cruising along at 7000 feet about ten miles from home and safety when there was a mid-air collision! A pilot in a bomber off our left wing lost control --- came up and crashed into the plane ahead. His propellers cut off that plane's tail --- it flipped and went down. Then a wing came off his plane and he crashed. Just then, our number two engine caught fire. We put it out and <u>made a good landing</u> <u>with three engines. Two bombers and crews were</u> lost due to carelessness; only 24 missions to go!"

Practice Missions --- We took a B-17 up for a test flight and later practiced "black-out" landings. Near mid-night, a German fighter (ME 109) attacked one B-17 while it was in the landing pattern. They are getting bolder! The next day we practiced flying in close formation and let-downs through the clouds. Later, we were supposed to 'home-in' on a radio beam from a station near our field and peel off and let-down through the clouds. Five of us in a row homed-in for twenty minutes. We knew it was too long, but we let down anyway and came out over the North Sea a few miles from the Holland coast! <u>German had jammed the radio beam we were following</u> <u>and were leading us straight into enemy territory!</u> Five more minutes and we would have been easy targets for a dozen enemy fighters waiting for us to come to them! Our gunners checked and manned their guns as we made a mad dash for home.

SECOND MISSION 10-2-43 Emden, Germany Target was a large transportation center in northern Germany. We flew in the high squadron at 23,000 feet. There were 180 bombers on the raid and we had P-47 protection. My navigator's seat in the plexiglass nose gave me a clear view of the sky as we started our bomb run. We flew into a lot of flak over the target – right at our altitude, none of our squadron was hit. However, this flak really scares you to death when you're flying into it. It looks so pretty and harmless, just black smoke floating in the air – but it's filling the sky with shrapnel! We bombed through the clouds on the lead plane's Pathfinder radar. Enemy fighters picked us up fifteen minutes after we left the target – did not hit our squadron, but one of our gunners got a burst at an ME- 109 that barrel-rolled under us. Two B-17s had to drop out of the formation with feathered engines. Things are getting serious! *Only twenty-three mission to go! "*

THIRD MISSION 10-4-43 Hanau, Germany Target --- the Frankfurt Rubber Works – biggest in Germany – 300 miles inland. Nine bomb groups and we were in the lead group. The lead navigator got lost and we bombed St. Dizier, France – it looked just like Hanau. Fighters (ME- 109) attacked us --- we hit a cloud of flak at the same time and were hit by flak --- a big hole in the wing. The ME-109 s peeled off one by one and came in head on – I got a good burst at one about 10 o'clock high with my nose gun. One B-17 feathered a couple of engines and dropped out of the formation. The Luftwaffe fighters lined up on him and probably got him. Later, we ran into more flak and more fighters came after us --- I think our gunners got a couple this time.

Coming home, we hit the Dutch coast and across the North Sea. One B-17 was shot up too bad to make it --- the crew bailed out over England before it crashed. We landed, checked the hole in our wing and found four more holes --- one just beside me, under the co-pilot's seat. We'll have to go back there!"

Note --- Flak Leave --- Crews periodically received three day passes off the base to relieve the stress of combat. Most guys packed a bag and headed for relaxation in London, although night-time German air raids and V-1 buzz bombs from bases in France were still bombarding the town. A few nights in the big city could help calm the nerves unless bombs hit too close. I remember my first pass. We were sitting in a large theater, when we heard nearby explosions and plaster began falling from the ceiling. It certainly broke a guy's concentration on the plot of the movie. Some airmen avoided London and the air raids. One guy said:

"I'd rather die sober in a bomber than drunk in a London night club."

On Joel's first night he watched a bombing raid a half mile from his hotel room. Six houses were blown away and the sky was lit up from the burning homes and the British flak guns blazing away at the attackers.

MISSION FOUR 10-10 - 43 Munster, Germany ---This was the "hottest" one so far - we got up at 0330--- took off at 1130, our secondary target was Hamm. We flew over Rotterdam and Amsterdam on the way in. Fighters caught us ten minutes before we reached the I.P. (initial point) to start the bomb run --- the group ahead of us had dropped demolition bombs on the business district and we followed with incendiary bombs. Flak was very heavy but we had clear visibility. Our bombs hit in a beautiful pattern

--- all concentrated and really worth the trouble for a change – this raid wiped out Munster --- we left a mass of flames and smoke behind.

However, the enemy fighters were waiting for us to come out of the flak and for fifty minutes we had a running fight with what seemed like a hundred German fighters. One bomber went down as soon as we left the target --- in all, we saw four B-17s go down but I think they got more! We saw some chutes open, but one went down in a spin – the last one was directly under us and I lost sight of it. Saw four ME- 109s explode and burst into flames. Our gunners claimed credit for one. Our P-47 escort picked us up after the excitement was over. A good raid --- Hitler must be tearing his hair now!"

Note --- Munster, in western Germany was a major railroad junction. Bombers also did saturation bombing on the center of the town to disrupt and demoralize citizens of the area. Germany had earlier bombed several non-military targets in England with same purpose. The English city of Coventry, a non-military target, was nearly destroyed. The Nazi attacks were strictly terror bombing of civilians.

Our P-47 fighter escort did not have the fuel range to escort us all the way to the target. More than 180 Luftwaffe fighters picked up our bomber formation as soon as the P-47 escorts had to turn back. Our bombers faced a day-long battle to the target and return. Luftwaffe fighters concentrated on the 100th Bomb Group and shot down several bombers on the way to the target; continued the attack on the return trip. The "Bloody Hundredth" lost twelve of their thirteen planes. The Eighth lost twenty-nine B-17 bombers and crews to flak and fighters on this Munster mission, but the worst was yet to come!

MISSION FIVE 10 -14 – 43 Schweinfurt Target was a ball bearing factory --- how we ever got back from this one, I still don't understand! Four hours over Germany and three hours under fighter attack. Flak over the target was like a cloud --- exactly at our altitude and very accurate. We were hit three times; tail, wing and plexiglass nose broken. Left England at 1330 and our P-47 escort left us twenty minutes inside Germany. When they left the 109's started attacking and continued for three hours. We were flying "Tail-end Charlie" in Purple Heart corner, carrying incendiaries. It was clear over the target and when we left --- it was a huge mass of flames 500 feet high. The whole town was burning. We saw two B-17s burst into flames ahead of us on the bomb run and three more bunches of chutes of seven or eight guys --- five minutes after we left the target another bomber crashed and burned. The Luftwaffe had everything up today --- JU-88, ME-10, and ME-210's --- The JU-88s were sitting out of our range and firing rockets at us. Another B-17 dropped down and two fighters dived after him --- twenty minutes later he came out of a cloud with engines smoking and the crew bailed out. Our number one engine ignition system was shot out and it sounded like a washing machine.

"I'm afraid things are going to be tough from now on---no milk runs!"

MISSION SIX 10-18-43 Durben --- Up at 0600, took off at 1000 and climbed to 27,000 feet --- left England at1330. The temperature at our altitude was 44 degrees below zero. The nose was completely frozen over --- couldn't see a thing --- my electric suit really worked well --- poor visibility and clouds all the way. The weather got worse and worse and when we were about 20 minutes from the target --- they scrubbed the mission and we turned around and came home! We might as well have gone on to the target --- pretty risky flying close formation in clouds. But this counted as a mission even though we didn't drop our bombs --- just as hard as a mission. I'm ready to do a raid --- weather or no weather.

10-20-43 MISSION #7 Durben --- Someone was praying hard for us today --- left England at1230 --- climbed to 28,000 feet and 44 below zero. We had an escort of British Spitfire fighters but twenty minutes before the target our number four engine ran away and we couldn't feather (stop) it. We couldn't hold our altitude to stay in the formation --- we had no choice we dropped down and turned back --- three minutes later four ME 109 fighters picked us up! We dove down to 12,000 feet trying to get away --- got into all the clouds we could --- did dives, climbs etc. but couldn't get up much speed with three engines and a strong headwind. The fighters came in on our tail, making several passes with machine guns and 20mm cannons --- keeping our gunners busy. They reported that they saw one fighter explode and another go down in smoke. Faber, our tail gunner, was wounded --- a 20mm cannon shell had hit the tail and he had slugs in his leg, buttocks and side. There was not much bleeding, so no first aid necessary.

We dropped our bombs in France in order to get more speed and zig-zagged for the coast, but flak picked us up and followed us for a few minutes --- did not hit us. We finally hit the English coast. We headed north for our field but our number four engine was now burning so we landed at the nearest field --- Dettling, an RAF fighter base five miles south of the Thames river near London. One tire flat and when we stopped rolling, the engine was really spurting out fire --- tried to put it out with our fire extinguishers but couldn't --- the field fire truck finally put it out.

Our bomber was riddled, must have been 200 – 300 machine gun holes in it and seven or eight cannon holes. I can't see how the tail and waist gunners got back alive. There were dozens of holes within inches of them. The fighters had attacked from the rear so most damage was in the tail section, but one 20mm cannon shell went through our bomb bay, just missing the twelve incendiary bombs we were still carrying! One plane in our squadron turned back ten minutes after us --- they haven't heard from him --- he evidently went down. Later learned that three gunners in our bomb group died from anoxia (oxygen loss) their oxygen tubes came loose and they didn't know it.

"Moral: Stay in formation even, if you have to get out and push!"

10-21 to 10-29 --- Called Great Ashfield to get a ride back to base --- the English treated us well --- tea in bed in the morning, tea at 1000, at lunch, tea at 1600, coffee after dinner --- a fireplace in every room. The RAF think "Forts" are great --- I showed about fifty guys through our plane. Our base sent a plane down for us --- took off --- buzzed their field and came home.

Rest, lectures, and practice missions --- no leaves or passes --- security leaks --- told the Germans knew the Schweinfurt mission was coming, that's why we had such high losses. Went to a couple of dances --- fog is bad, hangs right on the ground. Something is going to pop soon --- everyone can feel it in the air.

10-30-43 Mission #8 Ludwigshafen --- Got up at 0500—briefed at 0600 and took off at 0800 ---Target is in "Happy Valley" outside of Berlin --- the most heavily protected area in Germany with a mass of flak guns! Climbed up through fog and clouds to rendezvous with our group, but an hour later, they scrubbed the mission because of bad weather over the target.

Our field was "socked in" by the fog so they directed us to Docking, an RAF field 50 miles north. Our group broke up and we flew out over the North Sea and dropped our bombs. We came back to Docking and got down through the overcast to about 500 feet. We all got into the radio room and braced for the landing on the short sod field, but we made it OK. Three forts that landed ahead of us cracked up. Two went into a ditch at the end of the field and one couldn't get his wheels down and had to make a belly landing. Landed at 1400, lucky we didn't go on that mission, none of us would have had enough gas to look for an open airbase when we got home.

Note: the crew spent the night at the RAF base, flew their plane back to Great Ashfield the next and enjoyed a two day rest due to bad weather.

11-3-43 Mission #8 Wilhelmshaven --- Briefing at 0730 --- take-off at 0930 --- left England at 1130. Target --- the submarine pens and sub construction docks. Biggest raid so far -- over 1000 planes --- 600 B-17s and 400 B-24s. We had P-47 and P-38 escort fighter protection all the way, flak over the target was very accurate. Just after "bombs away" a Fort in the formation above us was hit in the gas tank (wing) and dove straight down, burning. Just before it hit the overcast it exploded into a million pieces. Nobody got out of that one! A minute later, another B-17 went down through the clouds with a German fighter on his tail. Ninety miles from the English coast, we found that the gas line to number one engine had been hit by flak and was losing gas fast! Ten miles later, it quit and we had to drop out of formation, lucky we were over the Atlantic and not Germany. Number two was spitting smoke, but we made it home ok on three engines.

"Red alert" and a lot of German bombers tonight! It was a good show ---flares, anti-aircraft guns etc. Just like a 4th of July display --- saw six German bombers burn and go down. They got our power supply so we had no lights.

11- 4-43 Mission to Ruhr Valley scrubbed-poor weather

11-5-43 Mission to Gilshenkirchen in the Ruhr valley --- had to abort-- Left England with the group --- poor formation and couldn't find a spot. Our number two engine was acting up at 29,000 feet, got to the Dutch coast --- lost all the oil in the number three engine, had to turn it off and "abort" --- came back on three engines and found a hole in our wing when we landed. Don't know where it came from – had not hit flak or fighters before we aborted!

The next five day days –took a 48 hour pass to London – came back – played touch football --- went to a couple of dances --- our plane was back in shape with two new engines and super chargers at a cost of $60,000 --- practiced formation flying, bombing range and another class in "ditching" procedures. Many shot-up or out of gas bombers returning from missions had to crash land (ditch) in the English Channel or North Sea. The life raft was stored above the bomb-bay in the radio room and a crew had three or less minutes to get out before the plane sank. Rescue boats saved some airmen, but many drowned or froze to death.

11-11-43 Mission #9 Munster --- A railroad center and 40,000 civilians --- took off at 0930 --- carrying thirty eight hundred pound incendiary bombs. We were flying number two position in the lead group, our P-47 fighter escort left us at Rotterdam, Holland --- nine German fighters attacked the group behind us. They got two Forts on their first pass --- they caught fire and exploded, two chutes came out of one. A few minutes later they got two more planes from the same group --- one exploded, the other one dove down.

After leaving the IP, our lead ship called us to take over the lead because they had lost their instruments. Munster had a large cloud over it, but we could see all the roads and rails leading into it. Finally, with three minutes to go, we leveled out on our bomb run and dropped our bombs. The entire formation behind us dropped their bombs on our lead. Flak was heavy and very accurate. Another fort went down over the target. Our ship was hit ten times and a piece of flak hit about two feet behind me --- tore up my jack-box and intercom!

We were really sweating out whether it was Munster we hit, however pictures tonight showed it was Munster; will find out more tomorrow."

11-12-43 This morning Tubby, our bombardier, and I got to go to Wing Critique. The Colonels, Majors etc. were very well pleased. They said our crew was evidently very much on the ball to be able to take over on such a short notice, with the target only five minutes away and still hit the target, even though it was covered with clouds. Reached the English coast and landed at 1630 (a nine hour flight.) Tomorrow, we go to <u>Division</u> Critique to tell the General how we did it! Tubby may get the DFC (Distinguished Flying Cross")

11-13-43 Went to a dance last night, slept till noon. This afternoon we test- hopped a plane. Forty of our group went to Bremen today, but for the first time we got to stand down. Only forty ships went and it was 52 degrees below zero at their altitude. Nine planes aborted due to bad weather. Over 200 fighters hit the formation at the target. Jennings flew our plane, 662, had to abort over Germany and got shot up pretty bad. They seem bound and determined to send us on raids no matter what the weather. General Hap Arnold said on the radio recently that there were plenty of replacement crews in the U.S. in case we needed them! Nice! We are going to start dropping time bombs that go off 15 minutes to 36 hours later. We had two more days for ground school and a practice flight.

11 -16-43 Norway Hydrogen plant --- Woke us at 0200, briefed at 0300 and took off at 0600. We assembled over the splasher (radio beacon) before daylight, but our number three engine went out. The propeller ran away and caught on fire! Not too large a fire so we stayed with the plane and headed for home. We started letting down through the overcast, but at 6000 feet, we hit a thundercloud and the plane went out of control. They got it straightened out at 1000 feet and rang the bail-out bell to abandon ship! Six guys went out the waist door. I got to the escape hatch in nose, but decided we were too low to jump. The pilots had things under control, so four of us stayed with the plane. The engine could have exploded at any time, but it didn't. We flew ten miles out into the Channel and dropped our six 1000 pound demolition bombs. Then couldn't close our bomb-bay

doors.--- hunted for 30 minutes for a field to land---finally landed at a P-47 field near Ipswich and put the fire out. We later got word that the six who bailed out were rescued.

Veterans History Project-Library of Congress

THE MEMPHIS BELLE

The crew of the Memphis Belle stationed with the 91st Bomb Group at Bassingbourn Airbase north of London, was one of the first to survive the required tour of duty of twenty-five missions. The boys on the Belle had flown from November 7, 1942 to their final mission May 17, 1943. The bomber received flak and bullet holes, had an engine shot out and returned from one mission with the tail badly damaged, but a crew member was never wounded. The B-17F bomber dropped sixty tons of bombs on enemy targets and the gunners were given credit for shooting down eight Luftwaffe fighters and five "probables." Lt. Robert Morgan and his crew were honored by a visit by the King and Queen of England before they were ordered back home. They were assigned to fly a 26th mission, which was a seventy-six day War Bond and Public Relations tour of 32 major U.S. cities. The Memphis Belle tour sold many war bonds and was a great morale builder for war- weary civilians eager to meet the ten men (boys) who had beaten the odds and survived the flak and fighters of the aerial war over Germany. That famous B-17 Flying Fortress will never fly again. The Air Force has declared it a national treasure. The plane was on display in Memphis, Tennessee for many years. My daughter Susie and I had the honor of boarding the Belle and she photographed me sitting at the radio operator's desk. I used that photo on the back cover of my first book, Through These Eyes. The famous bomber is now undergoing complete restoration and the permanent home of the Memphis Belle is the National Museum of the United States Air Force at Wright-Patterson Field, Dayton, Ohio.

U. S. airpower continued to grow as planes and crews were sent to Army, Marine and Navy Fighter groups. Bomb groups island-hopped to the war in the Pacific, while others flew the Southern or Northern route to the ETO (European Theater of Operations.) Eighth Air Force ground support units sailed over on the Queen Mary or other ships remodeled to transport troops. Later, aircrews to replace those who completed their tour of duty or were shot down were also shipped out on the Queen Mary. Our crew was booked for passage, November 4, 1944!

BLACK FRIDAY - OCTOBER 1943

American losses were very heavy in a September, 1943 raid, but the next mission to Schweinfurt on October 14th became known as Black Friday. The Eighth sent out 228 bombers and lost 60, which was a count of 600 airmen. Many of the 168 bombers returning to their bases in England carried dead or wounded crew members. A high percentage of those planes were severely damaged, some beyond repair. The disastrous losses of planes and crews halted the strategic bombing in the Ruhr valley for a few months and another call went out for more bombers and air crews. The Army Air Corps had been seeking aircrew volunteers from other branches of the Army, but now it was intensified. Replacement crews and bombers were desperately needed for the air war in Europe and I was in Amarillo, Texas, a VFT in Basic training for one of those vacancies

"Flak Alley" had become a "no-fly zone" until our Air Force leaders could solve a few problems. Allied bombers continued fighting their way to destroy closer targets with less flak protection and near enough to be escorted by P-47, P-51 or P-38 fighters.

CHANGES MADE

The combined losses of 60 bombers, their aircrews and the dead and wounded on returning planes in the October, 1943 raids was too costly. The results of the bombings did not justify the costs. Bad weather aided the Eighth in taking a two week break on long range missions into Germany. The heavy loss of planes and men was too high and for a while, missions beyond the fuel range of Eighth and Ninth Air Force fighter escorts were curtailed.

The Eighth continued to make changes and adapt new equipment to improve bombing results. They modified lead B-17s to use the Pathfinder radar equipment which had been used successfully by RAF bombers to bomb through the clouds. Eventually, heavy bombers were equipped with new methods of jamming or messing up the radar on German planes and anti-aircraft guns. Everyone knew the real solution: the mighty Eighth needed long range fighters to protect bomber formations from the enemy fighters. The Luftwaffe had air supremacy!

More bombers and aircrews were arriving to replace the losses. A new version of the Flying Fortress, the B-17G, was coming. More armor plate at crew positions was added and plexi-glass windows were added to staggered waist gun positions. The most important improvement was a remote controlled turret with two fifty caliber machine guns on the nose. The new turret's twin 50 caliber guns were a great defense against Luftwaffe fighter's head-on attacks on bomber formations. Diving down out of the sun from twelve o'clock high became a deadly risk for the Luftwaffe fighters!

Meanwhile the Luftwaffe added more firepower to their fighters. The Messerschmitt ME-109D became Germany's best fighter because of its speed and maneuverability. It had a 12 cylinder liquid cooled Daimler-Benz engine and a top speed of 350 MPH. The fighter had a range 0f 350 miles and operated well at high altitudes up to 32,000 feet. Two machine guns with 500 bullets per gun and a cannon with 160 shells made the ME- 109 a very dangerous enemy

The Focke Wulf FW-190 was another deadly foe. The heavily armed fighter carried two machine guns and four 20 mm cannons and one model was adapted to carry a rocket pod under each wing. The FW-190 could stay outside the range of bomber machine guns and fire rockets into the formation. Germany also reorganized their fighter groups to have more fighters protecting critical targets from daylight bombing raids. Late in the war, they would have the ME- 262 jet fighter. December, 1943 was a great date for bomber crews. P-51 mustang fighters were equipped with gasoline drop tanks and could now escort bombers! The odds in the air war were definitely tipping in favor for US airmen. Our bombing raids became more effective and Luftwaffe fighters slowly lost air supremacy due to loss of planes and trained pilots. Strategic bombing changed with the development of drop fuel tanks for new and improved Allied fighters. These auxiliary fuel tanks extended the range of our fighters; the gas in those tanks was used first and could be dropped when a pilot went into combat with the enemy. Fighters from the Eighth and Ninth in England and the Fifteenth in Italy could now escort and protect bombers deep into German territory. The improved P-51 and P-47 fighters became the "little friends" of men in the heavy bombers. By the early summer of 1944 Luftwaffe fighters gradually lost control of the skies and Allied bombers met less resistance in the destruction of Germany's factories, oil supplies and transportation systems. Allied ground forces marched across Germany, Russia from the east and the U.S. and British armies from the west. Hitler's dream of ruling the world was literally "blown away" and his Third Reich was left in the ashes! Millions of Germans died and the country was in ruins because of this madman's long reign of terror!

"War demands that you have the most effective killing machines!"

Hutch

Victory in Europe came at a high costs in dead and wounded. Many of those listed as Missing in Action were never recovered. U.S. airmen and troops are buried in twenty-six cemeteries in foreign countries. These countries have deeded land to the United States and Old Glory flies over the graves of 104, 366 heroes in the twenty American Cemeteries in Europe. Seventy-five percent of the 3,812 graves at the Cambridge, England cemetery are Eighth Air Force airmen. Cemeteries are also located in Belgium, Luxemburg, France and Italy.

S/Sgt Wilbur Lesh, our former ball turret gunner and T/Sgt. Lilbert 'Pick' Pickens lie among the 5,329 heroes in the Ardennes Cemetery in Belgium. (Graves may be located on the internet through the American Battlefields Commission.) My buddy, Wilbur Lesh is located in plot A, row 25, grave 7. The American Battlefields Commission maintains these cemeteries, however many Europeans adopt and place flowers on graves. Perhaps the thankful people of the countries we saved remember World War II much clearer than do citizens of our country!

"There were no atheists on those bombers and no foxholes in the sky!

Hutch

THE ROYAL FAMILY

The Royal Family never fled bomb-battered London for a safer place during World War II. Many well-to-do families fled to locations outside of London or evacuated their children to safety in Canada. King George VI and Queen Elizabeth, remained in the Royal Palace with daughters Elizabeth and Ann throughout the war. The Queen said the family would stay and support bomb victims and the men in the military. The industrial East End of London suffered from Germany's heavy bombing "Blitz" during the 'Battle of Britain.' The shipyards, docks and factories were prime targets of Germany's Blitzkreig to conquer England. The palace suffered bomb damage in 1940, but the Queen said, "I'm glad we've been bombed. It makes me feel I can look the East End citizens in the face." Adolph Hitler called her the most dangerous woman in Europe, because of her leadership and indomitable spirit in boosting British morale!

The Royal Family recognized the sacrifices of airmen of the RAF and Eighth Air Corps. They visited airbases on special occasions to show support and improve morale. For instance, they went to the Bassingbourn 91st Bomb Group air base to honor the men of the Memphis Belle, the first bomber to complete twenty-five missions. After the early death of King George in 1952, her daughter became Queen Elizabeth II and she became Queen Mother. The beloved "Queen Mum" remained active in public affairs, enjoyed great respect and a long life. She passed away March 30, 2002 at the age of 101.

QUEEN ELIZABETH II

Princess Elizabeth was crowned Queen Elizabeth II June 2, 1953. During the war, eighteen year old Princess Elizabeth joined the Women's Auxiliary Territorial Services as Elizabeth Windsor. She trained as a driver/mechanic and served as a truck driver. Photos in Stars and Stripes and Yank magazine showed her changing a tire and doing other duties to help the war effort. I realized that she was well protected (as a Princess should be) but she was a year younger than me and I liked the idea of a teenage Princess staying in London and doing her part for morale. I have always admired her as Queen Elizabeth II. She is the last surviving head of state, to have experienced the sacrifices of the Greatest Generation in World War II and she has kept her job a lot longer than I did!

The Queen, also a veteran, remembers those World War II days when freedom depended upon winning that war! She has visited the new World War II Memorial in Washington to lay a wreath to honor the sixteen million United States men and women who fought for freedom.

Well, to make a long story short, in 2006 I mailed her a copy of my first book, "Through These Eyes." Our 490th Group Historian, Eric Swain, is a Londoner and I thought she might like to know that a Brit is helping to preserve the history of the Eighth Air Force veterans who were there in WW II. Sometime later, I received a thank you letter from the Queen's Lady-in -Waiting. That framed letter now hangs on the wall of my den.

BUZZ BOMBS AND ROCKETS

The night of August 17th the Royal Air Force also launched a massive raid of over 500 bombers on the secret German V-2 rocket research center at Peenemunde, a fishing village on a peninsula in the Baltic Sea 100 miles north of Berlin. The entire operation was buried deep underground in concrete bunkers built with slave labor. This special RAF mission to destroy Germany's highly secret operation had been planned for some time. The British knew that Hitler's scientists were conducting rocket and flying bomb rocket research. New intelligence reports said Germany was close to developing cruise missiles to use against the Allies. The RAF made a second raid on August 25th which was successful and closed the Rocket Research Center for several months. The British had planned these raids for months. They were determined to prevent the deaths, suffering and damage rockets would cause to their homeland.

There were also underground V-1 bomb and rocket factories buried deep in the mountains of Southeast Germany. Again, slave labor from nearby concentration camps was used to do the digging and construction. This plant would also be manufacturing unmanned buzz bombs. It was time to "nip it in the bud" and save their country from missile attacks. Severe bombing raids were a major part of Hitler's tactics to terrorize civilian populations and convince people to surrender. Terror helped him conquer most of the small countries of Europe, but the English had refused to give in to Germany's intensive bombing raids during the Battle of Britain. The threat of buzz bombs and rockets had to be met, but unfortunately, Germany developed and used them against England and Belgium in the last year of the war.

RAF and US bombers pounded German underground factories to prevent their production. Germany didn't have the rockets until early summer of 1944. V-1 bombs were actually low-level flying bombs powered by liquid fuel. The V stood for 'Vergeltungswaffe' or vengeance weapon. The unmanned V-1 buzz bombs or 'doodlebugs' were launched at London across the English Channel from German bases in occupied France. The V-1 was used against Antwerp and other large population centers. The "doodlebug" carried 150 gallons of fuel, when it ran out of fuel it fell to the ground and exploded. One fact was sure, when you heard the noisy V-1 engine stop --- it was time to take cover! The 25 foot flying bomb carried a 1000 pound warhead, flew 400 MPH at an altitude of 2000 to 3000 feet and had a range of 150 miles. London was a prime British target and German launchers could calculate the amount of fuel needed to reach various targets. The "buzz bombs" could be shot down by fighters or anti-aircraft fire. More than 9,000 V-1 missiles were fired against England between June '44 and April '45, but only 2,400 made it to the target. RAF fighters shot down 2000, anti-aircraft fire got 2,200 and 278 were snared in the cables of barrage balloons. More than 32,000 of the V-1 bombs were built in underground factories in the mountain of southeast Germany at a cost of $600 per bomb. Slaves from the Buchenwald, Peenemunde and other concentration camps were used to build the underground factories and manufacture the bombs at various sites.

English Newspaper Story

The English people had endured heavy bombing raids during the Battle of Britain. The buzz bombs that began after D-Day were just another trial to endure until victory. This story appeared in the October 16, 1944 issue of the <u>Northhamtonshire</u> <u>Evening Telegraph</u>

THREE FLY-BOMBS DOWN
CASUALTIES AND DAMAGE REPORT

"During the night the enemy directed flying bombs against southern England, including the London area. A.A. guns were more than usually active on the East Coast. Projectiles, which got through the barrage fell in scattered areas, and at least three were brought down after heavy explosions. Casualties and damage to property, including a cinema, have been reported. A number of flying bombs were destroyed by the A.A. guns and fighters of the A.D.G.B. (Aerial Defense of Great Britain.) Ten people, most of whom lived in flats over shops, were injured, but no one was killed. Extensive damage was caused to a church, a school, a Post Office, a cinema and shops."

Note --- I recall my first night in Hut 29 at the 490th Bomb Group when someone called us outside to see a doodlebug. It was hedge-hopping low on the horizon west of the base. The noisy 'buzz bomb' was evidently running out of fuel, a few minutes later the engine stopped and it exploded harmlessly in farmer's field. However, a week later, one hit a theater in a small town near the base and injured several people."

V-2 Rockets ----- The 46 ft long V-2 rocket, was a different matter. It was a much more dangerous weapon and had a range of 200 miles. This monster carried a 2,200 pound warhead. The V-2 rockets were not used until September of '44, but Germany launched 3000 at major cities like London in the next eight months. Post war reports show that 5,700 V-2 rockets were made. The 27,000 pound V-2 was fired from a mobile launcher which made it difficult to find and bomb launching sites. The rocket reached a height of 55 miles before it plunged to the ground at 2000 miles per hour. There was no defense against such a rocket. It is estimated that over 5,000 died from V-2 rockets hitting London.

The British called them "Bob Hopes" .They said, "All you can do is, bob and hope it misses you!".

The V-2 was made at three secret locations and all were high priority targets for Allied bombing missions. The last V-2 hit London in March '45 before Allied troops captured all German launching sites and ended the threat of unguided rockets

Wernher von Braun was one of the top scientists working on the rocket research at Peenemunde, a peninsula in the Baltic Sea about 100 miles north of Berlin. This underground factory was built with slave labor from a nearby concentration camp. All scientists and their families were moved into this secret city to develop the new vengeance weapon. Allied bombing raids hit these heavily fortified underground rocket research centers many times. Our bombers could slow production, but were unable to destroy the underground factories. The threat of becoming prisoners of the Russian army closed them in 1945. All production at Peenemunde ceased when the Russian troops were getting too close and von Braun convinced the 500 or so scientists and their families to leave.

They disguised themselves as refugees, headed west and traveled for several days before they could safely surrender to American troops. Wernher von Braun and many of the others were asked to come to the United States to continue their rocket research. von Braun was later named head of the U.S. Rocket Research Center at Huntsville, Alabama and became the father our United States Space program.

Luckily, German scientists had not developed the V-1 buzz bombs or V-2 rockets during the Battle of Britain and the early war, but many people died and many buildings were destroyed by these guided missiles between June, 1944 and March, 1945.

"Germany had developed the first military cruise missiles, but they were too late to save the Third Reich"

Note --- On my first pass to London in the winter of 1944, I was surprised to see so many London families moving into the subway stations (Tube) at night. They carried in bedclothes to sleep on bunk beds provided by the government. When all the cots were taken, latecomers found sleeping space on the concrete floor. Londoners had been following this routine since the Battle of Britain in1940. Germany started launching the V-1 buzz bombs on June 13, 1944 (after D-Day.) The unmanned V-1 buzz bombs came every night and there was no telling where they would fall. Camping out in the Tube every night had become an accepted way of life. I could see the wisdom of moving into the subway. The Tube made a great bomb shelter and the noise of the trains was soothing compared to that of air raid sirens, bombs and anti-aircraft fire. On top of that, the subway got quiet when the trains stopped running at 11:30 pm. Of course our crew was foolhardy, so we boarded the subway and moved on to the Red Cross Rainbow Club in Piccadilly Circus to get rooms in one of their hotels. We were awakened several times by the sound of exploding bombs. I have a vivid memory of sitting in a London theater when a buzz bomb landed in the neighborhood. We were pelted by falling plaster as the film was ended and the organist made a quick exit from the orchestra pit!

1943 - Queen Elizabeth, Princess Elizabeth and King George VI talk with a pilot and General Doolittle during a visit to an 8ᵗʰ Air Force base

The Queen talks with the "Four of a Kind" crew of the 379ᵗʰ BG after their return from a mission.

SANDRINGHAM HOUSE

17th January, 2006

Dear Mr. Hutchinson,

The Queen wishes me to write and thank you for your letter, with which you enclosed a copy of your memoirs.

Her Majesty was pleased to receive this record of your experiences as a young airman, serving in the Eighth Air Force during the Second World War, and was touched by your recollections of the months you spent stationed in this country.

The Queen was interested to learn of your eighteen combat missions with the 490th Bomb Group based at Eye airfield, and thought it kind of you to pay tribute to the assistance you have received from Mr. Eric Swain in the preparation of your book.

Her Majesty appreciated the thoughtful sentiments expressed in your letter and the good wishes you have conveyed, and I am to thank you again for your kind thought for The Queen.

Yours sincerely

Annabel Whitehead

Lady-in-Waiting

Mr. J.L. Hutchinson

One of our 490th BG planes in a flak-filled sky over the target.
We had to fly into those deadly skies to drop our bombs.
Airmen said, "The flak was so thick you could walk on it!"

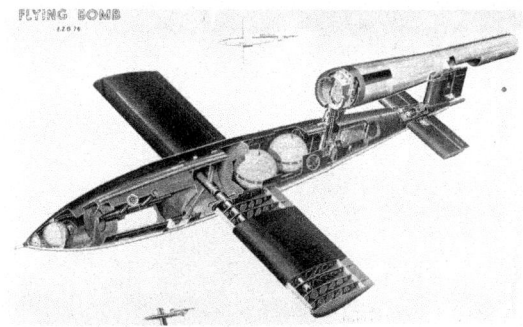

V-1 rockets buzzed noisily because of the rapid pulsing of its simple jet
engine, thus the nickname buzz bomb or doodlebug. Wikipedia

V-2 rockets were transported on a Meillerwagen which could
lift it to an upright position for launching. Wikipedia

German 88mm anti-aircraft (flak) crew of ten could fire fifteen shells per minute.
Photo provided by Hein Tlustek Sr.

CHAPTER FOUR

SNUFFY SMITH'S MEDAL OF HONOR

May 1, 1943 was the day S/Sgt Maynard "Snuffy" Smith became a hero and earned the Congressional Medal of Honor. While flying his first mission as a B-17 ball turret gunner, S/Sgt. Smith became one of the thousands of unlikely heroes who performed remarkable feats of bravery to survive.

Maynard Harrison Smith joined the Army in 1942 at the age of 31. He completed basic training and immediately volunteered for Air Force aerial gunnery school to gain rank and pay. Gunners earned their stripes much quicker before going into combat than buck privates in the infantry. After completing gunnery school at Harlingen, Texas, and combat crew training he was shipped overseas to a B-17 base in England and assigned to the 423rd Squadron of the 306 bombardment Group at Thurleigh Airbase.

Smith was older than most air crew member and the guys in his squadron considered him stubborn, obnoxious and a 'goldbrick'. He was quickly given the nickname, 'Snuffy' after the popular hillbilly comic character. Dubbed a 'misfit' for an air-crew; it was six weeks before the 'rookie' was assigned to fly his first mission. 'Snuffy' was 5 foot 4 inches and weighed 130 pounds; the perfect fit for a ball-turret gunner on the veteran aircrew of Lt. Lewis Johnson, who was flying the 25th and final mission of his tour of duty.

The U-Boat (submarine pens) at Saint-Nazaire, France was the target for the 306th Bomb Group on May 1, 1943. The heavy concrete 'submarine garages' over the water protected German U-Boats coming in for repair or supplies. Airmen had named the area 'flak city,' because of the numerous German anti-aircraft guns! However, the bomber formation was able to drop their bomb-loads and avoid enemy fighters by hiding in clouds. At that point, the raid was successful and almost a 'milk run,' however, a navigational error by the lead navigator led the formation into disaster. The formation leaders thought the formation was over the coast of England and let down to 2000 feet to land before they discovered they were over the heavily armed city of Brest, France. The formation was immediately hit by thick flak and German FW 190 fighters! Six Forts went down and flak hit Lt Johnson's bomber. The flak ruptured fuel lines and started a fire in the middle of the plane. Lt. Johnson remained at the low altitude and headed for home, aware of the fire, but striving to avoid 'ditching' in the sea. It was his last mission and he hoped to make it to an airfield in England.

Snuffy's ball turret lost power and the enter-com went dead. The waist gunners had to 'hand-crank' the ball up so he could escape into the waist area. He crawled out of the turret to find a wounded tail-gunner on the floor and the radio operator and both waist gunners preparing to bail out into the sea because of fires in the radio room and waist section. The three veteran crewmen then bailed out. Maybe 'Snuffy' couldn't swim or maybe he just wanted to show up those guys for deserting the ship. He had decided to stay with the plane and suddenly, he was the only man standing in the rear half of the plane. The Luftwaffe FW 190's continued to attack the B-17, the tail-gunner was wounded and the fire was burning holes in the radio room!

S/Sgt 'Snuffy' Smith could have bailed out, but he stayed to fight the fire! He tended to the wounded tail-gunner, fired waist guns at attacking fighters and fought the flames with fire extinguishers and water bottles for almost ninety minutes. Lt. Johnson and the five men up front fought off the fighters until they could touch down in England. The fire had burned the frame of the bomber so badly that it broke in half on the runway shortly after it landed. Ground crews counted more than 3,000 flak and bullet holes in what remained of the bomber!

Lt. Johnson recommended S/Sgt Smith for the Medal of Honor. Meanwhile, he flew four more missions in the six weeks before the award was approved. Then, the hero overslept and missed a mission. He was given a week on KP for that 'goof up.' Snuffy was in the Mess Hall scraping out trays when Secretary of War, Henry Stinson, arrived to present him the nation's highest award, the Congressional Medal of Honor. Squadron officers quickly got the honored guest, dressed in full uniform in time for the presentation ceremony!

S/Sgt Maynard 'Snuffy' Smith was a hero that day in the deadly skies over enemy territory when he single-handily saved the lives of six members of his crew members by extinguishing the fire and enabling the bomber to make it back to England. He had earned his Medal of Honor and two Air Medals and he gladly received the salutes of his Air Force superiors and Generals.

S/Sgt Smith was the first enlisted airman to earn the Medal of Honor. He became a national hero, but continued his pesky ways by taking advantage of his publicity, sometimes insisting on the rule that officers salute him as a holder of the CMO. He was eventually assigned to ground duty and a desk job and in March of 1945, he was sent back to the states for parades and honors.

May was an important month in the life of S/Sgt Maynard 'Snuffy' Smith.

1. May,1911 birthday

2. May ,1943 first mission - earned the Medal of Honor

3. May, 1945 discharged from service

4. May, 1984 passed

Maynard Harrison Smith, S/Sgt in the US Army, is buried in Arlington National Cemetery in our nation's capitol. His tombstone carries the emblem of the Congressional Medal of Honor --- no mention is made of the nickname Snuffy!

Medal of Honor Citation: "For conspicuous gallantry and intrepidity in action above and beyond the call of duty. The aircraft of which Sgt. Smith was a gunner was subjected to intense enemy antiaircraft fire and determined fighter aircraft attacks while returning from a mission over enemy-occupied continental Europe on 1 May 1943 .The aircraft was hit several times by anti-aircraft fire and canon shells of the fighter aircraft, two of the crew were seriously wounded, the aircraft's oxygen system shot out and several vital control cables severed when intense fires were ignited simultaneously in the radio compartment and waist sections.

The situation became so acute that three of the crew bailed out into the comparative safety of the sea. Sgt. Smith, then on his first combat mission, elected to fight the fire by himself, administered first aid to the wounded tail gunner, manned the waist guns and fought the intense flames alternately. The escaping oxygen fanned the fire to such intense heat that the ammunition in the radio compartment began to explode, the radio, gun mount and camera were melted, and the compartment completely gutted. Sgt. Smith threw the exploding ammunition overboard, fought the fire until all the firefighting aids were exhausted, manned the workable guns until the enemy fighters were driven away, further administered first aid to his wounded comrade, and then by wrapping himself in protecting cloth, completely extinguished the fire by hand.

This soldier's gallantry in action, undaunted bravery, and loyalty to his aircraft and fellow crewmembers, without regard for his own personal safety, is an inspiration to the U. S. Armed Forces."

"Courage is not the lack of fear, but the ability to act while facing fear!"

The Bloody Hundredth

There was a wide spread belief that bombers of the 100th Bomb Group suffered extremely high losses because they were special targets of Luftwaffe fighters. Throughout the history of the Mighty Eighth Air Force in WW II there have been questions concerning the high loss of bombers from the 100th Bomb Group. Did Luftwaffe fighters really seek out and attack the 100th BG bombers with the big square D on the tail? Was the 100th jinxed or was the legend of the "lowered landing gear" true?

Michael P. Faley, author of 'High Noon Over Haseluenne' and Historian for the 100th Bomb Group, recently supplied me with information concerning the famous bomb group: "The group did not lose the most planes in the Eighth Air Force, but did have high losses of aircraft and crews on nine separate missions. As Group Navigator Harry Crosby pointed out, "When the 100th lost aircraft, we lost big!" Many factors contributed to the nick-name of the group. Bad formation flying gave enemy fighters an advantage; being in the wrong place at the wrong time or the right place at the wrong time; missions to heavily protected targets; flying in the unprotected Tail-end Charlie position." All the above is true and could account for the losses. However, is the legend true or was it just plain hard luck." My big question: "Is there any truth to the lowering of the wheels legend?

The answer to the question of the legend:

"Yes and no! The legend goes that a 100th BG aircraft, while signaling to surrender by lowering its wheels down, shot down German aircraft as they pulled alongside to escort them to a German airfield. The Luftwaffe was so incensed by this breach of aerial conduct that they singled out the 100th BG for destruction. Thus the high losses on subsequent missions and the 100th Bomb Group became known as the "hard luck" group! To a degree all of this is true!

August 17, 1943 - Target Regensburg: while facing the Luftwaffe's onslaught, Capt. Robert Knox, piloting the B-17 Picklepuss, had sustained serious damage to his plane which required a decision to either go to Switzerland or try to make it back to England. Capt. Knox and his crew decided to try for England --- alone! Stragglers were 'meat on the table' for the Luftwaffe and Picklepuss was immediately pounced upon by fighters! Lieutenant Ernest Warsaw, the navigator, related the following to me: 'The intercom was shot out, so we had no communications on the ship. We were taking a beating, the bail-out bell was rung and it was time to get out. I was going out the front hatch when I noticed our wheels were lowered.'

No one on the 'flight deck' (Capt. Knox & Lt. Whitaker) survived the final attack, so we'll never know for sure if Capt. Knox lowered the wheels as a sign of surrender or if battle damage caused them to come down. What is known is that the wheels were down and when the German fighters pulled up alongside the plane, the gunners shot them down. Did the Luftwaffe single out the 100th Bomb Group for annihilation after this event? That is up for debate! The 'Bloody Hundredth' certainly had its share of losses that would tend to validate the legend! Others say the rate of closure made singling out any one group prohibitive. Which is correct? When in doubt, print the legend!"

The 100thBomb Group suffered some of their heaviest losses during Black Week (Oct.8-14, 1943) in missions on some of the Germany's most protected targets. The group flew three days in a row to Bremen, Marienburg and Munster. They lost so many bombers and crews in those three days that they could only send up eight planes for the Oct. 14th mission to Schweinfurt. They flew with the 95th Bomb Group and Eighth Air Force losses were so heavy that it became 'Black Friday'!

Air Force statistics show that the 100th Bomb Group, based at Thorpe Abbotts, flew 306 missions between June 25, 1943 and April 20, 1945 with a loss of 177 bombers. The group arrived early in the war, earned two unit citations and stayed for the victory!

Note --- S/Sgt Van 'Ike' Wright of Bloomfield, IN was a tail gunner on the Lt. Richard Atchison crew of the 100th Bomb Group. His bomber, Sweater Girl, was shot down over Munster on his eighth mission, October 10, 1943. Ike bailed out and became a POW in Stalag 7A. He eventually ended up in Stalag 17 B at Krems, Austria. (See Ike's story in my second book, 'Bombs Away.') This was the POW camp where T/Sgt Robert Stahlhut, engineer on the Lt. McMahon crew of the 384th Bomb Group and 2nd.Lt. Corbin Willis, Jr., co-pilot with the 486th Bomb Group were also prisoners of war! Their stories report many of the same experiences.

Information for this story was made available from the archives of the 100th Bomb Group Foundation. My thanks to the 100th Bomb Group Historian, Michael P. Faley, author of "High Noon Over Haseluenne

Bailing Out

The B-17 Flying Fortress was built to deliver bombs to enemy targets heavily protected by anti-aircraft guns. Eighth Air force bombers faced attacks by Luftwaffe fighter groups on the way to and from their targets. But flying into a heavy field of flak over the target was the part of the mission that really taught a kid how to pray. Every member of our ten man crew prayed that our plane would make it through the flak field as we dropped our bombs. A direct hit on a bomber meant every man for himself and crew members had only a small chance of bailing out. Many pilots died while trying to control their doomed bomber long enough for the crew to bail out. The crew on a damaged Fortress had two choices: stay with the ship and try to make it to friendly territory or make a hasty exit into a frozen sky before the plane went down. Pilots informed the crew of the plane's condition and made the decision to hit the "bail-out bell". Daytime missions meant Mighty Eighth bombers usually flew at altitudes from 20,000 to 25,000 feet where temperatures ranged from 40 to 50 degrees below zero and crewmen wore oxygen masks to stay alive. Hooking a parachute to your harness and leaping into space was not an easy task. Exits were limited; there was a waist door in the rear for airmen behind the bomb-bay and a nose hatch up front for those men to drop through. The bomb-bay would be open if the plane was over the target. The pilots wore seatpack chutes, the rest the crew had the bulky chest packs. Many airmen did not keep them hooked to their harness because they interfered with their work. Sadly, a direct hit or explosion did not give a crewman time to locate and hook on his parachute. There was a story that one left-waist gunner reported that he was waving to his buddy flying the right-waist gunner position in the bomber flying off his left wing when it got a direct hit. He later swore that for an instant he locked eyes with his buddy who was flying through the air without a chute when the plane exploded.

I had no problem wearing my chest pack while I sat huddled at my radio desk with my flak helmet and forty-five pound flak vest. I prayed on every mission and believed God would protect me, but figured I should do all I could to help Him!

The 490th Bomb Group's February 6, 1945 mission to Chemnitz, Germany's marshalling yards (railroads) was a costly mission in terms of men and planes. Four planes were lost, but not from enemy fire. Three were due to mid-air collisions and one was caused by mechanical problems. Each mission required hundreds of bombers to climb into the dangerous early morning sky over England to assemble with their formations and join the 'bomber stream' as it flew out over the North Sea to assigned targets. Group assembly in the murky sky caused the loss of many planes and crewmen.

S/Sgt. Spencer E. Flynn, was two years ahead of me in Bedford High, but in my sophomore year we earned 25 cents guarding the bicycle racks during noon hour. Two-bits was a lot of money in those days and we could earn the grand total of six dollars a month. Spencer graduated in1942 and joined the U.S. Army Air Corps. He was trained as a gunner and engineer on a B-17 Flying Fortress and assigned to the Eighth Air Force. Spencer was a veteran of many combat missions in the early air war, but he died in a mid-air collision during group assembly over England in November, 1943. He is buried in the American Cemetery at Cambridge, England

One bomber went down during assembly over England after colliding with a bomber from another group. A second went down when it developed mechanical failure after takeoff and crashed at Darsham, about twenty miles from Eye. Waist Gunner, Sgt. George Erwin, wrote about his experiences in the490th Historical Record of the 490th Bomb Group. He told of the crash of his bomber "Lil Edie," piloted by Lt. Lawrence Flannelly.

Sgt. Erwin reported: "Our bomber had been hit on our first trip, but our ground crew had installed a new top turret. We took off and headed out over the North Sea to assemble with the 490th Bomb Group. We were up to about 15,000 feet and on oxygen when the plane suddenly shuddered and went into a steep dive. Sparks and flames were rushing past my waist window. I was pinned to the wall as the plane dived and my buddies were fighting their way to get to parachutes. I clawed my way to the waist door, pulled the release pins, kicked the door away and bailed out. I wasted no time pulling the ripcord. What a wonderful sight to see that chute open above me. I got quite a jolt when it popped open-------both my flight boots were flung off, leaving me with just my electric shoes on my feet. I watched the plane go spiraling down and saw the bombs fall out at about 10,000 feet and blow up a road and some fields. I had seen some chutes and later another chute came out. I prayed that they all had made it as I watched the plane, with fire streaking out behind it, make a half spiral and dive. It splattered itself across the English countryside as if someone had thrown a giant bucket of burning oil all over the landscape.

My parachute brought me down in a wheat field, and I remember kissing the ground and saying 'Thank you God.' I got up and realized I still had the ripcord D-ring in my hand and was wearing my oxygen mask with a long piece of hose attached. My three pairs of gloves were shredded to the fingers and the knees of my flight suit were torn through to the skin. I really must have worked hard to get out of that falling plane! The entire crew survived and we later learned the crash was caused by a defect in that newly installed turret. A leak had allowed oil and oxygen to mix and create the fire."

Jumping into enemy territory was job feared by all airmen, because boys bailing out of a doomed bomber over enemy territory faced tremendous odds of surviving and a very dangerous and uncertain future. In the first place, the odds were greatly against them in getting out of the aircraft. Once they escaped from the plane they had to free-fall to get out of the frigid temperature, avoid the flak and wreckage of planes in the sky and float down into enemy territory. It was a sure bet that they would not get a friendly reception from the people they had just bombed. Our instructions were to hide the parachute and avoid capture if possible. Downed airman might hide for a few hours or be hidden by partisan organizations; but in Germany a majority of them had a reception committee waiting for them when they hit the ground.

The women wanted the silk parachute and the men wanted the man! The Mighty Eighth had rained death and destruction down on them and they wanted revenge. Civilians attacked and maimed or killed the airmen before German soldiers could rescue them from the mob. Former POWs, reported that when they were captured, they saw bodies of Allied airmen hanging from trees near German interrogation centers! Guys that bailed out hoped they would be captured by regular army (Wermacht) troops and not the dreaded SS storm troopers or an angry mob of civilians.

German soldiers had orders to hold captives for interrogation and prisoner of war (POW) camps. Every airman was interrogated for information about his plane, equipment and airbase. The International Geneva Convention of 1929 spelled out specific rules for the humane treatment of military prisoners. Captives were only required to give name, rank and serial number and most of that information was clearly stamped on the "dog tags" hanging on a chain around their neck. However, it was a fight to the finish and German intelligence officers were under pressure to gain every piece of new information. The interrogation was usually conducted by an officer who spoke excellent English and the session often ended with abuse or threats of death. SS storm troopers held cruel interrogations, many of which ended in torture or death. Prisoners of war were to be treated humanely according to the rules of the Geneva Convention. Early in the war, it was evident that German and Japanese POW camps did not observe those rules and were guilty of inhumane treatment, including torture, starvation and atrocities. Their POW camps were in direct violation of the agreement they had signed in 1929. Leaders of both countries were hanged or imprisoned during "war crimes" trials held after the Allied victory

> *"Jumping into enemy territory was like jumping from the frying pan into the fire !"*

> *Hutch*

PRISONER OF WAR CAMPS

The Geneva Convention is a series of treaties adopted by civilized nations to assure proper treatment of prisoners of war and wounded no longer able to fight. This idea began in 1864 during the Civil War when the Red Cross was recognized as a neutral agency to provide aid and food to prisoners.

The Geneva treaty of 1929 was adopted in 1931 to set out details on the humane treatment of prisoners of war. Germany and Japan generally ignored all Geneva Convention rules in World War II. Post war trials punished many of the war criminals with death and long jail sentences for the atrocities their troops committed against prisoners of war and civilians during their reign of terror. A fourth treaty, was adopted by 194 countries in 1949 to update the first three, it calls for humanitarian treatment of prisoners of war, wounded and civilian victims.

Germany built more than a hundred POW camps early in the war. They were scattered throughout thirteen military districts. Camps were designated for prisoners from various enemy forces such as seamen, ground troops and air force. A Stalag Luft was controlled by the German Air Force, the Luftwaffe. Two of the largest camps were the Moosburg VII A and the 250 acre Stalag XVII B at Krems, Austria. The Krems camp, designed for 12,000, had records of 120,000 prisoners when it was liberated by Russian troops. These permanent prisons were constructed in 1939 and surrounded by double fences six and thirteen feet high. They were complete towns with facilities for thousands of military prisoners. The POW camps were very different from the concentration (death camps) for Jews, political prisoners and undesirable German citizens. Dozens of camps like Auschwitz, Dachau, Buchenwald, etc. had gas chambers and crematoriums to carry out the systematic program of killing all prisoners.

Moosburg POW Camp, Stalag VIIA was a permanent camp 40 miles north of Munich. Built in 1939, the eighty-five acre camp was designed to hold 10,000 prisoners complete with barracks, parade grounds and guard towers and facilities for 10,000 prisoners. It was liberated by units of General Patton's 14th Armored Division April 19, 1945. The camp held records on 130,000 prisoners from all allied countries. 80,000 were in the camp and thousands were assigned to more than 125 Work Kommandos (labor gangs.) These men did slave labor in factories, on farms or repaired Allied bomb damage to railroads and buildings.

Stalag 17B at Krems, Austria was even larger and also used slave labor gangs. POW camp conditions worsened and prisoners suffered from disease, starvation and over-crowding as Germany slowly lost territory, food and supplies. Most long term prisoners lost thirty or more pounds due to poor food and lack of it. Germans closed POW camps in 1944-45 as Allied troops advanced and prisoners were loaded into cattle cars and transported to another camp. When transportation was not available, prisoners were forced to make long winter marches to other camps. Prisoners were weak from starvation and many men did not survive the ordeal. Stragglers were beaten, shot or left to die beside the roads. Hitler had ordered guards to move prisoners to another camp or kill them when Allied troops got too near. Germany's POW camps were solid evidence of the cruelty and punishment approved by Adolph Hitler and Nazi leaders of the Third Reich.

"A man never completely understands Freedom, until he loses it!"

T/Sgt. Bob Stahlhut – POW

T/Sgt. Robert Fred Stahlhut of Indianapolis, Indiana was a B-17 flight engineer and top turret gunner in the 384th Bomb Group at Grafton Underwood. He was a bomb crew member of the Eighth Air Force early in World War II and his plane was shot down Labor Day, 1943. Stahlhut's story reveals many details of surviving as a prisoner of war. It was an experience he shared with over 25,000 thousands young airmen who suffered the same fate. I deeply appreciate the fact that he allowed me to include portions of his memoirs: **The Way I Remember It.**

OFF TO THE WAR --- Our crew completed combat crew training at Walla Walla and went home on leave. We returned to base and were assigned to fly a brand new B-17 Flying Fortress across the U.S. by way of Kearney, Nebraska and on to Syracuse, New York. We were to fly the Northern route to England and the first stop was Gander Lake, Newfoundland where we waited for clear weather before a night flight across the North Atlantic to Prestwick, Scotland. Every bomber was on its own. Our navigator spent the night taking readings with his sexton to make sure we were on course, the radio operator kept in touch with Kearney, while the pilots and I kept close watch for other planes. We broke through the clouds at dawn and the Mc Mahon crew landed in Prestwick in time for breakfast. I met my first Scotswoman in the chow line and was surprised when she asked, "Do you have any gum chum? When our crew left the Mess Hall, we were told to take our belongings out of the new plane. It was going to a Bomb Group, but we were headed to an advanced combat training school.

THE 384th BOMB GROUP --- We went from that school to the 384th Bomb Group at Grafton Underwood where we were put in the 544th Bomb Squadron. The enlisted men were quartered in a Quonset hut, a small tubular structure that slept 24 people, with three other crews. We took the bunks of a crew that hadn't returned from a bombing mission! Then we were shown around the base. It had a nice mess hall for combat crews only. We were given lockers at squadron headquarters and so on.

I remember the officer at the armament shop telling us that orders were, that no one was to carry side arms on a combat mission, but if we wanted one he would give us one before we left on a mission. His advice was not to carry one on raids over Germany. If we did take one when bombing targets in an occupied country, we should give it to the first friendly person we met, if we were shot down.

The 384th Bomb Group was made up of four combat squadrons: the 544th, the 545th, the 546th and the 547th. It also included a Sub-Depot Squadron, Military Police, Chemical Company, Q.M. Company, Firefighters and Weather Squadron, all were part of the 8th Air Force. The Group had started bombing Germany in June 1943 and by early August of 1943, had already lost over 20 planes , which added up to over 200 men, dead, injured or prisoners of war.

MY FIRST MISSION --- On August 15, 1943, I flew my first mission. One of the other crews had an engineer shot-up on the last mission so I was called on to take his place. My pilot also subbed on a different crew. It was a milk run (an easy raid). There was little flack and few fighters. Two days later, August 17, 1943 was the first anniversary of the 8th Air Force bombing of Germany (Daylight bombing). Prior to this all raids were done at night by the British to hold down casualties, so they wanted to make it a big one. Schweinfurt and Regansburg were to be the targets. The 8th Air Force was split in half. One half was to take one target (Schweinfurt) and return home, while the other half was to hit the second target and go on to North Africa. The Africa half was given the B-17s that carried the most gas. The newer B-17s had what was called Tokyo tanks in the wing tips, which gave them a lot more fuel.

Our group was to go on the shorter raid, so we ended up with the oldest B-17s in the 8th Air Force. They didn't even have enough planes for our crew, so we sat that one out. I was out on the ramp of the air field when the planes of the 384th started to come back. It must have been a rough one. Planes came in all shot up. Ambulances were running out to take men off to the hospital. One plane came in with wheels up. What a sight that was! It slid the full length of the field on its belly. And then of course, some bombers didn't return at all.

Several days later, our crew went on our first raid together. I don't remember much about it, except that we were attacked by ME-109 fighters and we saw a lot of flack. As we were approaching the English Channel, on our way home, one of the men in the rear of the ship called the pilot to say that we had a large hole in the horizontal stabilizer. The pilot sent me back to see how bad the damage was. I told the pilot it didn't look too bad to me. Not wanting to take any more chances than he had to, the pilot decided to slow our speed, leave the formation and make our way back to home base by ourselves. Further inspection of the damage when we were on the ground led us to believe that an antiaircraft shell must have passed through the stabilizer without exploding. Such an explosion could have taken off the stabilizer or maybe the whole tail.

It was about this time that the radio operator and I were given the rank of Technical Sergeant and we were able to squeeze in a 48 hour pass to London. I saw many of the sights like Buckingham Palace, Big Ben and the London Bridge. I also had a chance to see what it was like to see one of the largest cities in the world during a complete blackout. -

THE FATEFUL MISSION --- Labor Day, September 6, 1943 was our next mission, one I will never forget. We were awakened in the middle of the night. Briefing was the first step, (Remember, I said that we had the oldest B-17s in the 8th). Well, the briefing officer told us that many of our ships could not hold enough gas to make it to the target (Stuttgart, Germany) and back to our base without stopping along the way to refuel. We would be flying at about 20,000 feet, where it gets very cold, sometimes 40 or 45 below zero. This ship was older than anything we had seen in training. It was a B-17 E, with an old-type oxygen system that we had not used before and there was no place to plug in our electric heated suits (sort of like an electric blanket type deal, but a suit), so we had to dress very warm for the flight.

It was daylight by the time we got in the air. We climbed as fast as we could. Then came the test- firing of our machine guns and getting into formation for the long flight to Stuttgart. It seemed like a long time flying back and forth across the target before we dropped our bombs and headed for home. We were attacked by ME- 109s (Messerschmitt) along the way, but they pulled back when we were over the target because the ground fire flack was pretty heavy.

Something had knocked out one of our inboard engines, so the pilot, without warning the rest of the crew, dove for cloud cover! I came down out of my turret in a hurry. When the pilot saw the look on my face, he called the rest of the crew and told them that we were still OK, but he could no longer keep up with the formation on just three engines. We flew along for a while with three engines going and one propeller feathered, then the other inboard engine started acting up. It soon stopped, but there was not enough oil left to feather (stop) that propeller so it kept wind-milling. I transferred all the gas from the two inboard engines to the outboard engines. Since we were now left with only two good engines we were using gas much faster than four good engines would. Put that together with that they told us before we left England, there was no way we could make it back home. The pilot asked the navigator to let him know when we were over France. We wanted France because we had a better chance of evading capture in an occupied country.

WE BAILED OUT --- Soon the empty lights came on for the two outboard engines. The navigator said we were over northern France, so the pilot said that we should start bailing out. I never knew in what order we left, but bail out we did! The bomb bay doors were open so that's the way I went out. It was like the rushing of a mighty wind for a few seconds and when it quieted down. I pulled the rip cord and as I floated down I could see a parachute on either side of me, but then I saw a B-17 coming at me in a wide circle. Only two engines were running and it had a wind-milling prop on one inboard that was making it turn. It had to be <u>ours</u>! It made about half a circle before it struck the side of a hill.

Then it was my turn to land. The parachute I was wearing was a chest pack snapped in front on the harness, which left me hanging with my feet out in front instead of straight down. The first to touch the ground was my feet and then the base of my spine. I was knocked out and I don't know for how long. When I awoke some man took me to hide in the woods. He left and then the Germans came.

It wasn't until many years later that I read what the Air Force had to say about that day in its "History of the 384th Bomb Group."

OFFICIAL REPORT OF THE MISSION (MACR) "Our bombers had as their objective today the large German industrial city of Stuttgart, in the southwestern part of the country. However, an overcast sky obscured the target from the wind in which the 384th's planes were flying and the Fortresses passed over the city without dropping their bombs. Targets of opportunity were selected on the return trip, although the seriousness of military damage resulting is doubtful. Captain Raymond Ketelsen, who led the formation, deposited his bombs on a German farm community, while another ship dropped their demolitions in a forest. The bombing was done helter-skelter, more to lighten the loads of the planes, than to inflict destruction. Gas tanks were running low after the long flight over the breadth of France into Germany proper. When the Group reached the French side of the English Channel, practically all peeled off and made for British territory in order to get under the wire of rapidly emptying gas tanks. Crews dumped guns ammunition and anything else that was detachable from the planes to lighten them for better mileage. Some planes landed at emergency fields. However, when it was time all planes should have been accounted for, five were still missing. Some were believed to have landed in Switzerland and parachutes were seen over France. Still others may have gone down over the target. The flack at Stuttgart was intense.

"Crews of missing ships-544th Sq. 2nd Lt. James J. McMahon, pilot, 2nd Lt. Rudolph P. Froeschle, co-pilot, 2nd Lt. Lesta E. Shackelford, navigator, 2nd Lt. Arthur H. Dinnodorf, bombardier, T/Sgt. Marcus A. Carr, radio operator, T/Sgt. Robert F. Stahlhut, engineer, S/Sgt. John W. Tripp, ball turret gunner, S/ Sgt. George J. Kemp, tail gunner, S/Sgt. Scheley H. Jessup and S/Sgt. James E. Savage, waist gunners."

THE CAPTURE --- The Germans who captured me made me sit at the bottom of a ditch until they could get transportation. The first stop was the Gestapo headquarters where they asked a few questions, nothing too serious to this point. Then it was off to the jail in Metz where I was put in a single cell overnight. While I was there I didn't see any other POWs.

The next morning I was put on a passenger train and taken to

Frankfurt. Another crew member, Jim Savage, one guard and myself were in a compartment. When meal time came, the guard pulled out a sausage roll, his knife and some bread and made us some sandwiches. Soon we were at Frankfurt and we were walking down some steps in the train station when a little old lady came up to us. She shouted something at me, which I couldn't understand and then she spit at me. Once at the Dulag-Luft camp in Frankfort, I spent several days in a holding cell and then was sent to the interrogation center. After a talk with those "friendly fellows", I was put in solitary for the next 14 days. During that time, they called me back for another chat about five or six times and each time I saw a different man, but the questioning was always similar. He would offer me a cigarette and be very nice, but as I refused to answer his questions, he would get angrier and threaten me. Turning me over to the Gestapo was his favorite threat. Not letting me out of solitary was another good one.

My wallet, wristwatch, a pack of cigarettes, escape kit (included maps, compass, emergency rations) had been taken from me before I was put in my cell. For meals, I was given a hot drink (they called it coffee), a piece of bread sliced about half the thickness of our bread, with a little margarine on it for breakfasts, a bowl of barley soup for lunch, then the breakfast meal was repeated again for super. The room was very small with a bed made of wood (no springs, no mattress, no blankets and no pillow.) When I wanted to go to the bathroom I had to turn a little handle that dropped a flag down on the outside of the door. The guard would come (at his leisure) and take me. He would then hurry me until I was back in the cell. There was no such thing as washing or brushing my teeth. The window in my cell had bars and shutters. When those shutters were closed, it was so dark, I could see nothing. I could hear voices in the cells next to me, but I never tried to make contact. I kept thinking they might be Germans, trying to get prisoners to slip and give them some information.

On my 14th day of solitary I was again taken to be interrogated. The man said, "I'm going to send you on to a permanent camp. We now have all the information we need about you." He proceeded to show me a list of 10 men, our group and squadron numbers. I didn't let on that two of those names were wrong. That told me that two of our crew had not been captured. I was then taken to a camp nearer the center of Frankfort. It was another holding camp, but unlike the first one, it was a very nice place. Meals were served four times a day in a mess hall. We could even take showers. I was told that representatives of the International Red Cross were brought to this camp to see how well prisoners were being treated.

STALAG 7A --- Next, a bunch of us POWS were put in a box car for shipment to Stalag 7A. I had the misfortune to suffer from dysentery on the trip (we called it the GIs). There was no place to go but the open door of the train. Under normal circumstances it would have been embarrassing but I didn't seem to care. A German doctor gave me some powdered charcoal to eat and it took care of my problem.

That night the British bombed near us. The train stopped and the guards got out of their car and went into the ditch. Our door was locked, but we couldn't have gone very far if we were able to escape. They had taken our shoes from us before we left Frankfort. The next evening we went through the same thing again. Our train was not hit either time. The next day we were taken into Stalag 7A, near Mooseburg. It was there that I was photographed and given German dogtags. Each camp had its own series of numbers. Mine was Stalag 7A 113517. This camp was guarded by the German army (Wehrmacht). Our Air Force enlisted men had been trying for nearly a year to get them to send American Air Force POWs to a camp guarded by the Luftwaffe (German Air Force). Since we were "Army" Air Force, they were treating us like army.

I was there only a short time when they put all 1,500 American Air Force enlisted men in "40 and 8" box cars (that's 40 men or 8 horses) and sent us to Stalag 17B, near Krems, Austria. Some thought escape might be easier from 7A so they traded places with prisoners from other countries. I knew of two Russian POWs who would be going along with us. A Polish American stayed close to them and tried to teach them English as best he could. Pronouncing their new names and serial numbers was the first thing they had to learn. It's not hard to understand, but how they made it through the picture check, I never knew. There were even Americans trading identities with other Americans. Only Air Force men were being moved. The Ground Force men would stay. (I didn't see the Russians again for about a year and by that time they could speak English as well as any of us.)

During our trip to Stalag 17B, attempts were made to find a way to escape. At last a door was forced open between the cars, but while we were waiting for a good place to jump off, we came to the Danube River. Just across the river was the end of our journey. We were unloaded and marched the rest of the way to the camp. The first meal was, as I remember it, pumpkin soup.

STALAG 17B --- Stalag 17B was a large camp, run by the army, but they put all the American Air Force enlisted men in the far corner with Luftwaffe guards. The prisoners in the camp were permitted to go from one part to another, but not the Americans. There was a large double fence with patrolling guards and dogs between us and them. All the enlisted men from our crew, with the exception of George Kemp, who was never captured, were put into barracks 36A. Believe it or not, the inside of that barracks looked a lot like the set of "Hogan's Heroes". Each barracks held about 150 men. A barracks chief was elected and someone was appointed to divide up any food that came to the barracks.

Much of the time we had Red Cross food parcels, food that was sent to us by the American Red Cross, through the International Red Cross. This was part of the agreement signed by the Germans at the Geneva Convention. The Germans started sending this food to a kitchen and mixed it with the soup they were feeding us. Sound good? Not so, many times their potatoes were rotten and if there was any meat it was likely to have worms in it. It was a waste of good American food. A huge cry went out from us, so the Germans running the camp started passing out the parcels to us. Each of these parcels was supposed to last one man one week. As the Germans handed them out they would jab each can with a bayonet. That was so we couldn't store up a supply of food for an escape. When we took them to our barracks, the first thing we would do was spread some margarine in those holes. This would keep the food edible longer.

Red Cross parcels usually contained a pound can of powdered milk, a can of fish, a can of corned beef or spam, a can of powdered coffee, a D ration bar (chocolate), a block of cheese and three packs of cigarettes. We formed small groups to make it easier to cook and divide our food. Jim Savage and I kept our food together all the time we were there. Bread (that's what they called it) was sent to the barracks once a day. It was not sliced. It was cut into pieces, maybe six or eight men to a loaf. If it was fresh it didn't taste too bad but let it get old and it did not mold, it got hard as a rock. You could pound a nail with it.

Since there was only a small stove in each barracks and little or nothing to burn in it, the kitchen would send us hot water each morning to make coffee with. The hot water, soup and boiled potatoes were sent to the barracks in a big wooden bucket. It looked like a whiskey keg cut in half with two holes located across from one another. A wooden pole was then put through the holes and two men would carry it. When the kitchen had anything for us they would send a runner to each barracks. Now and then we would get some meat, like the time that bombs had killed some oxen nearby. There were times we were told that the meat we received was from horses. There was no money in the camp, so the barter system became a method of trade. Everything was valued by how many packs of cigarettes it was worth. Trade was conducted between the prisoners and the guards that came into the camp. Guards brought things into the camp for trade without their officer's knowledge. They hid it in the metal can that was part of their gas masks.

Trade was also conducted by Americans with other nationalities. I mentioned the double fence. Such a fence was all around the outside of the camp. About 10-15 feet inside the double fence was <u>a single strand of barbed wire</u> (known as a warning wire) mounted on top of posts, about a yard high. In the area between the double fence and the warning wire were signs posted. In the center at the top and bottom the word WARNING was printed in large letters. Between was printed:

"ANYONE CAUGHT TOUCHING OR CROSSING THE WARNING WIRE WILL BE FIRED UPON WITHOUT WARNING".

One day an American was trading with a Russian in the next compound. The American threw some packs of cigarettes to the Russian but they didn't all make it across that second warning wire. The Russian thought he could beat the German guard so he jumped the wire and grabbed the cigarettes but the guard was too fast for him. He didn't make it back. The Germans left his body out there as a warning, long enough for all of us to see.

Note--- Sgt. Van T. "Ike" Wright of Bloomfield, Indiana (tail-gunner with the Bloody Hundredth) was a POW in Stalag 17B at this same time. His story in my second book, "Bombs Away" also tells of this event and a later one when an insane prisoner crossed the 'trip wire' and was killed by guards! He also described the sadistic treatment of the starving Jewish prisoners on their 'death march'. I arranged for Bob and Ike to meet at a POW Veterans' meeting at Crane, Indiana in 2009.

HUNGRY FOR NEWS --- The Germans didn't permit us to have radios in the camp, so some of the men traded with guards to get the parts necessary to make crystal sets. It was not necessary to buy the wire needed for antennas, because it was plentiful in the many heated suits that were worn by men when they were shot down. We had an information system all our own and those gathering the news would not report anything as fact unless two or more crystal set operators received the same report. It would be written up each day and someone would go from one barracks to another to give it to the men. When the news man would come in the barracks, he would look around the room for Germans. If none were sighted, someone would call out, "At ease, the news." Then a table would be slid into the center aisle for the news man to stand on and he would give us the news of the day. Many times we could hear that someone like Churchill or Eisenhower said that the war would be over in six months. That was a report everyone was ready to believe.

NEWS OF THE INVASION ---When at last the invasion of Europe came (June 6, 1944), we heard it first from the German guards. They said, "We will throw them back into the sea." They were never able to get the job done. While many of our countrymen never made it beyond the beaches, others kept coming. Hand-made maps were soon posted all over the inside of the barracks. We followed the progress of our liberators as they slowly came toward us. I thought the Germans would quit fighting when their homeland was invaded, but they kept at it for another eleven months.

With a new bunch of new prisoners that came into camp one day, was a man named Fred Wagner. His crew had shared the Quonset hut with our crew back in England. Every new prisoner has to tell his "Shot down story" a few times. Here is his: Fred had only a few missions to go before he would go back to the states on rotation. While returning from a bombing mission over Germany, the bomb bay doors would not go up automatically, so the engineer went to the bomb bay to crank them up by hand. When the walk around the oxygen bottle he was using ran low on oxygen, he asked that another bottle be brought to him. Fred, being the nearest man took a fresh 'walk- around' bottle into the bomb bay. He disconnected his own oxygen, thinking he would be back in time to hook up again. Instead he passed out from lack of oxygen and fell out the open bomb bay doors. He came to in time to pull his ripcord and floated to the ground. A few days later, the rest of his crew completed their twenty-five missions and went home without him. Fred spent the rest of the war as a guest of the Third Reich.

THE ESCAPE ---Life was going on day by day when one day an American was brought into our camp. The next day when the Germans came back to get him from the barracks, he was nowhere to be found. The story I heard was that he had escaped many times from other prison camps and this time he was being sent to a concentration camp. Since no one knew where he was, the Germans became angry. The Luftwaffe ordered us all outside. While they were giving us a "number and picture check," the barracks were searched. They kept us out all day. The next day it was the German army's turn. Then the third day the Gestapo took over. Wagonloads of our things were taken from the barracks, but they never found that American. These events became known in the camp as "the three day picnic."

One day a squad of guards came to one of the barracks and tried to take the men out of the camp. None of the Germans spoke English and the only thing our men could make out was that they were going to a Keno. Since no one knew what a Keno was, they didn't want to go. Some went out the windows. Others ran away when they got outside the barracks. Those who went with the guards came back in a couple of hours. They had been taken to the guards' part of the camp where they had been made to view a movie. I got to see several of those movies. None were in English, though. They were French films with German captions.

It seems the Geneva Convention said that POWS were to be given money while they were being detained! So they could buy things at a PX. Since we had no PX, this was our captor's way of trying to comply with the Convention. I wish we would have had a place to buy things. I was not able to brush my teeth for over six months and my beard got quite long.

The Geneva Convention required that leather soled shoes be given to POWS. The way the Germans supposedly complied was to take wooden shoes and tack pieces of leather on the bottom. Lice and bed bugs were a big problem. To combat this, the Germans sent us to the de-lousing facility about once a month. A whole barracks would go at one time. Hair cuts came first. (That's clippers over the top). We didn't have to worry about our hat sliding off for awhile. Those bristles would dig right into a knit hat. Next was the shower and while we showered our clothing went into a gas chamber. (The gas made them stink for a week). We could not linger in the shower because they would shut the water off soon after we got wet. They were not so fast about the clothing though. It would be several hours wait and there were no benches or seats in the waiting room. We just stood around with no clothing on. One day this all came to an end. Some fellows who didn't want to get their hair cut put margarine mixed with sand in their hair. The teeth on the clippers flew. Those guys were made to shower first and then some new clippers were brought out and they were given the burr. But that was the last time any of us were given a haircut.

A year had gone by and we had seen little bombing, since Austria was so far from any American or English airbases. When the Americans and English started getting bases in France and Italy, things did pick up a bit. It was the English at night and the Americans by day. I remember one night the air raid siren sounded and most of the men ran outside to the slit trenches. (It was not uncommon for many of the men to ignore the sirens and continue with what they were doing.) These trenches were dug in the compound behind the barracks, in a zigzag fashion so one could get protection from any direction. They were rather narrow and about

6 to 7 feet deep. As we were out there watching the show we could hear two airplanes. We never saw either one but we could tell one was a British plane by the unsynchronized propellers and the rapid fire of his .30 caliber machine guns. Then came the loud drone of the German plane and the slow but loud boom-boom of his cannon. If either was shot down that night we did not witness it. The show we watched from the trenches were flares dropped by the British to show planes that would follow, the way to the target. When the target was lit up with many flares, it was referred to as a "Christmas tree". Once the bombing began, the fires started by that bombing would keep things lit up.

MENTAL STRAIN --- Mental strain was a problem in the camp. One night a man in our barracks went crazy. He started yelling, but he was soon calmed down by one of the other men. The barracks next to us had a man try to jump out the window after curfew. He would have been shot since there was a camp rule that did not allow anyone on the grounds after curfew. One time a man, in broad daylight, ran to the fence and started to climb over. When the guard leveled his rifle some of the guys called to him and told the guard that the man was sick in the head. That did no good. The guard shot the fellow anyway. Another night we heard gun fire and when I heard an infantry man in our barracks yell, "Hit the deck" that's just what I did. We soon heard Germans running around outside. It seems that two of our men tried to escape and were shot. Stray shots also got a fellow in his bunk in the next barracks. The next morning we could see blood in the snow where the two were stopped.

Despite all the bad things that happened, there were many good times. Take the time we had been out of food parcels for some time when rumor came that a box car had come into Krems for us. It was not food at all, most of it was <u>toilet paper!</u> The YMCA had sent along some sports equipment. Most of it was allowed but the Germans cut up all the baseball bats because they didn't want us to have any clubs.

Since we were all Sergeants, we did not have to work outside the camp. We passed the time by playing a lot of cards. Some would play poker all night after parcels were handed out. I always hated to lose, so pinochle, euchre and contract bridge were my games. Did you know there are at least fourteen different kinds of solitaire? We would play so much at times that I would dream about cards at night. There was a time in late 1944 when the most seriously injured prisoners of each side were exchanged. We were happy for those who got to go home, but we would have liked to have gone home with them. I can't remember the exact date, but in early April 1945, we began to hear the sound of big guns to the east of us.

ON THE MOVE --- The Germans told us that the Russians were entering Wien (Vienna) and that they were going to move us to another camp north of Linz. We packed what we could carry. I made a pack out of the tops of two winter undershirts, crossed the arms and sewed up the neck. I was pleasantly surprised to see that it worked quite well. Many of the things that had been collected over the last year and a half were burned before we left. For the next month or so we were on the road.

The Germans divided us into groups of about 500 each. There were over 4,000 of us American POWS by that time. Each group had only a few guards. We could have slipped away rather easily, but I felt that while there was danger either way, the safest was to stay with a large group. (I have heard since, that Hitler had given orders that all POW's were to be shot). We had also heard that the SS was patrolling around us to catch anyone who got "lost". One morning after spending the night in a barn, we were talked to by an SS officer. It seems, someone in our group stole some chickens. He did not look kindly on that practice and he advised us not to let it happen again. There were some threats made but since he only spoke German, we didn't take him too seriously.

The first day on the road was one of the worst. Most of us tried to carry too much, so the road was littered with overcoats and other things that became too heavy to carry. We were given a bowl of soup to eat in the evening. We had brought as much Red Cross food as we could save and carry, so we would dig into that a little. Cigarettes were the main thing we used to trade. One guy in our group used some cigarettes to trade for some eggs. He and his friend took out a pan, started a fire and got ready to fry them when he discovered that the eggs were hard boiled. I had another bout with dysentery (GIs) so I went on sick call. The Doc, 'an American officer', had set up a shop at a house along the way. A woman there asked

me where I was from. When I told her "America" she said, "Oh Canada"?
I was surprised that she didn't know more about the U.S.A. but I guess
she was partly right.

When the news of President Roosevelt's death reached us, the next
question was, "Who is President now?" Most of us were prisoners before
the last election so we didn't know who was VicePresident. One of the
newer men said that he remembered a man named Truman was running
for Vice President when he left the states.

We were rounding a curve one day when three of our guys, in front
of me, left the road and went under a small bridge. I did not think the
Germans saw them, but when we took a break a little later, we heard gun
fire back in the direction of the bridge. We finally reached the Linz area
and could still hear the sound of the big guns, so instead of going north
to the new camp, the Germans took us across the Danube through town
and then west. The bridge had some of our unexploded bombs lying there.
We guessed that they were preparing to blow up the bridge by putting the
bombs on top of their explosives.

The Germans had warned us before we got to Linz that the people
there were eating grass because of the food shortage and since they had
been bombed, they would not be friendly to Air Force men. I had been
wearing an RAF hat until that time, so it had to go. We walked right down
the center of the main street.

Only one other time had I seen this gang so quiet. That was the time
we passed a group of Jews going the other way. They looked like the
walking dead. Some had on good business suits. One man was straggling
and the SS man would jab him with his bayonet. This man appeared so far
gone that he just turned around and smiled. I'll never know what happened
to him, but I can guess.

We were on the road about a month when we came to a pine forest. The
Germans had sent a group of Russian POWs ahead to clear a path so fences
could be put up. They herded us into this area and we knew that this was
the end of the line. We set up lean-tos or anything we could make. Snow
would still fall at times so we wanted some kind of shelter. One group of
guys was even using a hatchet to make a log house. We had to walk out
to the road when we wanted to get water. Just past the road was a bluff

overlooking the Inn river. By climbing down the side of this bluff we could find springs pouring down to the river. The guards didn't seem to worry that we might escape. After all, where would we go?

AMERICAN PATROLS --- One day some fellows came back from the bluff saying they had seen American patrols across the river. We continued to see them for several days so a delegation of <u>prisoners and guards</u> was sent over to see if they could come get us. The American officers told the Germans that they couldn't take us until the next day, so the guards remained on duty another day. They could have run now, but where would they go? The next day some jeeps came up the road, and the Germans were taken away. The German food stopped at this point and we got nothing from the Americans for several days. Some of our men started walking to the nearest town for food, so I went along to get some for Jim Savage and myself. The name of this town was Brenau, the birthplace of Adolph Hitler. An American soldier gave some food to me and another fellow and we headed back. This soldier said he was in the 13th armored division of the 3rd Army. While we were walking along we saw Russian Ex-POWs digging up seed potatoes in the fields to get something to eat. We stopped at a farm house and asked a lady for a drink of water. The lady seemed surprised that we wanted nothing more than water. Jim Savage had stayed behind with our things. Shortly after I got back, the Americans came in with trucks and hauled us to an abandoned factory southeast of Brenau. Straw was placed on the floor so we had a nice dry place to stay.

THE TIDE HAD CHANGED --- The factory had a wall around it and we would sit on top and watch the German soldiers come walking down the road in small groups, still carrying their rifles. When they reached an American soldier posted at a crossroad, they turned in their weapons and continued down one of the roads. They would go on until they would come to a stockade. There they would be interned until they could be interrogated. It was a little sad to see these men, who just a few days before, had been soldiers defending their homeland against invaders. Now they would be prisoners, just as we had been. I found out later that most of them were sent to their homes soon after they were questioned.

One day while we were waiting for transportation to fly us to France, we were entertained by USO troops. They asked at one point if we had any requests. Someone called out, we want to hear that song, Don't Fence Me In

The USO man didn't think we would want to hear a song like that, but we had never heard it. All we had heard was that it was a popular song in the states.

The American Air Forces soon started taking us out. When it was my turn, a bunch of us were loaded on a truck and taken to an airport. On the way we went through Brenau and across the Inn river. The bridge was down, (I don't remember hearing them blow it). The American engineers had put in a pontoon bridge.

THE WAR IS OVER --- We had to stay at the airport over night. That evening I heard Winston Churchill say on the radio that the war was over. The next day while we were waiting near the landing strip, I saw a small German airplane land. An MP jeep drove out and the Germans handed them their side arms. The Germans were then taken to a holding facility. We were flown to France and then trucked from the airport to camp Lucky Strike, which was located outside of La Havre, France. On the way we stopped for a break and saw an Army Red Ball Express supply truck, being stopped by an MP on a motorcycle, "Where do you think you are going, to a fire?" said the Military Policeman, well, if we didn't know we were free before, we knew it when we heard those words!

At Lucky Strike we had a reunion with the officers from our crew. Because they were officers and we were enlisted men we had been imprisoned in different camps. Our pilot, who we hadn't heard from, had been caught in southern France sometime after the rest of us. He was trying to get into Spain at the time. After a brief reunion, we were given a shower and new uniforms. The first meal I had at Lucky Strike wasn't enough, so I got back in line for some more. An officer came up from behind and tapped me on the shoulder. He said, "Haven't you gone through the line once?" I told him that I had. He said he would like to let me eat as much as I wanted, but someone had eaten so much that it killed him and they were being more careful now, so it was "Sorry, no seconds."

HEADED HOME --- Soon we were loaded on the SS le June headed for home. Our first stop was Liverpool. Then we joined a convoy for the USA. It was nice to see that Statue of Liberty when we came into New York Harbor. Some say there was a band to greet us. I don't remember one. We went on a ferry boat and then by train to Camp Kilmer, New Jersey. After that it was Camp Atterbury and then home for 60 days.

POW stories by Bob Stahlhut, Ike Wright and Corbin Willis paint a very clear picture of the mistreatment and suffering endured by prisoners of war in WW II German POW camps.

2ND LT. CORBIN WILLIS – POW

Major Corbin B. Willis Jr. submitted memoirs of his Air Force experiences to the Veterans History Project of the Library of Congress as a record for his children and grandchildren. The complete article tells the life of a career airman who enlisted in as a buck private in 1941 and rose to the rank of Master Sergeant before he entered the Air Cadet program. June 1944, he was 2nd Lt. Corbin Willis, flying the Northern route to England as co-pilot of a B-17E with the Lt. Albert Pierce bomber crew. He was stationed with the 832 Bomber Squadron of the 486th Bomb Group at the Mighty Eighth at Sudbury. A base I once visited to see my old Radio School buddy, Keen Umbehr. (See 'The Life of Riley in Through These Eyes')

Major Willis served in both WW II and Korea and logged over 3,300 hours flying time in many types of planes. His story is extremely interesting and is available on the computer at the Veterans History Project. I recommend it to all. I chose to include excerpts from his memoirs of his experiences as a German prisoner of war.

FLYING FORTRESS DOWN --- November, 1944 the Lt. Albert Pierce crew was flying its 22nd mission. The target was a factory and a military complex at Magdeberg, Germany. The formation was flying at 27,000 feet near the front third of the 1500 bomber stream. Flak knocked out two engines and the oxygen system while they were over the target and they dropped down to 4,500 feet to try for an Allied base in France. However, they were hit by more anti-aircraft fire as they passed over Cologne and one engine was on fire. The order was given to bail-out before the plane exploded. The wounded radioman had been bandaged and given a shot of morphine. He was unable to bail out, but a waist gunner held on to him and pulled his parachute ripcord after they jumped together.

Lt Willis said, "While descending, I looked down to see where I was going and saw a large field with a lot of people gathered on one side. It was so quiet I could hear the wind whistling past my ear and the people shouting below. I pulled the chute lines to drift away from them, but my chute started oscillating back and forth. I hit the ground on my back which numbed my whole body and I was dazed when I got to my feet. I hardly got to my standing position when a farmer hit me square in the back with a spade (shovel) and toppled me forward. I started to get up and was hit in the face by fists and knocked down again. I was so dazed I have no idea how many times I was hit, but suddenly the crowd was stepping back and I was being protected by a German Tank Corps soldier with a sub-machine gun. He ordered the crowd away from me. Some of the farmers were screaming at him and he struck at least two of them to get them out of my vicinity. ---The soldier walked me about a half mile a put me in a wire enclosure --- It gave me a chance to recover from the beating I took from the farmers. I had black eyes and a swollen jaw. Later I was marched to a local military sub-station and searched. Everything was taken away except the clothes I was wearing. ------

The nine men on our crew landed in the area, but only five of us had survived. Four of our crewmembers were killed on the ground by the angry civilians. The wounded radio operator was killed on a stretcher while on the way to the hospital."

Note---The airmen were locked up, and transported through various interrogation stations before arriving at Stalag Luft III south of Berlin.

Willis writes, "We started our day at sunup --- and stood our roll calls—"appalles" —as they were called. It would take a good hour to finish roll call for the 7000 plus POWs—after roll call we started our breakfast and our tea – They gave us bread --- made of sawdust and potatoes. It could be stored in warehouses for years without a problem. It tasted like sourdough bread and was only really potable when toasted --- so we had toast and ersatz (imitation) jam and margarine. The tea came from food parcels we sometimes received from the Red Cross.

Four men had to share any of the eleven pound boxes of food sent by the Red Cross. The Germans also punctured all cans so prisoners had to eat the food before it spoiled. This prevented prisoners from hoarding food for an escape attempt. However, the "barrracks committee" would sometime approve a good escape plan and help hoard food or sell it to guards for money for the escapees.

"Our rooms were small and held eight to ten men. Our beds were stacked two or three high --- we had one long table with benches and a wood stove for heat and cooking. The beds had wooden slats to keep you from falling through to the lower beds. We were issued two horsehair blankets, a pillow and a straw mattress. Speaking of mattresses, I had a legacy from my interrogation cell in Weise. I got the scabbies from the mattress in that cell. The only remedy was to shave my head and use a sulfur and glycerin solution daily for weeks on end. The cold got to my head and I had to wear a stocking cap, even to bed.

Those bed slats I mentioned served another mission. The grate of our stove could be lifted at night for a crew to enter a tunnel being dug under our barracks; the bed slats had to be used to shore up the sandy soil --- when it was my turn to give up my bed slats, it required using one of my horsehair blankets as a hammock nailed to the sides of the bed to support my weight. I remember I was losing weight rapidly and had little real strength, so when I was given ten nails to hold the blanket in place, I was able to pound in only seven and that was the end of my strength. I sat on the floor and actually laughed. It struck me so funny that I didn't have the energy to pound ten nails in place! The tunnel construction also required all of us to sew extra pockets to hold sand and dirt that had been from the previous night's work on the tunnel. We would walk around the parade grounds each morning letting out a little sand and dirt to mix with the graveled parade ground. ------ On one of my many trips on the parade grounds I noticed a lot of dandelions. Back home, my Mother used them in salads, so I took a large washbasin and collected it full to eat. Everyone was curious when food was involved, so when they saw our group this salad, we all shared and after that there wasn't a dandelion left on the parade ground! Later I discovered a lot of snails in the wooded area where I walked to gather firewood, so I gathered 52 of them in my wood sack and we divided them into two groups. The first day we boiled them --- they were horrible and slimy --- you could squish them out of their shells and eat them--- we did eat them. The following day we fried them in tallow from a candle and they were delicious---they tasted like fried shrimp. That was the last time I found a snail to eat! Another time, the camp commandant's dog disappeared and we all shared in dog meat soup --- the Commandant searched the entire compound for that dog, but didn't even recover it's collar --- don't know if that was eaten or not! ---- As the days got colder, I lost most of my body fat and my hips became nothing but bones. I had to sacrifice my sweater's warmth to make a doughnut shaped pad under my hips so I could sleep at night. Sleeping on my back created snores and loud disapproval --- I fashioned the doughnut, so I could sleep at night without a lot of pain."

Note --- Mail Call was one of the big events and POW's did receive some packages and mail. However, the Germans withheld much of it to keep morale low. Sacks of mail were found in the camp after the war.

"Many letters were shared because so many of us never received any letters while in prison ------- I for one did not receive any mail--- until I arrived in the USA. I was listed as Missing in Action. The telegram sent back to my parents and wife ---- reported the four crewmen killed by civilians and said the fate of the other crewmembers on our B-17 (Smokey Stover), was unknown because the bomber blew up."

Note-- 2nd Lt. Corbin Willis had been reported to be dead and so he served his POW time as Kreigegefangelin #8780 without mail. He was a man listed as dead by the Eighth Air force and his family. Willis said after his release he was able to get hold of his POW records. His identification card photo, taken when he was captured, showed his black eyes and swollen jaw from the beating by the civilians. He has kept it as a memento of his ordeal. Allied troops were moving rapidly across Germany toward Berlin in the spring of 1945 and the Stalag Luft III POW camp was in their path. The camp was closed and 7000 prisoners were forced to march to another camp. For many, it was a death march. The Willis story continues:

"The Russian armies were advancing --- toward Berlin and we were in their path ---so all 7000 were put out on the road to march toward Munich a (couple of) hundred miles I think. We started out in a column of four wide, but finally it dragged back for miles as we had little strength to fight the sub zero weather and walk for any distance. We had to stop often and when we did some POWs fell face down in the snow and we had to revive them and get them on their feet to keep them from freezing. My best friend had to be constantly helped and it used a lot of my reserve strength to practically carry him at times.

We had only the food we carried and that ran out in about three days so I survived on a box of sugar cubes (8 oz) for 6 ½ days. We stopped at a large glass factory and after giving us hot water for tea –they couldn't get a lot of us started walking again, so we got to spend two days there to help recover from our shuffling walk. ----- We moved on and passed a lot of refugee civilians fleeing from the front lines. Some of us gave them food for they were starving and pulling carts loaded with their household goods --- ironic isn't it?"

Note --- The march ended at the Mooseburg, POW camp, Stamlager VIIA – 40 miles north of Munich. Many men were lost and there were rumors of prisoners who couldn't keep up being shot by the guards. The camp was over-crowded and held an estimated 133,000 men. The Germans ran out of food, stopped feeding the prisoners. General Patton's tank column saved the day; they liberated the camp on April 28, 1945, two days before Germany asked for a truce!

"The liberation didn't come cheap, for many POWs died in the fighting to take over the camp --- Adolph Hitler had ordered all POWs executed and the German Army that guarded our camp would have done it, but the German Air Force would not allow it and took over. They later surrendered the camp without a fight, but German SS troops fired from their compound and the returned fire from Patton's tank column hit POWs in their barracks and killed some of them"

General Patton's Chief's of Staff's son was in our camp and the first tank through the gates was his --- he carried his son in his arms out to his tank. --- Gen. Patton came into camp riding in the back seat of his jeep --- what a target with his chromed helmet and pearl handled pistols. The General looked us over and saw our physical condition---so he told his supply officer that each man would have a square meal out of 7th Army rations --- he was told prisoners could not eat solid food --- it would kill us with kindness --- so he ordered soup kitchens set up --- the soup was too rich and it killed some POWs --- he allowed the Red Cross canteens to come in with doughnuts and coffee and that killed a few more POWs.

Finally, they realized experts were needed to advise on what to feed us, so they airlifted us to a location where they could control our diet, until we recovered enough to survive.

Note --- An office was set up in the former Commandant's office to prepare the flight lists. Willis volunteered as a typist and was able to find his POW records. He also was given a pass to go in or out of the camp. He later used that pass to visit the concentration camp at Dachau and see the crematoriums used to burn the bodies of millions of Jews murdered in the Holocaust. He said, "You could smell the camp for ten miles and the sight was unbelievable."

A Dead Man Returns Home --- POW Corbin Willis came home and learned of events that occurred during the six months he was believed to be dead. The American POWs were flown to Camp Lucky Strike near Le Havre and fed a diet of many rice dishes because rice is one of the easiest foods to digest. The starved POWs faced a long period of adjusting their stomachs to solid foods. Eventually they boarded a ship for a perilous voyage back to the USA. They arrived at Camp Kilmer New Jersey and all the men wanted to call home. The lines to the telephone booth were very long.

Willis said, "I finally got a telephone and tried to call my wife in Washington D.C., but our telephone had been disconnected --- I called my parents in Denver and got my Mother --- she did not believe it was me, so the operator in New Jersey, who placed our calls for us, --- finally convinced her it was not a hoax. My Mother proceeded to cry for about eleven long minutes before I could get a word in edgewise. I asked her about my wife, but she lied and told me she was not sure of her location, and I should to come home to Colorado --- I boarded the train, after getting new uniforms ---I weighed 121 pounds --- down from 165, so the uniforms only lasted a few weeks before I outgrew them.

I arrived in Denver in about three days by train --- my Mother told me that my wife had remarried in my absence and had started a family ---- that was the most painful experience I had as a POW --- I had accepted all the experience of combat and being a POW --- but was not prepared for that shock! My Mother and Father hovered over me day and night to try to make me happy and I finally accepted the fact of the situation and set out a course for my future --- I filed for divorce from my wife under the only statute allowed under Colorado law, adultery. The boy was born in my name because the other marriage was null and void --- the father, upon remarriage, had to adopt his own son. These are some of the tragedies of war that take a bite out of human emotions!"

Note --- ex-POW Corbin Willis recovered from the damage that had been done to his mental and physical condition and became a finance officer and pilot. He flew 57 combat missions in Korea as flight leader, was later a test pilot and later piloted B-29 bombers, KC-97 tankers, F-121 Fairchild transports in Newfoundland and C-54s in Arctic Resupply. He retired in 1961 with 3,000 hours of training and combat flying.

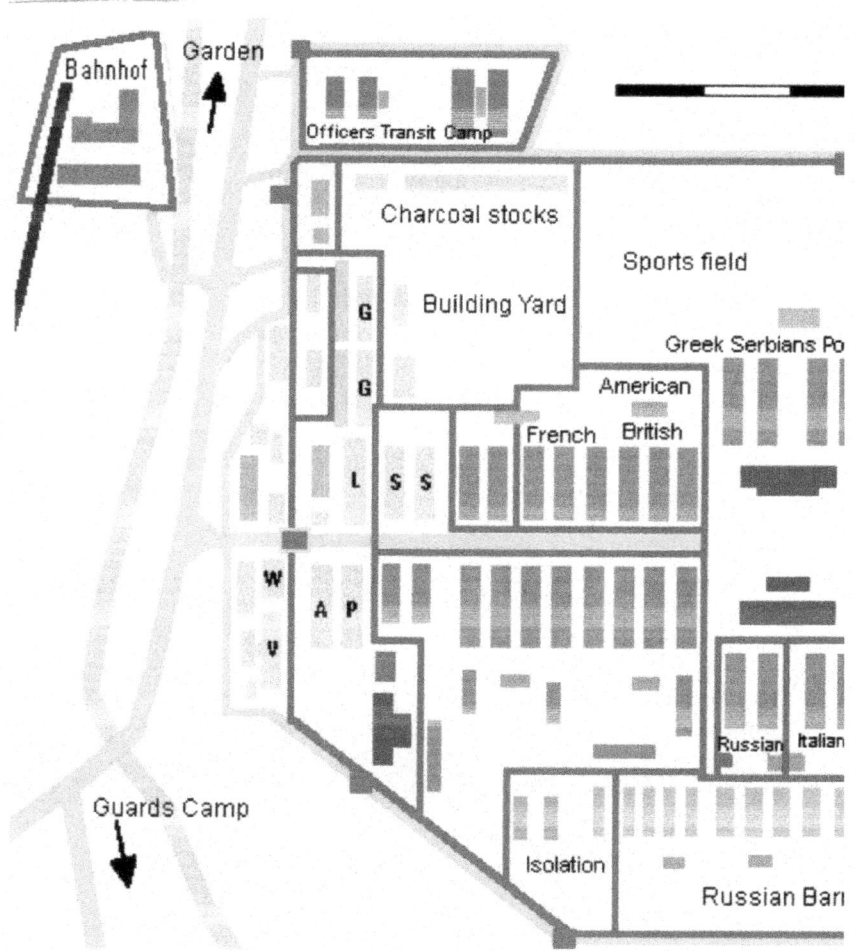

Garden

Bahnhof

Officers Transit Camp

Charcoal stocks

Sports field

Building Yard

Greek Serbians Po

G

G

American

French British

L S S

W

A P

U

Russian Italian

Guards Camp

Isolation

Russian Bar

Moosberg prison was built in 1939 to house 10,000 men, but was greatly over-crowded by war's end. POWs were segregated and received different treatment because of rank and nationality.

Badger's Beauty, a B17F of the Bloody Hundredth Bomb Group, crash landed in Normandy on October 4, 1943. The crew survived; five evaded capture and five became prisoners of war. Courtesy of the 100th BG Foundation

Oct 14, '44 – A flak shell exploded in the nose of this 398th BG bomber at 27,000 feet in a bomb run over Cologne. The blast killed the Toggleer and destroyed the cockpit instrument panel except for the altimeter and magnetic compass. Pilot 1st Lt. Lawrence de Lancey and co-pilot, 1st Lt. Phillip Stahlman dropped to 2,000 feet. Protected by two P-51 fighters, they managed to fly the plane without instruments. Lt. deLancey was awarded the Silver Star and navigator, 2nd Lt. Ray Ledoux, the Distinguished Flying Cross for exceptional skill in bringing the bomber and crew safely back to England. Lee Ann Bradley 398th BG Historian

Feb. 1, 1943 - A German fighter crashed into Lt. Kenneth Bragg's 97th BG plane and despite a 16 ft gash in the waist and tail section, he went on to the target to drop his bombs. Crew members used parachutes to tie control cables together and brace the plane's frame until they made it back to base. The tail section collapsed after a safe landing! USAF

CHAPTER FIVE

MISSION TO PARIS

This B-17 navigator describes a mission on November of 1943 when Paris was still occupied by Germany. The German Air Force (Luftwaffe) controlled the skies and Eighth Air Force losses were high. This mission was one year before I arrived at the 490th Bomb Group. During that year Allied forces had launched D-Day and chased German troops out of France. What a difference a year makes. The Templeton crew's first mission was December '44 and we were bombing Berlin!

The navigator's story: "Our target was another ball-bearing factory in the center of Paris and only one wing was going on this raid. Our group led this one and we flew the number two position in the lead squadron. We were "loaded for bear" with six 1,000 demolition bombs in the bomb-bay. We took off at 0630 to rendezvous with the group, but it was 1030 when we left England. The formation was flying at 23,000 feet. It was 35 below zero and we had a high tail-wind. Our escort of about eighty P-47 fighters joined us and we were over at Paris at 1115. We had flown from peace to peril in less than an hour and a half. Paris was completely covered by clouds; the only thing visible was the Eiffel tower sticking up through the clouds. One bomber was hit by flak over Paris. It dropped down and crashed into a bomber in our formation and both went down; I saw only three chutes. We headed home without dropping our bombs and were hit by over a hundred Me-109 Luftwaffe fighters. I got three good shots with my nose gun. One B-17 went down in flames. Five minutes later a fighter knocked out another Fort and followed it down. A third bomber went down and I saw three chutes before it crashed in the forest below. We reached the channel and another bomber dropped out of formation with two feathered engines, but got back to base later.

German fighter pilots had new planes and attacked our formation from out of the sun. Our P-47 escort fighters were a big help and had a lot of dog fights with our attackers. We lost six B-17s and had to drop our bombs in the Channel before we landed shortly after noon. It was a short mission, but definitely not one to build our morale!"

"Combat missions are hazardous to your health"

FLYING THE SOUTHERN ROUTE

The Army Air Corps used two routes, southern or northern, to fly planes across the Atlantic to combat areas in Europe and Africa. The season, destination and weather conditions determined which would be used. Both routes were dangerous and many planes and crews were lost in crossing, especially on the Northern route to Labrador, Iceland, Wales and England. Crews relied on their navigator and good weather to cross the North Atlantic safely.

The Southern route went to the West Indies and Brazil before crossing the Atlantic to North Africa. Some crews stayed with the Fifteenth Air Force and others flew north to England. Ground personnel went by sea as did replacement crews when bombers were not needed. Our crew went over on the Queen Mary, (my first ocean cruise) because they already had the planes. We were needed to replace boys who had completed their missions and/or the wounded and dead!

The 490th Bomb Group was one of the later bomb groups formed to beef up the Army Air Corps. The air war over Europe badly needed more aircrews and to destroy Hitler's Third Reich. Heavy losses in 1942-43 demanded more planes and crews.

The official birthday of the 490th was October 11, 1943 when the Mountain Home Army Air Base was established on the western plains at Mountain Home, Idaho. A small cadre of 52 officers and 72 enlisted men moved into tar paper barracks that were definitely not adequate for winter in Idaho. The leaders organized four squadrons (848-849-850-851) to receive air crews and B-24 Liberator bombers. The group was under-manned, but training and organization continued with seven aged bombers. Only two or three planes were flyable at any one time. Mechanics and maintenance crews gained valuable hands -on experience keeping them in the air. Training continued and the group gradually grew until February 1944 when 41 air crews arrived to bring the 490th Bomb Group to full strength of flying personnel. The group now had the airmen, ground crews and support units of a true bomb group. Seventy-two shiny new B-24 Liberators were delivered to the base in March. The Idaho weather cooperated and the group got in 634 hours of final phase training flying time for combat crew training in formation flying and eight simulated missions. During the final weeks a simulated Wing formation of 58 bombers proudly soared above several southern Idaho cities. By the end of March, the 490th Bomb Group of 412 officers and 1,696 enlisted men stood ready for overseas combat duty.

Orders for the group to prepare for overseas movement (POM) were received and on Easter Sunday, April 11th, the ground echelon boarded trains for a cross continent trip to New York. We later learned that our boys marched aboard a luxury liner, the Nieu Amsterdam, (converted to a troopship) and sailed for England with 8,000 other troops. Meanwhile, the air echelon loaded duffle bags and personal effects into their bombers and left the base in flights of twelve for the air base at Lincoln, Nebraska and four days of inspection and processing for overseas duty. Morrison Field, Florida was the next stop where pilots were briefed for the first leg of the flight overseas. The group took off at night; each pilot was handed his orders in a wax sealed envelope to be opened after an hour of flight. Everyone knew the 490th was flying the Southern Route to the war in Europe, but which part of the war? Were we headed for the Fifteenth Air Force in Italy or the Eighth in England? The opened envelope revealed the answer. The 490th Bomb group's destination was a brand new Eighth Air Force base at Eye, England!

The first leg was to Trinidad, British West Indies, then to Belem, Brazil. The third leg, some planes were sent to Natal and others to Forteleza, Brazil where planes and aircrews were prepared for a long night flight across the Atlantic to Dakar, West Africa! All planes made the it safely and the following day they flew across the Sahara desert to Marrakech, Morocco for a two day rest. Meanwhile the group's ground echelon had arrived at the brand new airbase in Eye, England (East Anglia) on April 26, 1944 and set up operations to receive the bombers.

In Morocco, crew navigators carefully studied the route of the last leg of the journey. The one day flight to England skirted over enemy territory and planes had to avoid flying over Spain, Portugal and France's Brest peninsula. The .50 caliber guns on all B-24 Liberators were loaded for combat and gunners were ordered to be alert for enemy fighters. Reality hit home and crews realized they were now in a combat zone! Two days later, April 28th, the first 490th bomber touched down on the runway at Eye! (Talk about timing!)

COMBAT MISSIONS

The men (boys) who flew daytime Eighth Air Force combat missions in WW II needed skill, nerves of steel and a faith that they would survive the hazards they faced in those deadly skies over Germany. A lot of thoughts go through your mind while you're plodding through the snow to a jeep or truck to take you out to your bomber. You've gone through briefing and you know the target. In a few hours you'll be soaring over the North Sea at 20,000 feet, at 20 below zero and on oxygen. You realize your life is going on the line and you may never see home again. With the optimism of youth you believe you'll make it, but you say a prayer to ask God's protection. Then, you toss your equipment into the truck and with a yell to the rest of the crew, "Let's get this show on the road!"

Thirty or so planes taxi out to the runway and line up for take-off. The roaring of the motors wake up all the Englishmen in the neighborhood, but they're glad the Yanks are here. You realize every B-17 is loaded with all the bombs and equipment needed for a mission to blow hell out of an Axis target. You also realize the enemy fighters and flak will be waiting to welcome you to the deadly skies over Europe!

There was a constant mental stress on aircrew members. We worried most of the night on the eve of a bombing raid, and "sweated out" every mission from take-off until landing. Most airmen feared flak worst of all because there was the reality of facing it over every target and unexpected locations along the way. Briefing sessions before a mission always included info on the safest route to and from the target. Aircrews relied on their pilot and navigator to avoid those hot spots, but many anti-aircraft guns were mounted on railroad cars, boats and river barges. Those mobile guns could raise havoc with a bomber formation. Flak was terrifying because there was no way of knowing when the sky would be filled with deadly exploding shells or who those iron slugs would strike.

Flak was sneaky, especially if the anti-aircraft gunners were "tracking" us! By the time we saw the puffs of black smoke from exploding shells, the sky around us was full of slugs of iron. It was even worse on our bomb-run to the target. We saw a sky full of flak that we had to fly into it to drop our bombs!! Flak brought death and destruction to our bomber formation as we opened our bomb-bay doors and released the bombs. We were always alert for an enemy fighter attack, but we could shoot back at them and our escort fighters could protect us. However, there was no defense against the flak barrage. Flak shrapnel could wound or kill crew members and a direct hit by an anti-aircraft 88 shell meant disaster. Severe flak damage to a bomber meant dropping out of the protection of the formation. Lone flak-crippled bombers became prime targets for lurking Luftwaffe fighters armed with machine guns, cannon and rockets. A crippled bomber's best chance of surviving was to be picked up and protected by some of our escort fighters until they could make it out of enemy territory.

Canon fire from enemy fighters could do great damage and a direct hit by a rocket would send an aircraft down in flames. There were seldom any survivors of a rocket blast. Every combat mission was a test of endurance and every crew member doing the best job at his position. The odds of a B-17 bomber completing a safe mission depended on luck, skill and the grace of God. There was no place for a crewman who was not in good mental condition. The crews on heavy bombers faced many hazards besides the actual mission. Examples include: crashes on take-off or landings, mid-air collisions, fire, engine or equipment failure, sub-zero temperature and anoxia (oxygen loss.) Combat fatigue was common and aircrew members sometimes "snapped" under the constant fear of death. Crews often flew two or three missions in a row. The common term was around the base was "flak happy," but we all sympathized, because we knew we might be the next victim of combat fatigue or a mental breakdown. Some boys endured unbelievable experiences in those dangerous skies of World War II. The guy who said he was not afraid, was either crazy or lying!

The Stars and Stripes, our army newspaper, printed daily reports and results of Mighty Eighth's bombing and fighter raids to show our successes in the war. We were always faced with the brutal statistics of the air war. Bombers that went down carried nine or ten men, so it was easy to count the casualties. Usually, the men (boys) listed as MIA (missing in action) were either dead or prisoners of war.

The Air Force recognized the fatigue problem and combat crews were given frequent three day passes to London or other recreational areas. Large R&R (rest and relaxation) centers were established in hotels or mansions for crews needing a week's vacation from the war! Airmen were keenly aware of the number of bombers and crews lost on each mission. Headquarters kept a special clean-up squad go to the barracks of crews that were shot down and move out all property and traces of crews that were lost. This "sanitizing" prevented looting and saved the missing crew's personal property for relatives. Most of all, it helped surviving crews forget their unfortunate buddies, but it was hard to ignore empty bunks!

Statistics report that a total of 350,000 men served in the Mighty Eighth during World War II. Approximately 120,000 were air crew members and only one crew in five completed their tour of duty. A total of 26,000 airmen were killed in action (KIA), thousands were wounded and 28,000 bailed out of disabled planes to be listed as MIA (missing in action.) Thousands of those guys served time in German prisoner of war (POW) camps, but many men were never located. The Eighth Air force had one of the highest casualty rates of any unit in the Armed Forces.

"A great number of American boys had their last night's sleep in a Nissan hut in England." Andy Rooney

Those figures explain why many airmen had the attitude expressed in the Bill Mauldin cartoon, when Willie turned to Joe and said:

"I feel like a fugitive from the law of averages!"

Non-Combat Dangers

There were many ways to die or be wounded in a combat zone, even when you weren't on a mission. Crashes, mid-air collisions, failed take-offs or landings, explosions, enemy air raids, bad weather, accidents, fire and equipment failures headed the list, but other freak accidents lurked in the background. Many boys died in mid-air collisions when aircraft were flying in close formations in combat and during practice flights. Ground crews worked around the clock to repair bombers and crews flew test flights to make sure the plane was ready for a long mission.

I remember one day, our Lt. Bill Templeton crew was testing a plane over Scotland and the number one engine conked out. We headed back to base and number four had to be "feathered." Now we were headed for Eye on two engines and Bill ordered everyone to put on parachutes and stand-by for the "bailout bell." I snapped my chest-pack parachute to the harness and joined the tail, ball and waist gunners in the rear near the waist door. Normally, I would have gone out the bomb-bay door, but we didn't want to open them and scare the people on the ground half to death. Through the waist window, we could see the black oil streaming out of number four and across the wing. Templeton and co-pilot Dale Rector, decided the two remaining engines could get us home and we landed safely. However, back at hut 29, Roddy, our engineer, told us that our number three engine was "acting up" when we entered the landing pattern!

Accidents from fueling planes to loading bombs, ammo and oxygen were a constant peril at airbases. Gasoline trucks of ground crews pumped gas into the wing tanks (2700 gallons capacity), washed the windows and checked the oil (148 gallons) on each bomber! Later, bomb-loaders on little tractors, towed trailer-loads of bombs down the runway to the hardstands, hoisted them into the bomb-bay of each plane and carefully hooked them onto their shackles. The bombs weren't armed, but all hell broke loose if one was dropped!

Rule #1: "If you see a bomb-loader running --- try to keep up with him!"

A bomb explosion at the 95th Bomb Group airbase at Alconbury in

1943, was a warning to all ground personnel. The group had flown only six missions when on the evening of May 27, 1943 ground crews were loading bombers with 500 pounders for the next day's mission. No one will ever know how it happened, but one B-17 exploded and blew the bomber and its ground crew to bits; leaving only a giant crater in the airfield. The disastrous explosion killed nineteen men and wounded thirty-five others. Shock waves killed men standing many yards away, while men resting on the ground survived. The blast destroyed four nearby bombers, crumpling or breaking them in half. Eleven others were seriously damaged and required months to repair. The loss of so many highly trained ground personnel and planes was a serious set-back for the airbase. The 95th Bomb Group later moved to Horham airbase (June 15, 1943,) it was the first group to bomb Berlin. (March 4, 1944) and flew a total of 320 combat missions and lost 157 aircraft, but one of their greatest losses was in that tragic accident early in the war.

Note --- I have a rare connection to the 95th BG because three of its members later became a part of my life: T/Sgt. Doyle Byers, Radio Operator-gunner became my brother-in law; my daughter married the son of S/Sgt Ralph Alexander, ground crew mechanic; Lt. William "Ed" Charles, navigator became a golfing buddy and later told me stories of his experiences. I inherited a copy of the Group's History album.

Air raids on London were frequent early in the war when Germany had bomber bases just a few miles across the English Channel in occupied France! The blast of the air-raid sirens was a warning of German bombers (buzz bombs later) in the sky and time to take cover until given an "all clear." Black-out curtains covered all windows, autos drove slowly without lights and nobody lit a cigarette outside.

Long range missions required bombers to make early morning take-offs. Planes lined up in the dark, revved-up all four engines and took off in close intervals, striving to get airborne before reaching the end of the runway. Nobody in the neighborhood slept when three squadrons (36 planes) left on a mission!

Pilots were challenged to get a loaded B-17 into the air. The total weight was about 55,000 pounds. The plane alone weighed 34,000 pounds plus a crew of ten, ammunition, 9,000 pound bomb-load, and full fuel tanks in each wing. The pilot had to rev his four engines for maximum power to roar down the runway and get airborne in time. Small wonder that engine failures accounted for many accidents before or after take-offs, causing planes to end up in the mud at the end of the runway or take-off too low and crash in some farmer's field.

Note --- From the diary of a member of the 100th Bomb Group at Thorpe Abbotts: "Beautiful weather today, but no mission, the PFF (pathfinder or radar dome) plane that was to lead the mission today took off at 1000 hours and crashed in a sugar beet field from low altitude on the first turn out of the traffic, near Eye. The crew of thirteen was killed and cremated along with three British civilians working in the field. The aircraft was said to be on fire --- pilot apparently tried to make it to Eye where a new runway is under construction --- was about 3000 yards short. Plane was loaded with phosphorous bombs, which accounted for the intense fire; most of the bodies were found in the radio room; probably braced for a crash landing."

One Colonel in the 100th who had seen too many accidents, submitted the following report concerning early morning takeoffs in the winter to his superiors: "Low clouds and icing conditions make pre-dawn take-offs and assembly in formation difficult, especially in layers of overcast before sunrise. Weather conditions (overcast) average 500 feet at our base. In spite of these handicaps our planes complete assembly and leave for the coast on time,although, many aircraft fail to get to their assigned location in their own group and some fly with other formations. First and Second Division planes assemble with the Third division. Pre-dawn take-offs in good weather are feasible, but bad weather take-offs should be limited. Too much combat efficiency is lost when planes can't make their assigned positions. Also, take-offs that require an immediate climb with a heavy load through thick overcast and heavy icing conditions are not practical. We could lose a whole formation."

Note--- I don't know what happened to that Colonel, but we were still doing those dangerous early-morning take-offs when I got there in November of 1944! We took off and climbed up through fog so thick (looking out the window in my radio room), I couldn't see our wing tips! The pilot spiraled upward in his own airspace, following a radio beam and we broke through the overcast to rendezvous with our group. Mid-air collisions and flaming crashes to the ground were not uncommon in those early morning skies over England!"

Bombers returning from missions faced many dangers:

1. Planes crashed and exploded landing with battle damage.

2. Bad weather sometimes closed an airbase and planes had to land at another field.

3. Belly landing due to landing gear failure

4. Running out of fuel and forced to ditch in the sea.

5. Wounded airmen dying on the long flight home.

6. Air raids and buzz bombs were always a possibility.

The above events and combat helped to account for the 26,000 deaths, 22,000 MIA (missing in action) and the heavy loses of planes by the Eighth Air Force. The aerial war of World War II was a monumental battle of men and machines that will never be seen again!

WEATHER HAZARDS

The "top brass" seemed bound and determined to send us up in all kinds of weather. Allied armies were fighting desperately in northern Europe and Italy. Our bombers and fighters were needed to support them on all fronts. Weathermen decided when was clear for bombers to take off, assemble over England and see the target when they got to Germany. Weather reports in those days were nothing like today. The weather forecasters gathered information by shortwave radio from various areas and ships at sea to make their prediction. Many evenings, the red flag was flying to alert the airbase for a mission. The next morning, hundreds of aircrews sat in bombers lined up on the runway waiting for the "go ahead" signal from the weather guys. Some mornings we sat on the runway for over an hour before, the mission was "scrubbed" (cancelled) and we went back to our hut for 'sack time' because we had been up since 0300. Other mornings, it was 'iffy,' but later we were cleared for take-off. We would take off with limited visibility, climb through a dense overcast into clear skies and head out on another mission. Too many men and planes were lost in mid-air collisions over England because of bad weather and poor visibility! One guy reported that General Arnold had said on the radio that there were plenty of replacement crews in the U.S. in case of heavy losses. I think he was just repeating a rumor, but it didn't do much for my morale!

One gunner, who had finished his missions, told us his weather story one dark and stormy night while we were huddled around our little Quonset hut stove trying to keep warm:

"On my fifth mission we were headed out over the north Sea when our number three engine caught fire and we had to abort and head back to base. We dropped down to hit a thunderstorm at 5000 feet and the fire went out, but the winds were so powerful that the plane went out of control! Our pilot fought the storm and got the bomber leveled out at about 2000 feet. He decided he was losing the battle to the strong winds and rang the bail-out bell to abandon ship. Five of the crew bailed out the waist door before we got any lower. I chose to stay with the plane during the storm because we were too low and the wind might destroy a parachute. Luckily, we came out below the storm and made it to an RAF field. The guys who bailed out were pulled from the water by British rescue boats and returned to base. Our crew and plane were ready to fly again in a few days."

The heavy snows of the winter of 1944-45 helped the German forces. Snowstorms kept Eighth Air Force planes grounded for over a week during the Battle of The Bulge that started December 16th. That bad weather gave German forces a great advantage when several divisions broke through Allied lines and overran our troops in Belgium. Snow and clouds kept our planes grounded many days and made flying missions difficult or impossible. Many mornings were 'zero visibility' and other times the guys on the ground crews spent thousands of hours cleaning snow from runways, hardstands and planes. Often, crews worked all night to get ready for a mission, only to have it cancelled. The work is best shown in a painting owned by the 398th Bomb Group titled "Clearing and Colder." Artist Jack Olson shows an aircrew walking to their bomber while a ground crew guy is on top sweeping off the snow. (see Bombs Away)

Once the weather cleared, the RAF and the Eighth sent thousands of aircraft to blast German troops and supplies. The biggest raid to date was Christmas Eve 1944 when we were part of a 12,000 plane mission. We said our bombs were Hitler's Christmas gift. January 28th was another bad weather day I'll never forget; it was the Lt. Bill Templeton crew's 10th mission. Only eighteen of the 490th planes made it into the air that morning before a snowstorm closed the base. Our little group joined the bomber stream on the Hohenbudburg mission. The flak was heavy over the target and our waist gunner, Robby Robinson, was hit in the head by a piece of flak. He would have died instantly, but his steel flak helmet saved his life.

DITCHING IN THE SEA

The thought of our pilots landing a 34,000 pound B-17 on water was one of my nightmares during my days in England. It was a routine that we had to review in training; something we practiced, but hoped we would never have to do it! 'Ditching' was the last resort, an often fatal attempt of a bomber crew to make it back to safety in a disabled plane.

Crews of combat damaged planes and those running out of fuel struggled to save their plane and land on friendly soil. This was especially true early in the air war when German troops occupied most of Europe. Pilots of damaged planes limping home with one or more motors shot out often gave crew members an option: bail out or stay with the plane to try to make it home with the distinct possibility of 'ditching' in the English Channel or North Sea. Airmen parachuting into enemy territory faced being killed by angry civilians or imprisoned in a POW (prisoner of war) camp for the rest of the war! Most men chose to stay with the plane and gamble on the odds of making over the water.

Ditching preparations included: Getting out of enemy territory; contacting Air Sea Rescue to give your location; reduce the plane's weight by throwing out all loose equipment, including guns and ammunition (with the proper tools the ball turret could be dropped), pull out the two inflatable rafts and the Gibson Girl emergency radio and pray for a calm sea. Crew members shed their parachute harness, checked their Mae

West life jackets, removed the radio room hatch and braced for a crash landing.

Pilots glided down to make a nose-up "pancake" landing on the water. The crew often had less than three minutes to scramble out of the plane into the inflated rafts and get away from their sinking bomber. A successful ditching required cranking the Gibson Girl radio to send out a pre-set emergency signal and avoiding hypothermia in the cold weather until Allied rescue boats arrived. Of course they were sometimes picked up by enemy boats and ended up as POW's.

Many planes were forced to ditch and men died in the freezing waters of the North Sea. Wounded men were often lost, others were trapped inside and went under with the bomber. Survivors were returned to active duty to continue flying combat missions. Planes were expendable, but the Mighty Eighth needed every available airman they could get! Ditching was seldom needed after Allied armies liberated much of Europe in 1944-45. Bombers with fuel, flak damage or engine problems could land at captured airbases in France or Belgium.

AN AIRMAN'S WEEK – JAN. 1944

Every heavy bomber carried a navigator; an officer trained to get the $265,000 plane and its crew to the target and safely home. This account of events from one man's diary during the in week of January 14-21, 1944 will give readers a better understanding of the mental and physical strain on airmen of the Mighty Eighth. Just imagine that you are this man. His experiences were common to thousands of Eighth Air Force crew members. Bad weather, fatigue and the fear of death took a heavy toll on the men (boys) praying to safely complete their required missions. The navigator's desk in the plexi-glass nose of the B-17 gave him a clear and wider view of the sky. He saw everything ahead, including the field of flak over the target or fighters attacking from twelve o'clock high. The navigator received a special briefing and had the latest information about our target and weather conditions. He was the officer the crew trusted to get us to the target and back.

"Day one --- Weather caused us to 'scrub' our missions on the last two mornings. Today's weather looked much better and we were briefed at 10:00 for a mission to bomb the same target, a German installation in France. This third time was a charm and we joined the formation in the low squadron at 12,000 feet. We were loaded with twelve 500 pounders. We reached the I.P (initial point) and peeled off by squadrons to start our bomb-run on the target. It was in an orchard and hidden by low trees. We made five bomb runs but never found the target, meanwhile they were shooting rockets at us from the ground. One Fort went down on the third run. I saw one chute open before the plane hit the ground and exploded. Enemy fighters came in on the fourth round and shot down two B-24s, no chutes opened! After the fifth run, we decided it was time to get out, so we left and brought our bombs back home. Landed at 1700 and no squadrons in our group had dropped their bombs.

Day two --- Ground school got 48 hour pass at noon and went to Ipswich. Back in time for a red alert tomorrow

Day three --- Up at 0200 and briefed for a mission to Frankfort in the Ruhr Valley. We were loaded with 36 incendiary bombs. The mission was 'scrubbed' and I took a 'liberty run' into town and went to a show.

Day four --- Got in some time on the Link Trainer this morning. A gas truck blew up on the flight line at noon and a B-24 crashed a few miles from here. They found five bodies in the wreckage, I think four bailed out. Worked out in the gym and played touch football this afternoon. Big red alert out for tomorrow. Never a dull moment in Jolly Old England!

Day five --- Frankfort, Germany again, population 500,000. We carried 38 incendiary bombs and flew in the #2 position to the lead plane in the high squadron. This was a 'Pathfinder' (radar) mission so the lead planes could see through the clouds. We were briefed at 0230 and took off at 0630 in the dark and had to climb through the clouds to assemble at 18,000 feet. Our group joined the bomber stream and we left the English coast at 0930.

We reached the I.P. (initial point to start bomb-run) on time and tossed out the chaff (aluminum strips) to throw off the flak guns. Dropped our bombs on the target and got past before they got the flak up. But about 100 fighters were waiting for us soon after we left the target. Those German fighters sure looked new and they were painted up in red and black. They hit the formations head on and also down through the groups. Our escort fighters did not show up and our gunners fought off fighters for about an hour on the way home!

One ME- 109 hit a bomber head-on, the fighter blew up and the Fort went down. Five minutes later Lt. Grey went down, five chutes opened. Ten minutes later another B-17 broke apart and went down and then another Fort turned over on its back and went straight down. Fifteen minutes later there was a mid-air collision when one Fort came up under another and cut off its tail section. We saw two bodies fly out before it spun down. The other plane tore its wing off and followed the first one down. We didn't see any chutes. Later another Fort pulled out of formation, one chute came out and the plane rejoined the group. Never did figure it out. Our P-47 fighters finally arrived to take on the 'bandits' and at 1330 we made it safely back to England

Note --- Some times, if an airman was severely wounded and could not survive the long trip home, the crew would bail him out, on the slim chance that he would get medical treatment from the enemy.

Day six --- Braunsweig, another large city 100 miles west of Berlin was our primary target. We carried twelve 500 pound demolition bombs. It was another 'Pathfinder' mission lead by our group commander. (One thing about the Air Corps, our top brass would fly missions with us.) We were up at 0200, took off at 0800 and left the coast at 1000. We encountered a large bank of clouds over Holland which we had to detour around to the north. Our fighter escort of P-47's and P-38's picked us up half way in and we flew through clouds most of the way to the target. This was a perfect set-up for mid-air collisions. The flak was light and we bombed through the clouds. Our squadron had to move over during the bomb run to prevent the high squadron from dropping their bombs on us! They had drifted directly above us! Luckily, a major catastrophe was avoided and we all hit the target. Scared the heck out of me!

Twenty minutes later, we broke out of the clouds. A damaged Fort dropped to the deck (low altitude) and was jumped by five enemy fighters, but our P-38's came to his rescue before they got him. Thirty miles out from the Dutch coast, we saw a German Air Sea rescue boat heading east to pick up a crew that had ditched in the North Sea. Landed at 1430. Our Squadron had lost one plane. He dropped out over the target and didn't come back. We are on mission alert tonight!!! "

"Air crews often flew two or three missions in a row;
the mental and physical strain was unbelievable!"

ESCAPE FROM HOLLAND

Citizens of countries occupied by German troops formed bands of Resistance Fighters (the underground) to sabotage enemy installations and to help airmen evade capture. Those members of the 'underground' risked their lives to help airmen reach friendly territory to be free to fight again! Hundreds of airmen 'walked out' of occupied countries because of those patriots. Late in the war, airmen carried small plastic covered cards of commonly used phrases in English, Dutch, Belgian and French. We were also given a paper with the American flag and phrases in Russian. (The Russian armies were moving so fast that we never knew where the Eastern front was located. Those cards were a Godsend to airmen who had to bail-out over enemy territory. I still have both of these items.

February 21, 1944 --- B-17 pilot's story of evading capture:

"It was my 24th mission; only one more to go and I would be home free. However, my life took a different direction in our bomb-run over Hamburg when flak knocked out two of our engines! With limited power, we had to leave the formation and drop down to fly alone. Ten minutes later, two German fighters spotted us, attacked head-on and knocked out another engine! We were then at 6,000 feet, flying on one engine and going down about 1,000 feet a minute. One of the dead engines was on fire; it could explode at any time. Meanwhile, the fighters were circling for the kill. I decided that even if we made it out of enemy territory, we would have to 'ditch' in the Channel and that would be suicide in the winter. I rang the bail-out bell over Holland and we all went out the bomb-bay.

I hit the ground, got into some bushes at the edge of a field, hid my parachute and waited to see if I had been seen. Later, I opened my escape kit to get my compass and silk map and started walking southwest. I knew

I was lost, so I took a chance and walked up to a isolated farm house. A friendly lady showed me where I was on the map and the safest way to get help from the Dutch underground. Four hours later I took another chance and talked to a Dutchman on a bicycle. When he realized I was an American flyer, he had me hide in a ditch. I laid there until he came back at ten o'clock that night and took me to a 'safe house' in town. Members of the Dutch underground (resistance fighters) were well organized to help downed flyers escape capture by the Germans who occupied Holland. These patriots had helped many airmen escape by traveling across France to Spain and freedom. The men and women of the underground used only their first name or an alias This was a safety tactic in case one was captured and tortured , he could not identify his comrades. They only revealed last names after the war.

My new friends kept me hidden for a week and gave me civilian clothes and a false I.D. card. I had become a druggist from Amsterdam. I traveled by train, following a Dutchman who guided me to safe houses along the way. Several times I was in crowds that included German soldiers, but I kept a low profile and moved away. Eventually, I walked across the Holland border into Belgium and hid a week in a haystack until a member of the Belgian underground guided me to the city of Liege. By then, the D-day invasion was on and they advised me to stay put until American troops arrived. They moved me around a lot and I spent a month in one house without looking out a window, but I was still free. I had been in enemy territory almost five months before American troops liberated the area. I was more than happy to climb into an U.S. Army truck for a ride to Paris and later to London. My last mission lasted much longer than normal, but the members of the Dutch and Belgian underground saved my life and I will never forget them.

I reported back to my base and got a new uniform, a promotion and all my back pay. But best of all – I got to go home!

> *"I'll never forget those unsung heroes of the underground who risked their lives to keep me safe"*

SWITZERLAND – OASIS OF PEACE

Nazi Germany conquered Denmark, Holland and Norway in the early spring of 1940, but allowed Sweden to remain neutral. Switzerland had been recognized as a perpetually neutral country in 1920 by the League of Nations, shortly after World War I. Pilots of crippled bombers who knew they could not make it back to England could land in the neutral countries of Switzerland or Sweden. Those planes were impounded and the air-crews were interned in camps for the remainder of the war. These two countries offered a safe haven for planes unable to return to base. They were 'islands of peace' in the middle a war that claimed the lives of millions of civilians and troops in the rest of Europe.

CO-PILOT'S STORY OF LANDING IN SWITZERLAND

"February 12th, 1945 we were up at 0400, met the gunners at the mess Hall and sitting in the briefing room at 0600. It was our 12th mission and we were ready to get on with it. Maybe the 'double twelves' was an omen. Whether it was or not, we were scheduled to fly. During breakfast, we learned that we were assigned to another bomber because our ship had been red-lined by the crew chief. That was bad news, because we all thought our Fort was part of our good luck and the 'scuttlebutt' in the Mess Hall said we were in for a long mission.

The 'scuttlebutt' was true. The lines on the briefing map showed a long flight across France into southern Germany. Our targets were ball-bearing plants and oil refineries. Good weather was predicted for the bomb-run and the intelligence officer warned of heavy flak. Our bombers would be full off gas right up to the 'Tokyo Tanks' in the wing tips. A relay of fighter escorts would protect the mission; P-47s to Paris, then P-38s would take us to the I.P. and P-51 Mustangs would guard us at the target and bring us back to Paris. But, there was nothing to protect us from the flak!

Various escape routes were pointed out for bombers in trouble (Airmen who bailed out had an escape kit with silk maps and a compass.) We hopped a truck for a ride out to our new shiny aluminum B-17G. The crew chief was ready to start the engines and soon all four were roaring. All gauges checked fine for: oil pressure, head temperatures, turbo charger rotation, manifold pressure and RPMs. The ignition systems were ok on all four engines and the pilot said we are ready to go.

Ground crews removed the chocks under the wheels and we taxied out to join the 'take off' line at the end of the runway. The control tower alerted us to get ready, the pilot set the brakes and revved the engines to full power until the plane shook. At the signal, he released the brakes and we sped down the runway as I called out the air speed. We hit, 70-80-90-100-110 MPH and we were airborne! The wheels came up and locked and we gained altitude as we spiraled up through the overcast to join our group circling overhead. Every B-17 bomb-bay carried 1,000 and 250 pound 'general purpose bombs and 100 pound incendiary bomb clusters. We joined our group formation and once all three squadrons were in place, we climbed up to join the bomber stream at the mission altitude of 26, 000feet. The escort of P-47 fighters joined us as we cleared the French coast. Our bomb group was the Wing Formation the 164 planes and we were off for Munich. At one point, I saw a wing of B-24 Liberators flying off to our left. The P-47 protectors were replaced by P-38s and we flew on to Germany where the P-51s took over.

Flying so long in close formation was a terrible strain on pilots and co-pilots. We always took turns flying and watching the sky for flak or fighters. The cockpit temperature was 27 degrees below zero and when a drop of sweat fell from our face (above the oxygen mask) it froze before it hit the metal floor and shattered on impact. We reached the IP and started the bomb-run. The radio operator was throwing out 'chaff" to foul up the radar, but the flak guns had already found us!

We heard it over the inter-com: "Flak at seven o'clock low"! ----Then "flak at seven o'clock high."

They were tracking us with radar, but we couldn't take evasive action on the bomb-run. We were locked on auto-pilot until we dropped our bombs. Seconds later, there was a loud explosion and smoke; the plane was shaking violently. The pilot took control of the bomber, struggling to keep us in position.

"Right Waist to co-pilot --- the number three engine is on fire!"

The pilot radioed for permission to leave the formation and told me to 'feather' the prop on that engine. Flak had hit the propeller hub. It cut the oil line and the oil spewing over wings caught fire from the re-hot exhaust pipes. The fire could take us down. We had a 6,000 bomb-load and plenty of gas in the tanks. We did everything we could to prevent the fire from spreading. We 'feathered' (shutdown) the engine, which shut off the oil and closed the cowl flaps. Mercifully, the extreme cold chilled the engine and its exhaust pipes --- thank God the fire went out!

We were out of the formation; a 'cripple' and a straggler and a perfect target for Luftwaffe fighters. We limped along on three engines and the pilot ordered the bombs dropped to lighten our load. Getting rid of three tons of bombs helped us gain a little power, but we all agreed that even if we escaped enemy fighters, we could not get back to friendly territory on three engines. We had two options; to land in enemy territory and be placed in a German POW camp or fly over the Alps, land in Switzerland (a neutral country) to be interned for the rest of the war. The crew chose Switzerland and the navigator gave us a new heading. Equipment, like the top secret Norden bombsight, radar identifier and most radios had to be destroyed. We kept the radio with the International Frequency Broadcast to get landing instructions from the Swiss. They directed us to a large pasture near a small town. We circled the field to check it out before making the final approach. The crew gathered in the radio room or waist to brace for a rough landing.

I read out the B-17's air speed as the pilot gave the orders;

"Lower wheels, high RPMs, full flaps!"

The Fort seemed to rise in the air as the flaps went down. The throttles were eased back and the plane sank slowly down. The pilot pulled back the throttles and the engines acted as brakes for the touchdown. The plane shook as we rumbled across the pasture until the brakes slowed us to taxi speed. We followed a guide truck to a stop and turned off the engines. A radio message told us to remain in place in the plane. We had landed in Switzerland, now what?

It wasn't a long wait! Swiss soldiers entered the waist door. Their green uniforms were styled like those of the German army, even the steel helmet. The leader, with rifle and fixed bayonet, came to the cockpit while the others guarded the crew. I reached for the red lever to lock the tail wheel, but he pressed the bayonet to my chest and said,

"Don't touch that!"

I think he thought it might be a detonator switch, anyway I didn't touch it! They let our crew get off the bomber and as I stepped down, he smiled and said. "Velcome to Switzerland!"

Eleven shot-up bombers landed in different places in Switzerland that day. The 110 aircrew members were all taken to Dubendorf by friendly Swiss soldiers, several of them spoke English. We were told the next day that we would be interned for the rest of the war. Two days later, we were moved by train to Adelboden, where the enlisted men were interned. The officers moved on to a camp at Davos-Platz.

"This crew would sit out the war, but they were saved
from death or a German POW camp"

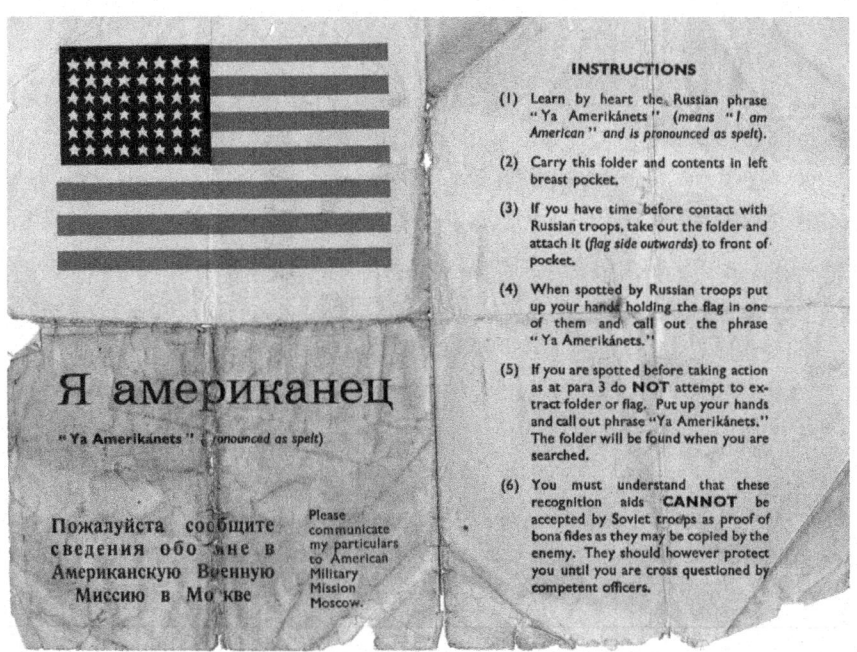

INSTRUCTIONS

(1) Learn by heart the Russian phrase "Ya Amerikánets" (means "I am American" and is pronounced as spelt).

(2) Carry this folder and contents in left breast pocket.

(3) If you have time before contact with Russian troops, take out the folder and attach it (flag side outwards) to front of pocket.

(4) When spotted by Russian troops put up your hand holding the flag in one of them and call out the phrase "Ya Amerikánets."

(5) If you are spotted before taking action as at para 3 do **NOT** attempt to extract folder or flag. Put up your hands and call out phrase "Ya Amerikánets." The folder will be found when you are searched.

(6) You must understand that these recognition aids **CANNOT** be accepted by Soviet troops as proof of bona fides as they may be copied by the enemy. They should however protect you until you are cross questioned by competent officers.

Я американец

"Ya Amerikánets" (pronounced as spelt)

Пожалуйста сообщите сведения обо мне в Американскую Военную Миссию в Москве

Please communicate my particulars to American Military Mission Moscow.

This identification paper was carried by airmen in case they bailed out and landed among Russian troops. Nazi troops had killed 200,000 Russians and they were out for revenge. You needed an ID to prove you were on their side! We also had a plastic card or phrases in other languages. These are among items I have kept for 67 years.

We flew at 25,000 feet with oxygen mask and heated suits. The 45 pound canvas covered steel flak jacket and a steel flak helmet saved the lives of many boys on bombing missions.

Blue Streak, a B-17 of the 486th Bomb Group, hit by flak over Merseberg, November 2, 1944 went down over the target while the formation was dropping bombs. USAF

Photo by waist gunner John "Rock" Doyle
20 yr old B-17 pilot, Gordon A. Glover of the 94th Bomb Group, 331st Squadron.
Flying at 25,000 feet; the oxygen mask, -40 degree temperatures and his seat pack
parachute made his missions even more difficult!
Photo and info submitted by his son Bill Glover, 2011

B-17 formation of the 381st Bomb Group take off for a combat mission
on a clear day. Note an airbase in the lower right corner.

CHAPTER SIX

GROUND CREW CHIEF

The Crew Chief and his mechanics were the unsung heroes who kept the fighters and heavy bombers of the Mighty Eighth in the air. They kept bombers flying and sweated out each mission hoping their 'bird' would return its crew to base. A bomber was only as good as the ground support units that provided the service and maintenance to enable it to fly eight hour combat missions at high altitude. There were forty-three American heavy bomb groups in England and each had 40 to 50 planes to be serviced and repaired. An Eighth Air Corps airbase needed a large number of mechanics and technicians to support those B-17 Flying Fortresses and B-24 Liberators for their high altitude missions.

Bomber pilots felt blessed with a good crew chief and mechanics who knew their business. A bomber with mechanical problems over enemy territory could mean the loss of the bomber and death or capture for the crew. A Crew Chief was highly trained and given lots of 'hands-on' experience before he earned the job of supervising a crew of mechanics to care for an expensive bomber. After basic training he attended aircraft mechanic school for five months and took shorter courses from electrical systems down to the automatic pilot. Every airbase had bombers to be repaired and serviced and Bomb Groups were expected to put up as many planes as possible for every mission.

Flyers sometimes called the support groups "ground-pounders," but they were respected by all crewmen, because they were the guys who kept us flying. In addition to the mechanics, there were armorers, bomb-loaders, radio and radar technicians, cooks, medics, parachute packers and other trained personnel required to support a bomber base. A bombing mission required at least thirty support people on the ground to keep ten men and a bomber flying.

The combat life of a B-17 was short, but there are exceptions to most rules, one 490th BG bomber, Alice Blue Gown, endured 87 missions!' Two Forts in the 379th BG at Kimbolton set endurance records, Old Gappy did 100 missions and Swamp Fire did 100 missions <u>without a mechanical failure</u>!

A bomb group's mechanics and technicians were the ground crews who kept bombers ready to fly. The Crew Chief and his mechanics devoted many hours to the maintenance of their bomber. They built "shacks" down near the repair hangers and flight line area in order to spend more time keeping their "bird" ready to fly. Duties ranged from repairing flak damage to fueling, loading, repairing and replacing parts to keep their bomber airworthy. The crew chief and his men often performed major surgery on their plane into the wee hours of the night. Indoor hanger space was limited and crews often replaced motors and major body parts outdoors; often working in the rain or snow. Motors, tail sections, wing panels, turrets and other parts were "cannibalized" from damaged planes unfit to fly. Many bombers flew missions with re-built engines, gun turrets and wing sections from the base airplane graveyard! Bombers with motor problems, new motors or body parts had to be flight tested before flying another mission. The Crew Chief and some of his mechanics went on these fights to check their work.

On those cold, dark early morning missions, aircrews climbed into their B-17 confident that their bomber was in top-notch condition. Ground crews warmed up the motors and made preflight checks on their plane. The ground crews' final actions, before we taxied out on the runway, was to remove the wheel chocks and give the pilot a thumbs-up sign. Then they rested and spent the day sweating out the mission; hoping their plane and crew returned safely. They were on the flight-line watching and waiting when we returned. As soon as we taxied back to our hardstand, the Crew Chief climbed into the plane to talk with the pilot and crew about any equipment malfunctions or mechanical problems during the mission.

Pilots used a checklist to test engines and instruments before takeoff and had an hour or so to check for unexpected mechanical or technical problems in flight during the Group Assembly over England or out over the North Sea. The pilot of a bomber with mechanical problems had to decide to continue the mission or "abort" and return to base before flying into enemy air space. A bomber that developed engine problems over enemy territory was an air-crew's nightmare. Mechanical failure left the bomber in a deadly situation. A loaded bomber with a dead (feathered) engine lost power quickly and was unable to keep up with the formation. The only option was to drop out and hope to hide in the cover of clouds or to be protected by escort fighters until they could land in friendly territory. Both choices were long shots and often failed. A lone bomber trying to make it safely back to base became an immediate target for Luftwaffe fighters. The odds of survival were greatly improved by late 1944 after Allied Armies occupied airfields in France and Belgium. Our crew came close to this experience this on our very first mission when an engine developed problems!

THE SWAMP FIRE SAGA

The B-17G Flying Fortress, Swamp Fire, of the 379th Bomb Group was literally a tough old bird, which set an endurance record of completing 100 missions without turning back (aborting.) because of a mechanical failure. It was the first B-17 to accomplish this feat.

Ground Crew Chief, M/Sgt. Dominick DeSalvo was presented the Legion of Merit for exceptional meritorious service as the Ground Crew Chief responsible for the maintenance of a heavy bombardment aircraft. DeSalvo credited the members of his crew for their hard work and dedication to keep the Swamp Fire flying. He then remarked:

"There isn't much of the original plane left. Not after 16 engine changes, 3 wing changes, a tail section changed and over 1,000 bullet and flack holes patches. In fact, although war damages have taken their toll on the original fuselage, she continues to be top dog in a league where the competition is pretty rugged! We were out in the elements all day and sometimes all night keeping her mission- ready and fit to fly."

Col. Lewis E. Lyle, Commander of the 379th Bomb Group, paid a compliment to all B-17 Flying Fortresses at the 100th mission celebration when he said: "No, there isn't much left of the original Swamp Fire, just the fighting spirit and tradition built into her and maintained by her ground and combat crewmen. She is an excellent criterion of the greatest bomber in the European Theater of Operations."

The record setting B-17G was assigned to the 524th Squadron of the 379th Bomb Group at Kimbolton, England in February of 1944 and flew its first mission on the 21st of that month. Swamp Fire completed its 100th mission without a mechanical failure November 1, 1944! Ground Crew Chief Dominick DeSalvo and his ground crew were assigned to the new bomber during its entire time in combat. They received full credit and honors for their remarkable service record. The bomber flew seventeen more missions, but on December'44, Sgt. DeSalvo declared the Swamp Fire "war weary" and no longer fit for service.

Note --- Swamp Fire researcher Richard Lewis of Elizabethtown, Kentucky is the son of S/Sgt. Elijah 'Lou' Lewis, tail-gunner on the first assigned crew. He writes: "S/Sgt. 'Lou' Lewis flew thirty-one missions on Swamp Fire and earned the DFC medal (Distinguished Flying Cross) Lewis says the collection of information and photos he has gathered tells the Swamp Fire story. It is a collaborative effort by family members of flight and ground crew members and especially those surviving veterans who took the time to explain and share their experiences.

The Swamp Fire was unique in that it had only one Ground Crew and two assigned air crews during the ten months it was in service. Various crews flew the new bomber for the first four missions and other mission crews took her up when the assigned crews were listed as 'standing down.' I have located at least ninety individuals who were on mission crews or 'fill-ins' for the sick or wounded on those other crews. We have the names of most of those who flew on Swamp Fire. Our stories come from diaries or official records. It has been our good fortune to have talked to some of the combat and ground crewmen. We have benefited from their input. Co-pilot, Byron Clark and crew chief Dominick DeSalvo attended a reunion in Seattle in 2011."

Swamp Fire's First Assigned Crew

Pilot -1st Lt. Joseph L. Korstjens;

Co-Pilot - 2nd Lt. Byron B. Clark

Navigator - 2nd Lt. Matthew J. Scianameo;

Bombardier - 2nd Lt. Harvey 'Herk' Harris;

Radio Operator-Gunner - S/Sgt. Edward J. Przybyla;

Waist Gunner - S/Sgt - Roy E. Avery Jr.

Ball turret gunner-S/Sgt Andrew Stroman;

Engineer/Top Turret Gunner S/Sgt. Berj G. Bejian;

Waist Gunner --- S/Sgt. John K. Rose;

*Tail Gunner ---- S/Sgt. Elijah W. 'Lou' Lewis;

Co-Pilot 2nd Lt. Byron B. Clark was the man who suggested the name Swamp Fire and the 1st Lt. Joseph L. Korstjens crew flew the bomber for its twenty-fifth mission on May 5, 1944. The crew completed 29 missions of their tour of duty (thirty-five missions) on the Swamp Fire and participated in the top secret 'Grapefruit Mission' to deliver blockbuster 'glide-bombs' on a high priority target.

Grapefruit Mission --- Grapefruit was the code name for a 2,000 pound glide bomb with a gyroscopic guidance system. The bombers were adapted with special release brackets under each wing so each B-17 could carry two of the 2000 pound top-secret glide bombs to the target. The Allied invasion of Europe was being planned and the Allies were seeking effective weapons to soften Germany's defenses. The glide bomb was a experiment assigned to the 41st Combat Wing comprised of three bomb groups ,the 303rd, 379th and 384th.

Eight days before D-Day, May 28th 1944, sixty Flying Fortresses took off on that secret mission, the target was Cologne. The mission was delayed until 1300 so the three formations might evade enemy radar as they followed a 1,200 plane raid into the Ruhr Valley area. The bomb-run procedure for glide-bombs was much different than a regular bombing mission. The formations flew at 20,000 feet, but were too release the flying bombs miles from the target. The bombers cruised at about at about 150 miles an hour, but the glide-bombs had to be released at 190 to 210 mph. Therefore pilots had to be on course and <u>dive</u> to 18,500 feet to reach the proper speed for releasing the flying bombs on the correct glide path to the target. Undetected by radar, the group released the 2000 pound glide-bombs thirty miles from the target

The Grapefruit formations launched 114 glide-bombs and almost half hit the target. Air Force General, Hap Arnold, was pleased with the results, however Allied leaders decided to cancel the experimental project and concentrate on strategic bombing raids prior to the invasion. It was later reported that the grapefruit mission confused German intelligence officers who feared the Allies had a new secret weapon for the invasion. One German newspaper's headlines stated that Cologne had been struck by suicide mini-bombers which could not be detected by radar!

SWAMP FIRE'S SECOND ASSIGNED CREW

> Pilot --- 1st Lt. Bruce E. Mills
> Co-pilot --- 2nd Lt. Carl A. Shedlock
> Bombardier --- 2nd Lt. James E. Whitney
> Navigator --- 2nd Lt. John E. McCray
> Engineer/Top Turret Gunner --- T/Sgt. Delmer E. Menger
> Radio Operator/Gunner --- T/Sgt. Joseph T. Cooper
> Ball Turret Gunner --- S/Sgt. James S. Boston
> Waist Gunner --- S/Sgt. Lucas S. Conner
> Tail Gunner --- S/Sgt. William A. Beddard Jr.

Pilot 1st Lt. Bruce Mills and his crew had finished their combat indoctrination classes and were ready for combat when they became the second crew to be assigned to fly Swamp Fire. Lt. Mills was not too impressed when he first saw the bomber. He later wrote in his diary:

"20 June 1944 – Got assigned a ship today, 42-32024 --- a B-17G with a new tail. We went out and looked at the Flak holes from yesterday's raid. It looked more like an olive drab colored F model that someone had put a new G model nose and tail section on. It already has more than 45 missions, but I hear it is heavily armored and has a damn good ground crew." Lt. Mills took command of Swamp Fire on his second mission July 6, 1944. He was the pilot of Swamp Fire on the hundredth mission on 1 November '44. That day, he wrote in his diary:

"November 1(Wednesday): My thirty-sixth mission. Got up at 06:30, briefing at 07:30, take off at 10:25 in Swamp Fire. Our Group Rendezvous was poor, clouds up to 20,000 feet. After forming the formation, I flew high diamond ---- the #2 engine blew up. It was "rebuilt" and we had about 2080 hours on it (we put on ten) --- we gradually fell behind the formation. At the English coast, we were ten miles behind, but I cut off a corner and gained on them. Now, #3 started acting up and so we reduced power to save it, sacrificing altitude. I knew we were sitting ducks out here with no support and was considering whether or not to abort the mission. I discussed this with the crew over the inter-com. Not a man wanted to return to base. The tail gunner's words still echo in my head,

"For the love of God Sir, don't turn this plane around!"

We hit the Dutch coast at 16,000 feet where we bombed transports under the clouds. The ships took off for the harbor of Ijmuiden, since they were just off the shore. The tail gunner reported mobile flak guns being brought to bear on us, so we peeled off and got the hell home!

We crossed the English coast, taking evasive action. Back at the field, I buzzed the ground crew tent and fired flares until we taxied onto the perimeter; 100 missions for Swamp Fire ---- Thirty-six for me!"

Note --- The 379th Bomb Group was not one of the early groups to arrive in England, but they set several records, surpassing Bomb Groups which had arrived much earlier. The men of the 379th served with distinction for two years seven months and 29 days. Their group was first to fly the thirty-six plane combat group with twelve planes in each squadron and first to use a straight-line flight on the bomb-run. The Eighth Air Force Operational Grand Slam, an award created by the commander of the Eighth Air Force, was presented to the 379th Bomb group in May, 1944. During the month of April the group had ranked first in all five categories of bombing efficiency graded by the "top brass." They were the only unit to ever win the Grand Slam.

The famed 379th Bomb Group flew 330 missions, and set an Eighth Air Force record of 10,492 sorties. The group dropped 26,459 tons of bombs --- more than any other unit. It led all other Mighty Eighth bomb groups in the total number of missions flown. The 379th carried out 330 raids between May 1943 and May 15, 1945, including the most un-escorted long range missions. Over forty-three percent (141) of the 345 bombers assigned to the Group were lost to 'flak and fighters.'

Two B-17 bombers of the 524th Squadron claimed individual fame: "Old Gappy," completed 157 missions probably more than any other Eighth Air Force bomber. (A Fort in my 490th BG completed 87 missions) "Swamp Fire" was the first heavy bomber to complete 100 missions without an "abort" (turning back with mechanical problems.)

Note --- Air-crews of 1st Lt. Donald D. Day and 2nd Lt. Joseph L. Wells, of the 524th Bomber Squadron, tied for the honor of flying the most missions in the shortest time frame. That record meant flying two or three missions in a row. The officers and men on those air-crews paid a high price in fatigue and mental stress.

The Swamp Fire was in the air on D-Day with the 'fill-in' crew of 1st Lt. Donald L. Day and so it happened that Swamp Fire's pilot on D-Day was --- D. Day! This crew, a mission crew, also flew the Swamp Fire's 50th mission to a target in France on June 22, 1944.

THE DONALD L. DAY CREW:

Pilot --- 1st Lt. Donald L Day
Co-pilot --- 2nd Lt. Ralph L. Vickery
Navigator --- 2nd Lt. Marshall Suloway
Bombardier --- 2nd Lt. Hoyt Edwards
Engineer/Top Turret Gunner --- T/Sgt. Paul .Yates
Radio Operator/Gunner --- T/Sgt. Blaine E. McIntyre
Waist Gunner --- S/Sgt. Donald R. Lesage
Ball Turret Gunner --- S/Sgt. Stephen J. Mc Cabe
Tail Gunner --- S/Sgt. Allen M. Whitehead

Swamp Fire's ground crew maintained the bomber throughout her wartime service, from changing engines to replacing gun turrets; it was all part of the job. They were the guys who worked many long hours in foul and fair weather to maintain and repair the famous bomber throughout its incredible combat record. Ground Crew Chief Dominick DeSalvo and his men were typical of the young men on ground crews who kept bombers and fighters ready for combat in World War II

MIKE PAPADAKIS - TAIL GUNNER

Mike was a B-17G tail-gunner in the 385th Bomb Group stationed at the Great Ashfield airbase near Ipswich. He relates some of his experiences in his 33 missions with the Lt. Ben Taylor crew in 1944-45. In a phone conversation with Mike, I learned that we flew missions to five of the same targets. His son, Gust, reports that Mike and his wife now spend their time between Warren, Ohio and Clearwater, Florida. Mike's crew flew their first mission on November 9, 1944 and completed 33 by March 11, 1945. His missions were on two different B-17G bombers, named Hot Chocolate and Hit Parade. Like many other bomber crews they flew almost every day the weather was clear, except for rest and relaxation breaks. Several times, they flew two days in a row and on two occasions they flew three days straight! That kind of duty; facing flak and fighters on long high altitude flights was an enormous strain on men and planes. However, the Eighth Air Corps had the task of destroying Germany's railroads and oil storage. The Fifteenth Air Corps in Italy had the same assignment and in early 1945, the Air Force made an all-out effort to take away Hitler's ability to move troops and weapons against our ground forces. Mike said, "The rest of the crew rarely saw the wounded after we landed. Planes returning to base with wounded men aboard fired red flares to be allowed to land first. Base ambulances raced to the plane as soon as it landed. The medic and doctors were in the plane when the props stopped turning. Ambulances whisked the injured or dead away and ground crews hosed out the plane The rest of the crew were given a ride back to the briefing hut for the required interrogation session. Coffee, cookies and a shot of whiskey were available before they were questioned on what they had seen during the mission. Intelligence officers needed to know where they saw flak or fighters. They wanted to collect as much information as possible to prepare for the next mission to that target.

I had a good buddy in my hut who slept in my top bunk. His name was William Boyd and of course, we called him Hop-a-long Cassidy. He had been grounded for a while because of sickness. They gave a temporary job in the laundry and he often had to wash the bloody flight suits of the dead or wounded. It was a terrible job and he begged to get back on a bomber crew. Eventually, they assigned Boyd to the crew of a bomber named "Ruby's Raiders." When the bomber was new, it was christened by Cpl. Ruby Newell, who was elected the most beautiful WAAC (Women's Army Air Corps) in the Mighty Eighth in 1944. The B-17G carried her name and picture. My buddy was really excited to be assigned to a replacement crew on the famous plane. However, after a couple of missions Ruby's Raiders had engine problems, so the crew got switched to another bomber. Coming home, they had to "ditch" in the English Channel and my buddy died on his third mission with that crew.

One mission, we were shot up pretty bad and had wounded on board so we landed at a field near Paris, about 20 miles from the front. I found a big hole in the tail just where my head might have been. That night I ended up on guard duty to protect our plane on the bomb-riddled airfield. Sometime after midnight, I saw ten to fifteen guys running across the field. A group of MP's (Military Police) were chasing and firing at the shadowy figures. As they ran past me, one MP yelled, 'Shoot the S.O.B.'s they're Nazi sympathizers and they blew up a plane last night! I was sure glad those MPs were on the job!

Another time our crew was on 'stand down' (we didn't have a mission) so we enlisted men decided to ride our bikes into town. We had a few pints of beer at a Pub before we returned to the hut around midnight. They told us our status had been changed and we <u>were on alert for a mission</u>! An orderly with a lantern woke us at 3:00 am and at 7:30 am we took off out over the North Sea with less than three hours of sleep. After group assembly, we were flying at about 26,000 feet and somewhere along the way I fell asleep and didn't answer an inter-com 'oxygen check!' The pilot thought I might be off oxygen and in trouble, so he sent a waist-gunner on a portable oxygen tank back to the tail to check on me! Our pilot was mad as the devil when he found out I had been asleep. He chewed me out royally over the inter-com and I knew I deserved it. He said I was supposed to be watching for enemy planes, not catching up on my sack time! I made sure I never let that happen again! However, there came a time when I really needed help. We were cruising along at 25,000 feet and about 40 below zero when my electric suit shorted out and burned my left arm. I beat it out, but knew I would freeze to death if I didn't get help. I grabbed my portable oxygen bottle and crawled to the waist area. The waist gunners quickly helped me change to a spare suit we carried in the emergency bag. I plugged my new suit into the rheostat and turned it on high to toast a little while before crawling back to my tail guns. It was just another accident that could really mess up your life on a bombing mission!"

5. One of my most dangerous missions --- we were flying deep into enemy territory and the engineer discovered that a bomb in our bomb-bay had come loose from one of its shackles and was hanging on top of the two below it! Col. Jumper, group leader, ordered our pilot to leave the formation --- an explosion in the middle of the group would have destroyed most of the planes. We had two P-51 fighters assigned to protect us, but we were flying way out from the formation and a sitting duck for Luftwaffe fighters. I felt like we were just "fighter bait" until we got rid of that bomb. Our pilot, Lt. Ben Taylor, called on George Burghard the ball turret gunner, to check out the mess in the bomb-bay. Wearing a portable oxygen tank, George manually released two lower bombs so he could free the one hanging above them. We dropped three bombs and closed the bomb-bay. The pilot worked our bomber back into the protection of the formation and we flew on to the target. Of course, our plane was short three bombs!"

"The tail gunner was the lookout and the stinger on the B-17"

TEMPLETON CREW'S FIRST MISSION

The Lt. William "Bill" Templeton crew arrived at the 490th Bomb Group at Eye, England shortly before Thanksgiving, 1944 (a year after I entered Radio School.) We were at Station 134 (code name Hangstrap) Squadron 848. Quonset hut 29 was our new home in the combat zone. Shortly after we arrived I learned that my best boyhood buddy, Chad, (in the infantry) had been killed in France.

Our crew finished bomb group training for combat in ten days and we were eager to start flying missions. The tour of duty had been raised from 25 to 35 missions and we figured we might as well get it done. It wasn't a long wait! Two days later our crew was alerted to fly its first mission and it was almost our last! The mission alert came in the afternoon, so we hit the sack early, but our nerves didn't let us get much sleep! The CQ (charge of quarters) woke us up at 0330 in the morning. The six of us (officers had a different quarters)) put on our long- johns, electric suits and all our heavy clothing before hiking through the snow to the Mess Hall and then on to the Briefing room for enlisted men (officers had a separate briefing.) The old-timers at the Mess Hall said this would be a long mission because we were up so early, maybe Merseburg, Munster, Regansburg or Berlin. After a good breakfast, we caught a truck to the Briefing Room for mission instructions and to learn where we were going to face death for the first time! Rumors were still flying when the enlisted men of all crews were assembled for briefing. Officers had separate briefings and we didn't see them until we got out to our plane. Our worst fears were confirmed when the briefing officer stepped up on the platform and pulled back a long curtain and to reveal a giant map of Germany. Our target was <u>Berlin,</u> the German capital, and one of the most heavily defended areas in Germany.

We were starting at the top, but what a way to break into the business! The Eighth was going to bomb Berlin for the first time since October, 1944 and the Lt. Bill Templeton crew had been invited to the party. We were briefed to expect 300 or more anti-aircraft guns and lots of Luftwaffe fighters. This was a maximum effort raid on Hitler's capital with the largest number of bombers to date. I guess they had been saving the big one until we got there. Flight lines plotted on the map showed the safest routes to avoid flak gun locations on the flight to the target and back.

Our formations would have the protection of a large escort of P-51 and P-47 fighters with extra fuel tanks for the long mission. Our target was technical buildings and labs in the northwest section of Berlin and we were to bomb at 11,000 feet. Alternate targets included railroad yards and oil supplies in and around Berlin.

After briefing, we joined the lines at the equipment and parachute huts before hopping a truck out to our assigned bomber on hardstand eight (parking space.) We weren't sure what the day would bring as we caught a ride out to our B-17G for our first mission. It was a cold snowy morning and I was shaking like a leaf, but it wasn't just from the cold!

We climbed into the bomber to check it out our flight positions. Ground crews had installed the guns, ammo and flak jackets. I got a radio check and made sure I had the current Morse code cards. The pilots started the engines at 0630, warmed them up, checked all gauges and taxied out to line up on the runway for our first mission. Loaded with bombs, ammunition and ten men, the plane weighed about 56,000 pounds on our take off at 0645. The 490th Bomb Group assembled on red and yellow flares at 11,000 feet. Later our group formation joined the bomber stream over the North Sea. The Templeton crew was flying in the "Tail-end Charlie" or "Coffin Corner" position at the rear of the low squadron which was a great place to be picked off by Luftwaffe fighters. The Roufs crew, who trained at Sioux City and came over on the Queen Mary with us, was flying in the element ahead. Experienced pilots were leading squadrons in the tight box formation which required bombers to fly close together to prevent enemy fighters from flying through the formation. New pilots brought up the rear where they had more room to make mistakes. However, they also had less protection from other planes in the formation.

Somewhere over enemy territory our number three engine developed a problem and began losing power. We were losing air speed and lagging behind the formation. This was a dangerous situation, a lone bomber over enemy territory was "easy money" for enemy fighters. It was a sickening feeling to see the formation gradually moving away from us. It was too late to abort and we would soon be a sitting duck for enemy fighters! Templeton, Rector and Roddy worked like mad to correct the problem. Our only chance was to get that engine running right or pray that one our own fighters would appear to escort us back to friendly territory, but there wasn't an escort fighter in sight. Luckily the engine regained power and we finally caught up and took our place in the formation. Later our pilot said he didn't radio for escort help because German fighters might intercept the call for help and get to us first.

That battered old war weary B-17 really gave us a scare!

The 490th formation reached the Initial Point (IP) and because we were in the rear, it was my job to reel out my trailing wire radio antenna to send that info back to our base. The formation started on the fifteen mile bomb run to the target. It was our crew's first flight into a sky full of anti-aircraft fire. The sky was filled with black smoke from the bursting 88 mm shells. We knew those shells were spewing thousands of jagged pieces of iron (flak) into the sky, just like a shotgun shell shoots buckshot at a rabbit, but this time, we were the rabbit!

The plane shook from close explosions and flak pinged on the plane. Our pilot could not take evasive action. The bombardier on the lead crew took control of the plane through the bombsight and automatic pilot to hold the bomber on a straight and level course and allow himself time to feed information into the bombsight. Thirty-six B-17 Flying Fortresses with bomb- bay doors open, followed their squadron leaders into a sky full of flak to drop their ten 500 pound bombs on the target. I saw one plane get hit and peel off out of the formation. Our squadron released the bombs, closed their bomb bay doors and tightened up the formation to prepare for fighter attacks as we headed for England. It was later reported that one of our lead bombers had been badly damaged by flak. It fell behind the formation and was shot down on the way home by a group of Luftwaffe FW-190 fighters. The crew was listed as MIA (missing in action.) The same fate we had escaped earlier in that mission!

Dozens of Luftwaffe fighters came up after us as we turned to fly out of the flak area and they were intercepted by our escort fighters. Our heavy bombers were escorted by more than 800 P-51 Mustang and P-47 Thunderbolt fighters P-51 escort fighters and bomber crews witnessed a terrific series of dogfights. Our gunners stayed on the alert and tail gunner, Ralph Moore, had a front row seat for all the action as we headed for England. The mission had been listed as a "massive effort" to hit Berlin. But, many years later, I learned that we were also bait to lure the Luftwaffe fighters into the range of our escorts fighters from the 357th, 479th and 355th Fighter Groups. Our fighters outnumbered the German fighters who suffered heavy losses which could not be replaced. The Luftwaffe was running out of fighter planes and experienced pilots. Our group bombed the target through clouds with the radar dome and we did not see the results. However, the next day a Stars and Stripes article reported that Eighth bombers also blasted a big munitions plant northwest of Berlin and U.S. fighters had shot down 80 German fighters. The Eighth lost 12 bombers and 22 fighters on this raid. Only one 490th B-17 went down. Our crew had an action-packed introduction to aerial combat over Germany! We landed at 3:30 p.m. and had to clean the machine guns, check-in our chest pack parachutes and equipment before going back to the briefing room. The Templeton crew had survived its first mission --- only thirty-four more to go! The poor performance of our bomber on that day taught our pilots the importance of making sure that in the future we had a plane that could get us to the target and back. We didn't need another scare like the Berlin trip!

At de-briefing we were asked questions about anything we had seen on the mission (where we saw flak or fighters etc.) The Red Cross girls were on hand to provide cookies and coffee. A shot of scotch was also available to help us relax. Some guys managed to get several shots and got so "relaxed" they could hardly walk! The trip to the Mess Hall was a treat because we hadn't eaten since that early breakfast so many hours ago. Hut 29 was a welcome sight and we were happy to crawl into the bunks we had vacated fifteen hours ago. "Sack time" was a precious commodity after a combat mission!

We were alerted for a mission the very next day. We repeated the previous day's activities, but again our aircraft developed mechanical problems. Our pilot aborted the mission and we returned to base. Lt. Bill Templeton's crew had learned a lesson on that first mission!

Our armorer, Bert Allinder flew in the nose as toggleer/nose-gunner on our first four combat missions because we flew without a bombardier. Bert dropped our bombs when the lead plane dropped this. On the third mission we thought Bert had been hit by flak over the target. When he released our bombs we only heard 'Bombs Aw_____! Then dead silence. He was back on the inter-com in a few minutes to report that he was OK. A piece of flak had cut the cord to his throat microphone!

"I would spend over 300 hours in a B-17 Flying Fortress before I left England!"   Hutch

147

BLACKOUTS FOR PROTECTION

Air raids on London were frequent early in the war when Germany had bomber bases just a few miles across the English Channel in occupied France! The blast of the air-raid sirens was a warning of German bombers (buzz bombs later) in the sky and time to take cover until given an "all clear." Black-out curtains covered all windows, autos drove slowly without lights and nobody lit a cigarette outside. England was 'blacked out' at night and Air Raid wardens patrolled cities and towns to enforce the rules every night from the Battle of Britain until the end of the war (1940-45). Blackout curtains covered doors and windows. Outside lights could not be used and headlights on all cars and military vehicles were covered with metal shades, only a small cross of light showed to warn pedestrians. Night driving was slow. Drivers needed to avoid accidents and pitch-black darkness kept them at a safe speed. Citizens understood that just the flare of a match could be spotted by enemy pilots. Air Raid wardens watched the night skies at night and air- raid sirens blared a warning when German bombers or buzz bombs were spotted. Allied fighters went up to intercept the deadly raiders. People scrambled for shelter in cellars, basements or bomb shelters, anti-aircraft guns were manned and huge searchlights pierced the night to help anti-aircraft gunners blow them out of the sky.

During the blackout at our airbase, we needed cat eyes to move around outside the hut. It was a weird feeling to walk among the shadowy outlines of buildings, unable to recognize the guys passing you on the street, so you can imagine our amazement on our first pass to London. You get an eerie, spooky feeling walking in the pitch black darkness of a strange city. It was kind of like those Sherlock Holmes movies. The ruins of bombed out homes and stores was a scary reminder of the bombings and the need for the black-out of one of the world's largest cities. I had been through air-raid drills back in Indiana before I was drafted, but London was another story. Bombing had destroyed large areas of cities and killed or wounded thousands. London's East End industries and shipyards had been especially hit hard. German air raids had dropped off by December of 1944, but the V-1 buzz bombs were coming in every night to blast the city. The guidance systems on the un-manned 'doodle-bugs' was not too reliable. They destroyed thousands of homes, terrorized people and lowered morale.

Note --- I remember our crew's first London pass. Our train pulled into Victoria Street station in the early evening. We had been told to take the subway (tube) downtown to the Red Cross Rainbow Club in Piccadilly Circus. Dozens of people were camping in the underground station. We learned that Londoners, especially those with children, moved into the underground each night. Families simply packed up blankets and bed clothes and moved down into the subway (tube) to sleep in government provided steel bunk beds along the walls. The children might bring a favorite toy. Many families had sent their children out of London to safety with relatives in rural areas. Some were sent as far as Canada or the United States. Thousands had died because of Hitler's air raids earlier in the "Battle of Britain." The noise of the trains was not as disturbing as air-raid sirens and exploding bombs, the trains stopped running each night at 11:30. The subway was a perfect bomb shelter for a safe night's rest when the air raid sirens went off. Suddenly, we all realized that spending our weekend pass in London was going to be a risky experience!

The black-outs were a life-saving protection against air raids and buzz bombs. However, Germany had the same 'black-out' problem, because RAF bombers pounded their cities every night they had clear weather! The Mighty Eighth bombed major targets in daytime missions. Germany became the victim of around- the- clock bombing.

STUTTGART – DEC. 16, 1944

The 490ᵗʰ bombed railroad yards at Stuttgart today in spite of the bad weather. It was our third mission and second in a row. The overcast was terrible and our pilots flew on instruments to reach the assembly area. It an eerie feeling to be flying up through clouds so dense I could not see past our wing tips. In other words, it was "visibility zero" and we had to put on our oxygen masks before we reached assembly altitude! We were a chaff ship and our waist-gunner, Bert Allinder and I threw 450 bales of the aluminum sheets out of the chute in my radio room during the nineteen minutes we were on the bomb-run over the target. Gunners could leave their post during the bomb run, because enemy fighters never followed us into the flak area, but they were waiting for us when we came out. Our bomb-load was ten 500 pounders with two 500 pound clusters of incendiary bombs. Flak was light and we hit the rail yards dead center. Our plane was also the group camera ship today. They had mounted a camera in the bomb-bay to record bombing results. We hit the target and took a good picture. The 490th was later complimented by General Partridge, head of the Third Division. Stuttgart was a seven hour mission, at 23,000 feet on oxygen and 35 below zero.

It was really great to crawl out of that bomber and go to the de-briefing session. The Mess Hall was a welcome sight after a day in sub-zero temperature. Now we could finally relax in a nice warm building full of hot food and coffee. Our last trip to the Mess hall was breakfast around 5:00 am; all food is good when you haven't eaten in about ten hours. We returned to our den in Hut 29 and hit the sack. Our hut buddies had managed to sneak more coal (coke) from the squadron storage bin and had the little stove fired up for us. They were on alert to fly the next day, so everyone crawled into the sack early and hit the lights. Our radio was down low and the Glenn Miller band was playing all our favorite tunes. We were snug and warm in spite of the snow and winter winds whipping around the hut. It was a treat to relax and thank God that our crew had survived another mission. Little did we know that our favorite band leader's plane was missing in that storm out over the English Channel!

THE GLENN MILLER STORY

Bad news travels fast and we soon heard the "scuttlebutt" about Miller's plane being missing. We hoped he would be found safe by the by dozens of planes and boats searching the English Channel and the route to Paris for his plane. The popular band leader with dozens of top ten records had volunteered for service and was commissioned a Captain in the Army Air Corps. Miller organized a band from many of his musicians already in the service. He soon became tired of playing the traditional marches and started playing jazzier arrangement like the St Louis Blues

March for the young airmen. The new marching music was approved by General "Hap" Arnold and in the spring of '44 the Glenn Miller Band moved to England to play the music GI's liked. It became a great morale builder as a radio program and performed dozens of live shows at airbases, hospitals etc. Gen. Arnold said Miller's Band brought a 'little bit of home' to the men of the Eighth Air Force. The BBC and the Armed Forces radio networks played records and broadcast his live programs. The German radio programs of Axis Sally (American traitor) and Lord Haw Haw, (British traitor) also played the band's records to get American troop to listen to their propaganda. We often tuned in to listen to the music and laugh at their lies.

December of '44 Miller was asked to take the band to Paris to give a Christmas Concert for Army commanders and troops. On the stormy afternoon of December 15, 1944, Major Glenn Miller boarded a small plane to fly a short hop to Paris to make arrangements for the band. A friend, Lt. Col. Norman Baessell, had invited Miller to fly over with him. They met that afternoon at the Twinwood RAF field in Bedford. The single engine Norseman C-4 plane had no parachutes and no wing deicers or navigation equipment. Despite the fog and heavy rain, pilot F/O John Morgan, took off and the three were never seen again. There was a five day search for the plane, but no the wreckage was found.

Miller's death was a great loss. Eighth Air Force commander General, Jimmy Doolittle said, "Next to a letter from home, his band was the greatest morale-builder in the European Theater of Operations."

Major Glenn Miller was gone, but the music never stopped. The band played on and the G.I.'s continued to enjoy songs like, Moonlight Serenade, In The Mood, St. Louis Blues March, String of Pearls and Little Brown Jug through the end of the war and back into civilian life. The big band music had great lyrics with tunes you could sing or whistle; songs to remind us of why we were fighting and the promise of a better life when it was over.

"Glenn Miller's music will never be forgotten by WW II veterans and members of the Greatest Generation!" Hutch

Swamp Fire's First Assigned Crew

Standing left to right: *Radio Operator-Gunner - S/Sgt. Edward J. Przybyla; Bombardier - 2ⁿᵈ Lt. Harvey 'Herk' Harris; Waist Gunner - S/Sgt - Roy E. Avery Jr. Pilot -1st Lt. Joseph L. Korstjens; Ball turret unner-S/Sgt Andrew Stroman; Engineer/Top Turret Gunner S/Sgt. Berj G. Bejian; Waist Gunner -- S/Sgt. John K. Rose; Navigator - 2ⁿᵈ Lt. Matthew J. Scianameo; *Tail Gunner --- S/Sgt. Elijah W. 'Lou' Lewis; Co-Pilot - 2ⁿᵈ Lt. Byron B. Clark;* *Kneeling left to right – Ground crew* *Rube Cohen- Armorer; William Riegel- Mechanic; James Abbot- Engineer/Mechanic; Henry Gerhart- Mechanic; Dominick Desalvo- Ground Crew Chief*

Dominick Desalvo (on the left) said, "We worked very hard at fine tuning those engines, patching her up and even improvised changes in her armor, because we wanted all that flew her to come back!"" Swamp Fire air crews benefitted from the skills and dedication of Ground Crew Chief M/Sgt. Dominick De Salvo and his crew! "- Richard Lewis

152

The Lt. Bruce E. Mills crew flew Swamp Fire on the 100th misson
Standing L to R --- 2nd Lt. James Whitney, bombardier; 2nd Lt. John Mc
Cray, navigator; 2nd Lt. Carl Shedlock, co-pilot; 1st Lt. Bruce Mills. Pilot; T/
Sgt Joseph Cooper radio operator/gunner. *Kneeling L to R* --- T/Sgt Delmer
Menger, engineer/top turret gunner; S/Sgt James Boston, Ball Turret gunner; S/
Sgt William Beddard Jr., tail gunner; S/Sgt Lucas Connor, waist gunner.

Tail-end Charlies' view of his bomber formation as they headed for the
target! The purpose of the mission and type of target determined the size of
bombs the armorers hauled out to hoist into their bomb-bay racks.

CHAPTER SEVEN

CHRISTMAS EVE 1944

It was December 22, 1944 and the lead-colored sky showed no sign of clearing when we stepped out of the mess hall after breakfast. In fact, there was the threat of another snowstorm. Europe and the British Isles were suffering record-breaking snows this winter. RAF and Allied planes had been grounded for five days because of snow and poor visibility. It was very frustrating to "stand down" when our troops needed our air support so badly. Ground crews had worked all night to clear the snow off the runways in case the weather cleared enough for a mission. The mechanics on the flight line said visibility was so bad that the birds were walking!

I'll never forget the Christmas season of 1944 in Jolly Old England, but things weren't so jolly that year. The Stars and Stripes reported more and more advances of the twenty-four divisions of German troops, and ten Panzer Tiger Tank divisions that had made with their surprise counter-attack the week before. They had broken through American forces, created a 'bulge' in our battle lines and surrounded our troops at Bastogne, Belgium. The Battle of the Bulge was raging and Allied fighters and bombers could not fly.

Clear skies were predicted for December 24th and the Allied Command ordered a major effort air attack. The largest air armada to attack Germany was in the air on Christmas Eve. I was a teenage radio operator on a B-17 Flying Fortress with just three bombing missions under my belt and this was not a Christmas Eve activity I would have chosen. However, I was only one of thousands of teenagers in our armed forces sixty seven years ago and nobody asked my opinion. Every air-worthy bomber and crew in the Eighth Air Force flew that day. On a normal mission, our 490th Bomb Group sent out 36 Flying Fortresses. This raid we sent up all four squadrons, 50 planes, to bomb a Luftwaffe fighter base at Frankfort, Germany. We flew at 25,000 feet with a bomb-bay full of hundred pound bombs and caught the German planes on the ground before they could get air-borne. We destroyed a hornet's nest before they could "sting" us." Other Eighth Air Force bombers headed for other strategic targets to cripple Germany's military. More than 2,000 Eighth Air Force B-17 Fortresses and B-24 Liberators flew that day. They were escorted and protected by more than 900 fighters as they carried out their strategic bombing missions. Targets included airfields, bridges, oil storage, communications centers, and railroad yards. Direct hits would prevent the German armies in the Ardennes from receiving fuel, ammunition and military supplies.

This air raid was so big that bombers were still heading out from England when the first groups were bombing their targets in Germany! I remember releasing our bomb-load over Berlin, sending a "strike report" back to base, and heading for home. We flew past a steady stream of other Bomb Groups heading into Germany. In addition to our heavy bomber raids, the Ninth Air Force tactical fighters and medium bombers were flying at low altitudes to strafe and bomb tanks, trains and enemy troops.

"Thunder is good, thunder is impressive, but it's the Light'ning that does the work" Mark Twain

Our bombers made lots of "thunder" over England every mission, but we saved our "lightning" for the German war machine. The 1944 Christmas Eve bombing raids helped our ground forces drive back the last German attack. It was the beginning of the end of World War II in Europe. The cost in lives on the ground and in the air was very high in the Battle of the Bulge. There are 14,000 Americans buried in the three American cemeteries in Belgium. Services are held Memorial Day for these men buried in a distant land, so far from home.

"Freedom is not free – thousands have paid for it!

General Castle's Medal of Honor

Col. Frederick Walker Castle, West Point Graduate, had worked for two years on General Eaker's staff to organize the Eighth Air Force in England. He requested combat duty in August, 1944 and was given command of the 94th Bomb Group at Bury St. Edmonds. Later, he was promoted to Brigadier General and appointed commander of the Fourth Bomb Wing, which contained four Bomb Groups, largest in the Eighth Air Force.

Christmas Eve, the Fourth Wing was selected to lead the Third Division on the largest Eighth Air Force raid to date to relieve our ground troops in the Battle of the Bulge. Bad weather had kept bombers grounded for several days and Allied troops badly needed air support. December 24, 1944, the 487th Bomb Group took off from Lavenham airbase with General Frederick Castle as command pilot in the lead plane. It was his thirtieth mission and he was Air Commander; leader of the war's largest raid of heavy bombers launched by the Mighty Eighth. The goal of this massive Christmas Eve mission of 2,046 bombers and 853 fighters was to aid American ground troops fighting the Battle of the Bulge in Bastogne and the Ardennes mountains of Belgium. Eleven German airfields were the targets for 1,400 bombers while others were to hit major communication centers, bridges and railroad yards west of the Rhine. Unfortunately, the number one motor on General Castle's B-17 developed a problem over Belgium and was unable to keep up with the group. He had to drop out of the lead position and lag behind the formation in enemy territory. The General could have dropped his bombs to give his plane more power to keep up, but the formation was flying over the front lines and he refused to drop his bomb-load on the American troops below. The lead group's P-51 escort fighters were late in arriving and his lagging, unescorted bomber soon became the victim of ME- 109 fighter attacks. Luftwaffe guns and cannon fire ripped the left wing, set the oxygen system on fire and wounded two crew members. Fire flamed from two engines and the Flying Fortress was in danger of exploding. General Castle took control of the plane and gave the bail-out order while he remained at the controls to keep the doomed plane level while seven men bailed out (five survived.) A third fighter attack hit the gas tanks in the right wing and the bomber went into a spin before he had time to bail out.

Brigadier General Frederick Walker Castle was awarded the Medal of Honor posthumously for his intrepidity and willingness to sacrifice his life to save members of his crew. His actions were in keeping with the highest traditions of the military service. He was the highest ranking officer in the Eighth to receive the Medal of Honor and the last of seventeen awarded to Eighth Air Force members. The Mighty Eighth lost fifty-six bombers that day, including General Castle's, but the mission was a great success and helped defeat Hitler's last offensive of he war. General Castle was buried in the American Cemetery at Henri-Chappelle, near Leige, Belgium; not far from the site of his crash on that cold Christmas Eve in 1944.

General Castle was the second Eighth Air Force General to die in combat on a B-17 Flying Fortress. Brigadier General Nathan Bedford Forrest III died June 13, 1943 while leading a raid on the submarine pens at Kiel.

Note--- The mission was the fourth for the Lt. Bill Templeton crew. My diary shows that they rousted us out of the sack at 0400, briefing at 0545 and take off at 0935. This was the Mighty Eighth's biggest mission of the war. We had to deliver a 'knock out' punch to Hitler. They said the Eighth sent up everything that had wings. We flew in the high squadron at 25,000 feet. The 490th target was the Luftwaffe airfield at Frankfurt. I threw out 'chaff' at two different points, once when we crossed enemy lines in Belgium and again at the IP (initial point) when we started the bomb-run. Our bomb-bay was full of hundred pounders. We had heavy flak and it put one big hole in the left wing. Our tail gunner sighted a German ME-262 jet on this mission. We landed at 1700 (5:00 pm.) and got back to our hut about 20:00 (8:00pm.) The mission lasted over eight hours, but we had been awake for 16 hours!

"It was a great Christmas Gift for the guys fighting the Battle of the Bulge in the Ardennes!" Hutch

S/Sgt. Robinson's Last Mission

The other crew members in our barracks were not on alert, but they had several missions under their belts and knew the dangers we faced in the early dawn. Soon the bravado of young airmen won out and the talk turned to where we were and what we had to do to get home alive. Survive thirty-five missions over enemy territory or get wounded and pick up a Purple Heart medal. No one wanted to earn that medal the "hard way," that was too final! Everyone realized that we had a tough way to go and the odds were that we all wouldn't make!

Jake, a ball gunner on the other crew, started the conversation with his imitation of a briefing officer as he unveiled the large wall map to reveal our It was January 28, 1945, in a cold and dreary England, and once again, snow had kept us "grounded" for almost a week. Our crew's first "lead crew" mission was to Sterkade-Rheine to hit oil storage tanks on January 20th. One of the guys had 'raided' the rationed coke bin again last night so we were warm and cozy in hut 29. That is, as long as we stayed huddled around the small coke stove in the middle of our home- away- from- home, which was a long way from home. The Templeton crew had been alerted and we were to fly another mission tomorrow, weather permitting. Lead crews carried four enlisted men instead of six. Our tail gunner, Ralph Moore, and ball turret gunner, Wilbur Lesh, had been assigned to the gunnery pool to fly with other crews.

A command pilot, bombardier, navigator and the Mickey (radar) operator were assigned to the bomb group's three lead crews at the officer's briefing session before the mission. The mission leader always flew in the lead plane of the middle squadron. The ball turret had been removed and replaced by the radar dome (Mickey) and the radar operator's desk was in the radio room across from my desk. Our co-pilot became our tail gunner and squadron fire control officer. Roddy, our engineer, was responsible for listing all aircrew members on our plane before take-off. Sometimes, he came back to tell us who our command officers were for the mission, but often I didn't know who was flying with us until the mission was over.

Jake's "Hillbilly briefing" went something like this:

"Now boys, I want you to pay attention up there, a feller could get killed flying around in one of them bombers. Them Nazi's is serious, we're dropping bombs on them and they don't like it. I think they're mad at us.

That's why you see all those little puffs of black smoke in the sky on the bomb run over the target. That flak is dangerous stuff! Them's 88 mm anti-aircraft shells explodin' and fillin' the air with iron slugs. You know, kinda' like giant shotgun shells. Now watch out for that stuff and good luck up there. Wish I could go with you, but I'm allergic to flak. Besides, I gotta' stay here to mark up this big map for the next mission."

Jake's plan was to make light of the coming mission and hope laughter would break the tension and allow us to get some sleep. It did help a little, but not much. After all, our crew was going and Jake's wasn't. The trick was to keep from worrying long enough to get in some sack time before we were roused us out of bed by the pre-dawn wake-up call. The night orderly let us sleep until 03:15 before he burst into the hut. We brushed the sleep out of our eyes, dressed in our warmest flying outfits, made sure we had our "lucky charms" and moved out into the snow. It was a two block hike down the company street for a good breakfast. The freezing wind helped hurry us along and we were happy to reach the Mess Hall. The large room was warm and filled with the odors of coffee, bacon and eggs. Air crews always got a hearty breakfast before a mission because our high altitude lunch was meager. It was either a C-ration, about the size of a "Cracker Jack" box, or a box of high energy candy. Either way it would probably be eight or nine hours before we had another hot meal after de-briefing. Mission crews jokingly referred to this extra special breakfast as "our last meal" and sometimes it was!

Trucks waited outside to take us down to the briefing room for information on the mission. We never knew our target until the briefing officer pulled the curtain on a huge wall map of Germany. Then the mystery was over and we knew where we were going, it was always bad news, but some targets were so much worse than others. Of course, we always hoped for the ones with the fewest flak guns and of course, the briefing was nothing like Jake's comedy routine. We always got a clear description of our target and a map of the safest route in and out of Germany to avoid anti-aircraft fire and fighters. All information was based on the latest reports from the Intelligence officers at Group Headquarters. However, there was an unknown factor in the flak information. The Germans had mounted anti-aircraft guns on trains and barges which could be moved to protect various locations.

The target for our tenth mission was the railroad yards at Hohenbudburg.

Blowing up Germany's railroads kept them from sending troops and supplies to the front. We picked up our equipment and parachutes and hopped on a truck to ride out to the "hardstand" (parking space) of the bomber we were flying on that mission. Take-off time had been moved back to 8:30 because the weather was still "iffy" and snow was in the air. The ground crews had worked all night to clear snow off the runway. We took off in a snowstorm and visibility was so poor that only eighteen of our twenty-five bombers were able to lift off before a snowstorm closed the runway. Our bomb-bay was loaded with twelve 500 pound bombs and we were headed up for our 10th mission.

Flak was very heavy on the bomb run over the target, and each crewman hoped his flak jacket and helmet would protect him from the shrapnel (flak) zinging through the sky. We had dropped our bombs and turned for England when Bert, called on the intercom from his waist-gunner's position: "May Day--May Day, Orville's been hit in the head, I've got to stop the bleeding now!"

A piece of flak had hit Robinson's flak helmet just above the right eye. He was down and wounded, but alive. The steel flak helmet had stopped the slug and saved his life, but its jagged edges had cut him badly. Our P-51 Mustang escort fighters were flying with our formation and no Luftwaffe fighters had been sighted in the area. Pilot Lt. Bill Templeton ordered Roddy to leave his top turret gun position to go back and help Bert with the bandaging. We were lead crew, so the Mickey (radar) operator and I had to stay at our desks. Rod was in a hurry when he came through the bomb bay and passed through my radio room with his portable oxygen bottle in one glove and a First-aid kit in the other. He only had a few minutes to get back to the waist gunner positions, plug in his electric suit and hook up to an oxygen outlet before he could help Bert. Those two guys did a great job taking care of Orville. The 40 below zero temperature froze the blood under the bandage and stopped the bleeding. A morphine shot eased his pain on the journey back to Eye. The situation became even more serious when I received a radio message warning us of a snowstorm approaching Eye. Robby was wounded and we needed to land and we hoped to beat the storm to our field. We were in a race and the snow won!

The big storm hit just as we were approaching the base. It was a sickening feeling to see that snowstorm sweeping in over the airfield below. It was like a giant white broom sweeping over the runways and then--- it was 'visibility zero'. There was no way we could land at Eye and no time to waste. Our eighteen planes were directed to stay ahead of the storm and land at another field farther away. We made it to that base just ahead of the snow. Roddy fired the red flares from his top turret to indicate we had wounded aboard. We were allowed to land early and an ambulance followed us as we taxied to a hardstand. The medics whisked Orville away to the base hospital. We had beaten the storm by only a few minutes.

The snowstorm continued and all 490th crews were trucked back to Eye, leaving our grounded planes buried in the snow. The weather cleared the next day and we were taken back to pick up our bombers. We had packed Robinson's personal belongings and were allowed to visit him in the hospital. Bert took him a piece of flak that he found in the waist area. It may have been the one that did the dirty work.

S/Sgt Orville Robinson was going to be ok, but our buddy from Eye would lose his eye. We said our goodbyes and boarded the B-17 to return to base, but Hut 29 was not the same without Orville. After ten missions, our buddy had earned an Air Medal, a Purple Heart medal and a ticket back to the USA.

A new waist gunner, Pvt. Dwight Parrish, joined our crew the next day. He was a former S/Sgt and gunnery instructor who had been "busted." Parrish won back his stripes after a few missions, because he was a very good waist gunner. We were a complete crew again and our game of life or death continued!

"Fate and a small piece of flak ended S/Sgt Orville Robinson's combat missions!"

Note --- Orville died in 2007 and lies in the Blue Bonnet Hills cemetery at Colleyville, Texas near Ft Worth. My granddaughter Stacy regularly jogs nearby. She and my daughter Susie recently located and placed flowers on his grave for me in honor of my buddy and waist gunner who protected us on our first ten missions sixty six years ago.

HOENBUDBERG- ENGINEER'S VIEW

Tech Sgt. Ellsworth Barr was also in our 848th squadron, flying as engineer/top turret gunner on the Lt. Adolph Barnes crew. The Barnes crew was one of the eighteen that managed to take off for the Hoenbudberg mission before the snowstorm closed our base on Sunday, January 28, 1945. Ellsworth also kept a journal of his missions (perhaps more detailed than mine.) I include the story of his crew's third mission, because as engineer he rode up front. His job and his seat behind the co-pilot or in the top turret gave him an entirely different view of a mission than my radio operator position, sitting at my desk behind the bomb-bay. I would have been even more scared, if I had always known what they knew and saw.

T/Sgt. Barr wrote: "The weather today was atrocious. We took off straight into a snowstorm and only eighteen of us managed to get airborne before take-offs were stopped. Over the target area the flak was intense and accurate. When we got to the IP, the bomb-bay doors would not open, but we managed to free them during the bomb run. Our bombs were one minute late. The flak seemed to be bursting right in the bomb-bay. We picked up fifty-six holes. Number one engine had was hit (it later had to be changed.) The cable to the prop governor was cut and we couldn't get more than 1950 rpm out of it. One of the push rod casings was smashed and there may have been other damage.

Number two engine had an ignition cable cut and oil was leaking from somewhere. There were holes in our two Tokyo gas tanks and a hole in one main tank. A piece of flak came through the plexiglass nose, cut the togglier's heated suit rheostat and knocked out the remote reading compass. A small piece hit our navigator in the seat of the pants. Another piece went through the radio room, almost cutting through two cables to the trim tab (to the tail) and missing the head of our Carpet (Mickey) Operator by inches. A large piece hit the tail gun position, but the armor plate around the tail gunner saved him. All in all, we were pretty well shot up!

Our bombing altitude today was 27,800 feet and our bomb load was twelve 500 pound GP (general purpose) bombs. The area around the target, a large marshalling yard (railroads) was as clear as a bell; considering the conditions, we should have wiped it out. We will have to check the Combat Library to see how well we did.

Co-Pilot 2nd Lt. Joel Johnson's Mid- Air Collision Story

March 17, 1945 thirty-five aircraft of our 490th Bomb group successfully bombed the railroad yards at Bitterfeld, Germany and were returning to Eye. The formation was flying about of 25,000 feet above Bad Camberg, Germany when there was a mid-air collision involving the Lt. Albert Stern and Lt. Robert Tennenberg crews. The following account of that accident so many years ago was provided by 2/Lt. Joel R. Johnson, Co-pilot of the Tennenberg bomber:

"We were clearing the target with a long curving sweep after an intense bomb-run. It seemed as if we had escaped any flak damage to our plane and our thoughts were on the long trip home. This was my twenty-third bombing mission over Germany. The day had been calm; however we were facing cloudy skies and poor visibility. In addition, the enormous contrails of the bomber formations ahead of us were making the sky "soupy." That's how I described it later in a letter to my younger brothers at home.

We were flying off the tail of the leader of the middle squadron, maybe fifty feet below and behind. We were an element leader with a plane on each side and another element flying under us. As usual my wrist watch was hung on a strap above the instrument panel where we could see it easily. Pilot, Bob Tennenberg and I usually exchanged pilot duties every fifteen minutes to off-set fatigue. It was about time for me for take the controls when in my windshield, I saw another B-17G. This was impossible. However, as soon as I saw it, we hit it!

The right side of the nose of our plane hit the upper turret of the other plane and our number three engine plowed into their radio room and conked out. At impact, the two planes flew together for a moment. I have always thought the number three engine propeller flipped their radio operator into the crushed-in nose of our plane, where he ended up on our navigator's table. Our number four engine's propeller finished the job of cutting the other plane into two pieces and setting our plane free! We came out of the collision at a much lower altitude and in a level condition. How did it happen? Since both planes had been flying in the same direction at a similar speed, the difference was that the other plane was inclined about twenty-five degrees, so its speed would have become slower than ours. I did not feel or hear the crunch. I was sitting ten feet from the impact and was temporarily stunned. I still feel it down the top center of my brain!

Our starboard engine propellers number three and four were bent and causing enormous vibrations in our plane. Tennenberg was busy trying to trim the plane and I was frantically working on the number three and four engines. I was afraid would we lose our right wing from the vibrations. I brought number four back to 700 RPMs and that stopped the vibrations. The number three engine was dead but the propeller kept wind-milling and would not "feather." It was so bad that I was hoping the engine would fall off or at least that the propeller would spin off the engine. Some of the crew wanted to jump.

Two nights before this mission, Chet (Chester) Deptula, our navigator and I rode our bikes to a pub off base. We had a couple of beers with two officers from another base and got to talking about flying. One of the officers, a major, told of dealing with a cranky propeller. He said to keep repeating the normal procedure over and over again. Well, I repeated the feathering procedure on number three engine maybe fifty to a hundred times and all at once it began turning to the feathering position and the vibrations stopped!

Chet Deptula, our navigator, came up to the cockpit from the nose. He was covered with blood and I asked him if he was injured. He said he was okay, but he had ended up part way out of the aircraft's nose during the collision. He had been wearing his flak suit and no parachute, but managed to pull himself back into the plane. He said John Gann, our nose-gunner, was injured, and he needed help to move him from the smashed nose back to the radio room. He then reported that there was a body on his navigation table! I got on the intercom and checked all positions. Everyone on our crew was accounted for and that's when I knew we had someone from the other aircraft on our plane. Deptula said there was a pair of legs on the floor in the nose. Later, when John Gann returned from the hospital in Belgium, he told us he thought those were his legs!

We were flying alone, but able to maintain our altitude by increasing the RPMs on the number one and two engines and holding 700 RPMs on number four. We had lost our air-speed indicator and there was another huge problem. We still had to figure where we were and how to get out of Germany. We were lost, in shock and over enemy territory. To have had this happen makes me shudder even today.

Tennenberg went back to the radio room to check on the crew and I put out several Mayday (SOS) calls trying to get a radio heading to an Allied base, but never got a reply. When Bob came back from the radio room, he suggested that we try to make it back to England, but I argued against it because no one knew how much damage we had sustained.

Then the third miracle happened! Off our right wing, about a mile away, we saw a plane that looked like one of our P-47 fighters. We were more than a little nervous, because Germany had a similar fighter, the FW 190. Luckily, it was a P-47, so we fired the red flares and alerted our gunners to let him come on in. We followed our "little friend" as he led us to safety. We finally spotted the field (A-92) in Belgium. The P-47 went in first and swept the runway to clear it for us. During the long approach, our flight engineer, Joe Pour, shot the remaining red flares to alert the airbase of our emergency condition and to signify that we had wounded on board.

We made a long careful glide toward the runway, because we knew we might not have enough power for another pass. We used flap control, RPM control and the feel in the seat of our pants so the engines wouldn't stall out. We didn't have a functioning air-speed indicator and this was literally the approach of our lifetime. Tennenberg made a perfect three point landing on the runway and we spun it off into the grass. The fire trucks and ambulances rushed out to our plane and the commanding officer of the field came out to take Tennenberg to his headquarters.

When I exited that plane in Belgium, I kissed the ground. I felt like I was grandstanding, but I still kissed the ground and I meant it! Several miracles had happened to allow my crew to be safely on the ground and

I deeply regretted the complete disaster for the crew of the other bomber. When things quieted down, I examined our plane and noticed chaff in the nacelles of the number three and four engines. Chaff was the aluminum foil strips that were scattered over the target to mislead enemy radar on the flak guns. That led me to assume that the extra body in our nose area was the radio operator, because chaff was a stored and tossed out from a chute in the B-17's radio room. One thing I should not have done was to charge back into our plane and look in the nose, because there was the torso on the navigator's table.

I stayed with the plane until the medics loaded S/Sgt John Gann, our wounded gunner, into the ambulance for a trip to a Belgian hospital. The Medics then removed the body of T/ Sgt George Delvin, (the radio operator from the other plane) from the nose of our plane. They said his body was rolled up like a ball. A 6x6 truck was sent out to our plane with instructions to take us to Brussels. My watch was left on the plane above the instrument panel. I asked the driver to stop by the hospital so we could visit John Gann. Then we stopped at the Officers Club. They were serving pork chops for lunch and I talked them out a full sack. I was told that the woman who gave it to me had cooked for German pilots who used this base before Americans took it over. Our crew hadn't eaten since five am, so we had a great snack on our way to Brussels. We found a place to stay, the crew, minus John Gann, got together in a small bar and tried to figure out what had happened to us. I remember Raymond Janisse, our ball turret gunner, saying that the tail of the other plane had split his machine guns and when he popped out of the ball-turret, his parachute opened and spread all over the waist area. The collision happened so fast that we had no answers to the question. We only knew that it was a day when we had faced death and survived!

Later, we caught a plane and returned to our base in Eye, East Anglia and when we entered our hut we found a clean-up crew packing all of our personal belongings. We had been presumed missing in action (MIA.) It was an eerie feeling. Among those in the clean-up crew was John Mann, our former ball turret gunner, who had been grounded.

Our mid-air collision was never discussed with us by anyone on base. I did hear a rumor that some pilots had asked to be grounded. I do not know why or how this accident happened. I do know that on March 17, 1945, "something happened" and I cannot explain it all. I know my mind froze on the moment of impact! No intelligence officer ever had a critique with me about this mission. Maybe, I feel guilty somehow, but I have thought about it every day for more than 24,522, days! "

As told by Major (Ret) Joel Johnson

1. Lt. Fred Seals, (Col. ret) present editor of the 490th newsletter, Bombs Away, was flying off our left wing. Fred writes: "*We were on the left wing and were covered with airplane parts. We landed in Belgi-53) airbase. I still get shivers thinking about it!*"

2. Harold Turk, tail gunner on the Stoval crew flying near us, said he would never forget the roar of the four engines of the stricken plane. None of the Stern crew survived as they were probably trapped in a spin as the plane fell.

3. Harry Thatcher on the Mackay crew, wrote: "*We were flying through contrails so thick that I could not see the wing tips of my own aircraft from my position in the ball turret Two planes on the starboard side of the formation collided in mid-air, blowing their whole formation apart.*"

4. George Devlin, radio operator of the Stern plane is buried next to his brother, James Devlin, in the American Cemetery in Ardennes, Belgium. James, a B-24 radio operator in the 15th Air Force, had been killed in action on a bombing mission over the Ploesti oil fields in Romania on October 13, 1944.

5. The Tennenberg crew flew seven more combat missions, including the April 19th, mission to Aussig, Czechoslovakia, when the 490th Bomb Group lost four bombers to Me-262 jet fighters

6. The crew also flew one "food drop" mission to the Netherlands.

7. Joel says, "Most of the Lt. Albert Stern crew was re-buried from Germany in the Netherlands. I have visited the cemetery in Ardennes, Belgium where the Devlin brothers are buried side by side."

Members of the Lt. Robert Tennenberg crew on March 17, 1945 was: Lt. Robert H. Tennenberg, pilot; Lt Joel R. Johnson, co-pilot; Lt. Chester A. Deptula, navigator; T/Sgt. Joseph Pour, engineer; T/Sgt. Edward L. Miller, radio operator; S/Sgt. Raymond R. Janisse, ball turret gunner; S/Sgt. John W. Gann, nose turret gunner; S/Sgt. Joseph D. Kennedy, waist gunner; S/Sgt. Alvin Wilhelm, tail gunner

Information provided by Major (Ret) Joel L. Johnson

S/Sgt John Gann's Story

S/Sgt John W. Gann, the youngest kid on the Tennenberg crew, was flying as toggleer and nose turret gunner on the day of the mid-air collision of the Lt. Robert Tenneberg and Lt. Albert Stern bombers while returning from bombing the railyards at Bitterfeld, Germany on March 17, 1945. The Eighth Air Force was doing "pattern bombing" and many bombers carried a toggleer/nose-gunner instead of a bombardier. The nose- gunner shared the bomber's nose with the Navigator. His job was to open the bomb bay doors when the group started its bomb run and when the lead plane dropped their bombs, he hit the toggle switch that released their bomb-load. The rest of the mission he sat at the remote controlled nose turret and searched the sky for enemy fighters that might be coming in from twelve o'clock high!

Sixty-seven years later John Gann tells his story:

"The sky was cloudy and filled with the exhaust of other planes in the formation, but Navigator Lt. Chet Deptula and I were glad our 490th formation was heading back to England. It was our 23rd mission and we were flying in the middle (lead) squadron. I was looking out the right front window when I saw a plane rising up into us from the right. I screamed as it crashed into our nose! The next thing I knew, I was sitting on the floor minus my helmet, intercom mike and oxygen mask. I saw my legs were cut off and lying across my lap! I was in shock and made no attempt to move or do anything at all, because I thought my legs were cut off and I couldn't walk. Then I had a near death experience as I stood at the bar of justice. All

168

my sins and shortcomings were revealed, but on the other hand the only good thing I had done was to write a letter to a friend of my Father.

My head cleared and I looked around, there was no plexi-glass in the crushed nose and freezing air was rushing through the plane. Our bomber was falling, shaking and losing altitude. I thought it was going to shake itself to pieces. I passed out again, but this time when I came to, the legs across my lap were gone and I realized I still had legs, but a big cut on my head! The shaking had stopped and I saw the air speed indicator. We were doing about 160 mph so I decided to move around and try to bail out. I tried to stand, but couldn't get my forty-five pound flak vest off. I literally tore the rivets out of the shoulder straps to get rid of it. I grabbed an oxygen hose on my right. I had been off oxygen too long and really needed that, but my lips froze to the hose. I pulled it loose and now my lips were bleeding as well as the hole in my head. The nose compartment looked like a slaughterhouse! I was freezing, but crawled around and saw my parachute pack on the floor. I was afraid it was going to fall out of the plane before I could get it. I grabbed it, hooked on my harness and for the first time, I thought I might have a chance to make it!

I stood half way up looked around. It was then that I and saw our navigator, Chet Deptula, hanging half out of the plane! He was holding on for dear life with his hands and feet inside the plane, but his body was outside the crushed nose. He was not wearing a parachute and was very near the wind-milling propeller of the number three motor! I stumbled across the nose, braced myself against the frame, grabbed hold of his chute harness and used all my strength to pull him back inside. Chet clipped on his chest pack parachute and we crawled farther back in the nose toward the escape hatch. Chet got the door open, but sat at the open hatch with his legs hanging out. I wondered why he waited, but then I saw our engineer, T/Sgt Joe Pour, who had crawled down from the flight deck to see if we were still alive. Joe told us not to jump because the pilots had the plane under control and we were going down to a lower altitude. My memory from that point is hazy. My legs wouldn't work, but Joe Pour and Chet Deptula managed to get me up out of the nose, though the bomb-bay, radio room and back to the waist area. They put me in an electric blanket from the planes "emergency bag" and after a while I began to thaw out a little!

By now we had dropped out of the group formation and were flying at a low altitude and didn't need oxygen masks. However, we were still in danger because a lone bomber over enemy territory is an easy target for German fighters. Our engineer, Joe Pour came back to give us a damage report on our Fort's condition. He said our plane was in bad shape, but we still had two good motors and a fair chance of landing safely in friendly territory. He made an inter-com check of all gun positions before telling us that the bomber that hit us had gone down and there was the body from that plane in the nose of our plane! A body of an airman from that plane had been drawn into our nose! It was then that I realized whose legs had been in my lap and that I had seen his torso on the navigator's table! I also remembered the marking on his jacket. I had talked to him that morning when we were cleaning our guns. He had told me he was going to London that night! I later learned that he was T/Sgt George Devlin, the radio operator on the Lt. Albert Stern crew.

I do not remember much of rest of the flight until the pilots landed our crippled bomber safely at a Belgium airbase which our army had recently liberated. It was amazing, our crew had survived a mid-air collision and we were safe on solid ground. I remember them taking me off the plane and the ambulance ride to the hospital on the cobblestone pavement. They put me on a stretcher and my first stop was an x-ray table. They cut off my clothes, put me back on the stretcher and carried me to another room. I was the center of attention lying naked on the floor as a man shaved my head with a safety razor. They sewed up the gash with a needle and thread and put me in a plywood bed with a very thin mattress.

Just about sundown the rest of my crew came by the hospital to tell me goodbye. They had been loaned a driver and truck to take them to an army airbase in Brussels where they could catch a plane back to England. Co-pilot Lt. Joel Johnson gave me some money, because I didn't have a cent. When they started to leave, I just lost it and began to sob and cry. Of course, I was a wounded teenager who had just survived a mid-air collision and I was being left on the continent all by myself. That was the straw that broke the camel's back. They called the nurse, she gave me a shot and I slept like a log.

How I experienced the hospital and hitch-hiked a plane ride back to England to rejoin my crew is another story."

Information provided by John W. Gann

Me-262 Jet Fighter

Germany had the only jet propelled fighters in WW II. Their most effective jet, the ME-262, became operational in November of 1943 and later in the war became a terror for our bombers and fighters. The ME-262 was a twin engine fighter with a top speed of 500 MPH, armed with cannon and rockets as well as 50 caliber machine guns. Everyone in the Mighty Eighth was glad it didn't become operational sooner. Hitler planned to use the new jets as bombers to hit England. He preferred his ME-109 and FW-190 fighters because they had been so successful defending targets against our bombers. Germany built 370 of the ME-262 s and late in the war the Luftwaffe redesigned them as fighters.

They were extremely fast and could riddle a formation with cannon, rocket and machine guns in a very short time. I remember that the 490th BG was attacked twice and we lost several bombers and men in each of those attacks. However, the world's first jet had several drawbacks and only about a third saw action.

1. It carried a limited amount of fuel and could only fly about 30 minutes.

2. Jet fuel was scarce.

3. It required skilled pilots and was very hard to control and land. Pilots were literally riding a plane with rockets on the wings.

4. Because of its speed, it had to make wide turns in a dogfight, our fighters could loop in behind and shoot it down. Our pilots called this tactic "The Luftwaffe Stomp."

Today, a ME-262 fighter is on display in the World War II section of the United States Air Force Museum at Dayton, Ohio. However, it doesn't look nearly as deadly as those attacking our formation with all guns blazing on March 21, 1945!

DEADLY PLAUEN MISSION

Lt. Bernard L. Painter's combat crew completed their training January, 1945 and prepared to fly the Northern Route to England in their spanking new B-17 Flying Fortress. The Eighth Army Air Corps needed bombers and replacement crews to blast Germany into surrender. In his diary, S/Sgt. Donald L. Becker describes his tail gunner position in the new plane after a shake-down flight.

"The take-off went smoothly --- I picked up my chute and crawled back past the retracted tail-wheel along the catwalk to the tail. Here is where I began to think: "This is mine, my own private little two-gun coffin of shining metal and plexi-glass, I checked out my newly made, oiled guns and the new N-8 sight. I had all the improvements in the latest model B-17 tail, but it was still a compact, cozy little coffin! What amazed me most were the pipes from the engines way back for heaters."

I spent the flight checking my guns, the sight, switches, oxygen stations (there were two in this one,) interphone and swinging my guns all over the countryside below. The field of fire has been increased from 30 by 30 degrees to 100 by 60 degrees. That's quite a morale booster after reports of seeing fighters standing off to the side and not able to fire, because the guns wouldn't go any farther."

S/Sgt. Donald L. Becker's combat diary tells vivid details of their bombing missions. I think the story of this crew presents a realistic description of the deadly missions faced by the young airmen on the heavy bomber crews of the Mighty Eighth. Aircrews of 1944-45 faced the same dangers as those in the early days of World War II in 1942-43. They did have fighter escorts to the target, but they also faced the Luftwaffe's new ME-262 jet fighter and heavier concentrations of anti-aircraft guns!

Note --- Lt. Painter's crew flew at the same time as my Lt. Templeton crew and we were on several of the same missions. Precision bombing was very important in the final months of the aerial war over Germany. British RAF and Eighth Air Force sent out hundreds of bombers and fighters on missions every day the weather allowed to bomb railroads, bridges and military targets to destroy Germany's ability to continue the war and to force Hitler to surrender. Allied armies had forced Germany troops back into its borders. The Russian army was invading from the East while British and American forces advanced from the south and west. The leaders of the Third Reich were cornered and fighting for survival! The Painter crew was assigned to squadron 350 of the 100th Bombardment Group, the "Bloody Hundredth" at Thorpe Abbots Air Base. February 20, 1945 the new crew flew its first mission and in the next month they had completed thirteen missions to some of the toughest targets in Germany!

Jet Fighter Attack --- March 3, 1945 Mission #6 --- Brunswick, Germany was the target of the 100th Bomb Group. S/Sgt. Becker's diary gives a graphic description of this sixth mission. Tail-gunners had a panoramic view of all the action behind the formation, while pilots, top turret and the guys in the nose saw what was ahead. Pilots relied on tail-gunners for the location of flak bursts and/or fighters behind the formation.

Note ---- I was on two 490th BG missions when we were hit by enemy fighters (ME-109 and ME-262), but I didn't see too much of the attack. My radio operator position was in the middle of the plane. I had only two small windows and the overhead hatch to catch the action around our plane. The guys on the guns saw it all! S/Sgt Becker's diary gives us details of an attack on his formation by Germany's newest weapon; the ME-262 twin engine jet fighter:

Diary entry --- "Mission #6 Brunswick --- The day started at 2:15 A.M. so we awoke with the expectation of another long haul close to the Russian lines --- we were briefed for Brunswick which appeared to be a 'milk run'(easy mission) on the surface with only 90 flak guns and no mention of fighters. We took off at 6:30 and were assigned to the lead squadron --- to lead the whole 8th Air Force throwing chaff (aluminum strips to foul up radar on the flak guns.) We had another bombardier flying with us so Herby sweated us out on the ground --- maybe that was the start of our bad luck. We flew the North Sea to approximately the Norwegian border and then into Germany. We encountered no flak so we felt safe regardless of our vulnerable position --- we had a whole group of fighters covering us --- The trip was uneventful to the I.P. (initial point) when a terrific barrage of flak started boxing us in and our fighters disappeared --- Our lead ship called out to spread the formation into an echelon, making us a dead duck for enemy fighters! We started evasive action and were on the bomb-run --- bomb doors open and things were popping --- excitement and tenseness reigned. I glanced out to 5 o'clock (behind) and there six fighters --- seemingly riding cover so I didn't pay much attention – they looked like P-51's with belly tanks, which were our fighter support. Painter was yelling "call out the flak" so he could go thru evasive action --- I looked back to 9 o'clock (right) and called out some close bursts --- looked back to 5 o'clock and those P-51's gave a burst of speed and exploded in all directions midst of the jet trails --- they were Germany's new jet fighter --- the ME-262! Before I could get my wits about me they were in on us and completely out of my line of fire! One was no more than 15 yards off my tail --- I could see the Jerry's face and every detail of the secret ship --- I was in a cold sweat, paralyzed with shock but I swung my guns as far as I could out of reflex action but it was too late --- he kicked his rudder and was blazing away at our lead ship at point-blank range of 20 yards with all cannons and guns --- I was the only one who saw him --- so I called out the fighters madly, but it was too late --- our lead ship right alongside, burst into flames and blew up before my eyes --- suddenly the jets were gone as fast as they came --- leaving a crowd of muddled, dumbfounded fliers burning with the sight of the screaming wreckage plummeting towards the ground --- I looked back at 6 o'clock and another "Lady" plunged earthward like a rock.

We'd been missed by the enemy's perfectly planned attack by a bare few feet --- our formation routed and scurried for cover in the main group formation --- collisions were missed by inches in the mess of blind aircraft. They didn't attack again, but our bombs never fell because our lead ship never toggled his out --- we rode on back with the crippled formation of damaged and crippled aircraft, dazed and shaking. The attack came at the psychological moment before 'bombs away' when everyone was busy and concentrating on the flak and hiding in flak suits. Our formation was spread and protection from gunners was weak and almost nil. The fighters picked PFF (radar) ships with no ball turret and came in on the tail-gunner's blind spot.

That was the closest enemy airplane has been to me and I never want to see one again, especially a deadly jet with 30mm cannons! Only two ships out of a thousand saw the remarkable attack --- one is a pile of wreckage and flesh somewhere in Germany and the other man is writing this diary --- Others in our crew saw the attack as it was ending, but I saw it all the way and was helpless. Just a few seconds difference and I could have saved ten men's lives --- it almost drives me crazy to think about it --- but it wasn't mine or anyone else's fault so there's no use thinking about it --- I really need my shot of whiskey when we landed --- only I'm still shaking and I can't erase the picture of that German fighter within arm's reach and that bomber blowing up right next to us --- it was quite a mission to earn my Air Medal on and I think it's deserved too!"

March 15, 1945 --- Mission No. 11 --- Berlin (Wittenberg) --- "Today at our briefing, when the curtain was pulled, the lines on the map ran straight to "Big B!" The screams and moans were loud and numerous. Berlin was the terror of the heavy bombers because it was so well protected. But our target was fifteen miles north of Berlin, just missing their 400 flak guns, but still remained the terrific fighter menace with the Defense of the Reich Staffel up against us.

It was a grueling nine hour flight, five of which were on oxygen at 25,000 feet and 50 degrees below zero. Our primary target was obscured by low clouds, so we had to go to the secondary target, Wittenberg which had eight Flak guns. We were much relieved when the lead crew radioed to Painter where we were headed. We were on the bomb-run when all hell broke loose. We were hit once and my head crashed against the plexi-glass window --- I was stunned --- then we were hit again and again --- I died four times, I was without a flak suit or helmet and a dead duck if shrapnel hit me. But then the light but perfectly accurate flak barrage was over and we were clear. When we landed we had ten hits on our ship, ranging from the size of a grapefruit on down. We were all ok although Mac, Painter, Rabbit and I had had close calls. When we landed, the red flares (wounded aboard, bring ambulance) were going off like the Fourth of July as planes limped in with wounded, dead engines and severe battle damage. All-in-all in our squadron, four men were killed --- eight wounded. My pal, another tail-gunner, had his leg blown off and bled to death. Of all the places we've been --- it had to be a place with only eight guns to raise hell

--- passing all those at Berlin, Munich, Frankfort and Hanover --- now I'm really getting flaky!

Note --- The Lt. Painter crew's 13th mission to Jena was not too rough, but getting home was another problem and they almost had to 'ditch' their plane in the English Channel because of zero visibility. However, they flew through the heavy fog and landed safely.

S/Sgt. Becker's last diary entry was --- "the coast of England suddenly loomed up and it never looked so beautiful before and the crew went wild with joy. We landed with a few more gray hairs and about a cupful of gas in each engine --- God what a relief! Old No.13 came off O.K. --- but someone was sure looking after us!"

Note --- Mission 14 ---March 21, 1945 --- The Lt. Painter crew was shot down on this mission to Plauen/Ruhland, Germany. Their formation was attacked by Luftwaffe ME-262 jet fighters at 9:40 a.m. over Leipzig, Germany. De-briefing reports after the mission said the bomber was hit by fighters, the left wing caught fire. The B-17 exploded and crashed and eight men died; Lt. Painter, pilot, bailed out and became a prisoner of war. July, 1945, he filed a MACR (Missing Aircraft Report) with the following info: ---"Fifteen minutes from the target our number one engine failed (turbocharger) and we had to drop out of formation to salvo our bomb-load and gain the power to keep up with the formation. However, we were attacked by ME-262 jets before I could rejoin the formation. The jets shot out our number two engine, the nose and the plane's controls. --------- I gave the order to abandon ship and bailed out at 18,000 feet."

S/Sgt Donald A. Becker of the 100th Bomb Group, was killed in action March 21, 1945. Sadly, he met the ME-262 jet fighter he had dreaded so much since his sixth mission! In this attack, he joined the thousands of other Eighth Air Corps airmen killed in action (KIA) over Europe. He and his buddies were buried in Freiberg, Germany. Later, at the request of his parents, his remains were returned to the United States in 1950. He now lies in the Zachary Taylor National Cemetery in Louisville, Kentucky --- seventy-five miles from my home.

Note: The information for this story was made available from the archives of the 100th Bomb Group Foundation. My thanks to the 100th Bomb Group Historian, Michael P. Faley, author of "High Noon Over Haseluenne"

MY DAY OVER PLAUEN

I flew on that same mission and it was also our crew's, fourteenth! My diary entry: --- Awakened at 0200, breakfast and briefing by 0300. Take off at 0612. We were on oxygen five hours of this seven and a half mission. Our target was the railroad marshalling yards at Plauen. The Lt. Bill Templeton crew, squadron 848 of the 490th Bomb Group formation was leading the middle (lead) squadron. Major Cochran was mission commander and our command pilot. Our co-pilot, Lt. Dale Rector rode tail-gunner position as Squadron Fire Control officer. Our 490th formation had 38 aircraft and we flew at 21,000 feet Major O'Dell, was command navigator, I forget the name of the command bombardier, but he had to be good because all planes in the formation would drop their bombs when our lead plane reached bombs away! We took off at 0612, assembled at 8,000 feet on red and yellow flares and joined the stream of 2,200 bombers sent to bomb German airfields, oil storage and railroad centers.

This was a tough mission, lots of flak and we were hit by a group of ME- 262 twin engine jet fighters. They hit the low squadron about twenty minutes before we reached the IP to start the bomb run. There were tracer bullets and flak puffs everywhere. Two of our 490th bombers were shot down and a third was lost when a jet crashed into it after being shot down by 490th gunners. Ewing Roddy, top turret gunner, and waist gunner, Bert Allinder later swore that they were firing away at one fighter bearing down on us when it peeled away before firing. Perhaps the pilot ran out of fuel or ammo or was chased away by our P-51 escort fighters. Gunners in our group were given credit for downing one jet that crashed into one of our bombers.

God had smiled on us again and our bomber was spared serious damage or injury. I don't know how near the 100th BG was flying to our 490th BG, but now, 66 years later, I know that Sgt. Becker and I were on the same deadly mission that day over Plauen.

BOMBERS DOWN!

The March 21 1945 mission to Plauen was the Templeton crew's fourteenth mission and we were leading the middle squadron with mission commander, Major Cochran, as command pilot. The ME-262 jet fighter attack on the Plauen mission was very costly for our 490th Bomb group. Three aircraft were lost from the low squadron in less than three minutes. The following stories from the 490th Bomb Group (H) Historical Record are first-hand reports from the Plauen mission.

Lt. Elmer Buckner of the 850th also flying in the low squadron wrote: "ME-262 jets came at us out of an overcast sky about 0900 hours to make tail-on attacks on our low group. They shot down three ships in a space of three minutes. Lt. William Audette's plane (848th) had the rudder shot off; Lt. Herman Ballard's (850th) ship was on fire and the Lt. John Schultz bomber (848th) was raked from nose to tail by cannon fire from a head-on jet attack. I got a good view of one Me-262 as it as it passed under my left wing. Our gunners poured lead at the jets and shot one down. It just blew up and crashed into the Shultz bomber. We finally got to Plauen dropped our 1000 pound bombs on the rail marshalling yards and returned safely to Eye with several flak holes in our ship."

Bombardier 2nd Lt. George Gilbert was flying in the Lt. Audette plane of squadron 848 and the crew was listed as (MIA) "missing in action." USAAF notification letters were sent to all next of kin almost two months later. May 16, 1945 Mrs. George Gilbert received one of those letters, however by that time her husband had been rescued and was safe in friendly hands. In 1978 he wrote the story of his 30th mission to be included in the 490th Historical Records.

"It all started off as just another mission. Briefing was at 05:00 hrs and we took off at 07:00. It was routine to the IP (Initial point) with no flak. Suddenly, out of nowhere, we were attacked by ME-262's and on their first pass our vertical stabilizer was shot off. The tail gunner, waist gunner and radio operator were all killed. On the second pass both of our starboard engines were set on fire and it was time to get out. I helped navigator Lou Havare, bail out then the ship went into a dive. At about this time the fire hit the fuel tanks and the aircraft exploded! The force of the explosion blew me out through the plexi-glass nose. Capillaries in my nose and ears burst and my chest-pack chute hit me in the mouth. I looked like I had gone 15 rounds with Mohammed Ali! A P-51 followed me down, and if I knew who the guy was I would buy him a drink.

I was captured as soon as I landed and placed in the local combination jail, city hall and school building at the edge of town. Children climbed up on the ledge outside my window to look at the American monster and I certainly must have looked like one. The next day I rode on a baggage train and was turned over to the Infantry. I spent most of the day watching some German soldiers fixing shoes. While I was there, they brought in Lou Havard and Ron Johnston. We were guests of the Germans until we were freed the 6th of May. I went into the hospital at Camp Lucky Strike for leg surgery and returned to the states in June. Sometime after the war, I learned that our ball turret gunner (Sgt. Ted Chapin) had also bailed out." Engineer and top turret gunner, Sgt. Charles R. Johnston also gave his version of events for the record:

"Because our squadron had strayed from the main formation, we were intercepted by ME-262s near Dresden and our ship took some crippling hits. Both starboard engines were on fire and the skipper ordered us to abandon ship. I had a jet in my sights at the time and he was up on our tail for the final kill. I waited until he was roughly 600 yards out and then opened up with both of my 50s until I had run out of ammo. He went down; I claimed the kill and bombardier, George Gilbert, confirmed it. At this time I decided to bail out. We were at 25,000 feet, so I did a "free fall" and didn't open my 'chute until I could recognize things on the ground. I landed in a very tall tree in a forest. I scarcely had time to slip out of my parachute harness before several members of the German Home Guard were at the base of the tree pointing their rifles at me and urging me to come down. I had a wound over my left eye and a broken ankle, the young German officer had his men put me in a cart and haul me into town. On a table in the building where I was taken, I saw the dog-tags the Germans had taken from Lt. Audette and Lt. Ankenny (pilot and co-pilot.) Later I was taken to a nearby town and turned over to the Burgermeister who had a very low opinion of American flyers. I was placed in a cell with Havard. The next day we were marched to Dresden, about ten miles away and turned over to the regular German army where we were joined by Gilbert.

I went on "sick call" with German soldiers and the doctor dressed my head wound and bandaged my broken ankle. Later, the three of us were moved about 130 miles to Weimer for interrogation.

The start of our journey was by public street car across the city to the Dresden railway station. When we arrived at the station the townspeople came after us shouting, "Morderen auf frau and kinder!" (Murderers of women and children!) The sergeant escorting us ordered his men to aim their rifles at the mob and herded us into an empty box-car for protection until he was able to get us on the train. After interrogation I was separated from Havard and Gilbert and sent to a POW camp hospital near Nuremberg. Not long afterwards American forces liberated the camp and I was flown to Paris where I finally got a leg cast and my head wound treated."

RODDY'S LUCKY DAY

T/Sgt. Ewing Roddy, our crew's engineer, became top turret gunner over enemy territory. It was a short hop from his seat behind the co-pilot to step into the turret. It was the Templeton crew's 14th mission and the target was Plauen. A welcoming committee of Me-262 jets was there to meet us! We were really lucky to have fighter protection, but the 50 caliber machine guns of all gunners in the formation got a good workout that day.

Rod's recollections, "That day I had test-fired my twin 50 caliber guns out over the North Sea and the shells jammed! I had a mess on one gun's base-plate. I wasn't sure of the temperature, but I took off my gloves to fix those 'cockeyed' shells and my thumbs froze to the greasy base-plate. I pried them loose, but years later back in Pennsylvania, they had to take my faint thumb prints six times before I got my gun permit! It was a good thing I got that jam fixed, because I needed both guns before we got to the target!

We were leading the lead (middle) squadron when we were hit by the jet fighters. During the attack, they shot down three bombers from the low squadron. Flak was really heavy over the target, but we hit the Plauen railroad yards.

It was really crowded in the turret when I was rotating around, so I only clipped one side of my chute pack to the harness. I didn't have room to hook both sides so it always hung down on my side. When we landed back at Eye, I tossed my harness and chest pack parachute out the nose hatch before I jumped down

A mechanic yelled, 'Whose chute is this? It's a good thing nobody had to use it!'

I looked down and the guy had his finger stuck in my parachute pack up to his knuckle. A piece of flak had hit my chute and it would have been riddled with holes and therefore useless. A chute full of holes is one thing you don't want if you have to bail out. Then I realized how lucky I had been that day. I didn't have to bail out and my parachute had stopped a chunk of flak that was headed for my belly!"

Lt. Tennenberg crew photo with Ground Crew chief before their mid-air collision from files of 490th Historian, Eric Swain
Standing L-R: Unknown, Lt Chester Deptula, navigator; Lt Robert Tennenberg, pilot; Lt Joel Johnson, co-pilot; T/Sgt Ed Miller, radio operator; Sitting L-R: S/Sgt Ray Janise, ball turret gunner; S/Sgt Alvin Wilhelm, tail gunner; S/Sgt John Gann, nose turret gunner/toggleer; S/Sgt Joseph Kennedy, waist gunner; unknown; T/Sgt Joe Poor, engineer/top turret gunner
Information by Shari Garvin, daughter of Alvin Wilhelmt

The Templeton crew flew the lead squadron (middle) to hit the Ansbach rail yards on February 22, 1945. Photo taken after we completed our twelfth mission and earned a second Air Medal. Kneeling left to right: Sgt. Dwight H. Parrish, waist gunner; T/Sgt Ewing G. Roddy, engineer /top turret; T/Sgt James Lee Hutchinson, radio operator/gunner; S/Sgt Bert Allinder, armorer/ waist gunner. Standing L to R: 1ˢᵗ Lt. Bruno P. Conterato, navigator; 1ˢᵗ Lt William D. Templeton, pilot; 2nd Lt Dale F. Rector, co-pilot. Our tail gunner, S/Sgt Ralph Moore and ball turret gunner, S/Sgt Wilbur Lesh had already been assigned to other crews. The Command pilot (mission leader), bombardier and radar operator are not shown. The Templeton crew flew eighteen combat missions, fourteen as lead crew and a prime target for fighters and flak! We also did two Mercy missions and earned a total of three Air Medals. The Stars and Stripes

CHAPTER EIGHT

New York　　London Edition　　Paris

THE STARS AND STRIPES

Daily Newspaper of U.S. Armed Forces　　in the European Theater of Operations

VOL. 5　No. 30—1d.　　WEDNESDAY, Dec. 6, 1944

Daily French Lesson
Est-ce direct pour l'Opéra?
Ess deerekt poor lopayra?
Is it a thru' train to the Opera?

Berlin Raided by Heavies

Luftwaffe Loses 80 in Air Battles

Eighth Air Force fighter pilots slugged it out with the Luftwaffe in the skies over Berlin yesterday and shot down more than 80 enemy fighters.

More than 800 Mustangs and Thunderbolts covered more than 550 Fortresses and Liberators of the Eighth in attacks on industrial targets in the Berlin area and railway yards at Munster.

Berlin was last attacked by Eighth heavies on Oct. 6. The capital was once the most heavily-defended area in the Reich.

The 357th Fighter Group, a P51 outfit led by Maj. Joseph E. Broadhead, of Rupert, Ida., bagged 20 Nazi craft, while the 479th Fighter Group, another P51 unit led by Lt. Col. Kyle L. Riddle, of Decatur, Tex., knocked down 16.

Maj. William Hove, P51 squadron commander from Crookston, Minn., in the 355th Fighter Group, reported shooting down 5½ Jerries.

Pound Tegl Munitions Plant

Fortresses, comprising the bulk of the bombing force, pounded the Tegl munitions plant in the suburbs northwest of Berlin and other objectives in the capital itself.

Several formations bombed visually through breaks in clouds.

RAF Lancasters in daylight yesterday blasted the railway yards at Hamm.

Losses from Monday's large-scale operations by the Eighth were 12 bombers and three fighters.

Monday night RAF heavies dropped more than 3,500 tons of bombs on the important railway and industrial centers of Karlsruhe, in the upper Rhineland, and Heilbronn, 40 miles east. RAF heavy bombers sent over Germany starting in the afternoon numbered 1,150.

Ninth Air Force Marauders, Havocs, Invaders and fighter-bombers flew more than 15,500 sorties in November, attacking over 100 of the fortified towns and villages which constitute the German defensive system east of Aachen. Eleven bombers and 119 fighter-bombers were lost.

Meanwhile, complete reports of Tuesday's assault on Berlin, the first in two months, showed 91 German fighters shot down by Eighth fighter-pilots. U.S. losses were 12 bombers and 22 pursuits, but at least 11 of the fighters and some

650 Heavies Pound Reich

More than 650 Fortresses, escorted by upward of 550 Mustangs and Thunderbolts, resumed the offensive against German rail and industrial targets Friday.

The heavies struck at Hanover and Kassel, key points in Germany's battered rail routes to the Western Front. Kassel, a tank-production center, was last hit Dec. 4.

Eighth's losses were four bombers and two fighters. There was no enemy fighter opposition.

Italy-based 15th Air Force Forts and Libs also bombed rail facilities yesterday, pounding the yards at Innsbruck, northern terminus of the Brenner Pass, as well as strategic targets at Linz and Salzburg in Austria and Rosenheim and Amstetten in Germany.

This short item describes the mission of April 15, 1945 when the bomber carrying Wibur Lesh, our former ball-turret gunner, was shot down over Aussig, Czechoslovakia. He was the third of four Lesh brothers to die in WW II.

This was The Templeton crew's first mission and we got a full report of the action that day. The article also said that 1,150 RAF Lancaster bombers blasted railway centers and industries Monday night with 3,500 tons of bombs. The article concluded with a report that Ninth Air Force twin engine fighter-bombers flew more than 15,500 sorties (raids) attacking a 100 enemy fortifications in November. Eleven heavy bombers and 119 fighter-bombers were lost!

Yard Birds

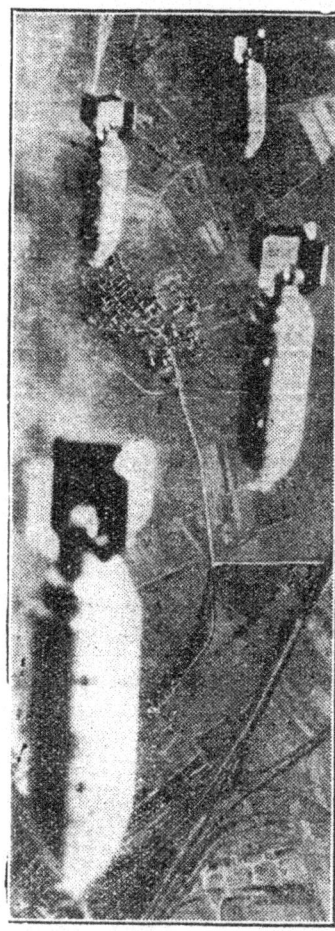

USAAF Photo

Bombs falling on Germany is an old story with Eighth AF crews by now. For the record, here's a dramatic shot of the raid on the Friedburg marshalling yards Dec. 4. The yards can be seen directly under the nose of the largest bomb. Objectives of this and similar Allied raids, together with a map of the Nazi railway system, are told on page 4.

900 Heavies Hit Berlin, Hanover Plants

The 8th Air Force aimed twin blows yesterday at Germany's inner circle of war industry and what may be its last remaining industrial trump card when over 400 Fortresses bombed war plants in suburban Berlin and more than 500 ranged over Hanover to hit factories and railroad marshalling yards.

Significantly, ack-ack gunners in Berlin and Hanover yesterday threw up a stiff umbrella of flak, indicating that the Nazis, in expectation of savage attacks yet to come, may not yet have stripped their vital industries in central Germany.

Some fliers over Berlin, where tank, armored vehicle and weapons factories were attacked, reported particularly heavy barrages of ack-ack fire, besides thick clouds, which made bombing by instrument necessary in most cases. Clouds also covered Hanover, where the targets included plants making half-tracks and other armored vehicles.

Some 350 Mustangs shielded the bombers yesterday, but ran into no enemy fighters, a further gauge of the effectiveness of the 8th's and the 15th Air Force's recent saturation assaults on German airfields and plane factories

NO. 2 HANOVER DEC. 15
MARSHELING YARDS

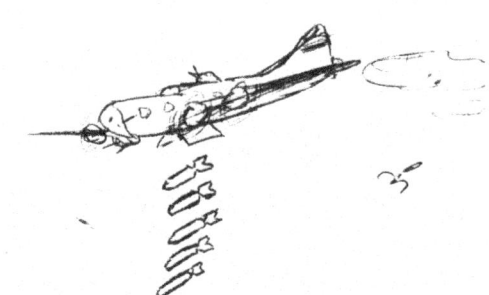

Plane Mission!
Author's Diary 3-21-'45

Stuttgart Rail Yards Bombed

Bad weather confined the weekend's activity by the Eighth Air Force to an attack Saturday by a small force of Fortresses, escorted by P51s, on the Kornwestheim railyards in the northern suburbs of Stuttgart. Three bombers were lost.

The Kornwestheim center is one of the two main marshalling yards in the Stuttgart area. The other, at Unterturkheim, just south of the city, was bombed and severely damaged Dec. 9.

Forts and Libs of the 15th Air Force Sunday carried out an assault on synthetic-oil plants at Blechhammer and near Odertal in Silesia. Escorting Mustangs and Lightnings encountered their first sizable formation of enemy fighters in weeks over northern Moravia, engaging in over 50 dogfights.

More Railyards Struck

Other B24s, ranging Austria, struck at rail yards at Salzburg and other targets at Wels, 15 miles southwest of Linz.

Mediterranean RAF heavies attacked motor transport in Jugoslavia, and others dropped supplies to British troops in Greece.

A Reuter dispatch said 300 German aircraft operated over the U.S. Ninth Army front Saturday night.

Meantime, it was announced that all of the tracks of the important Innsbruck railyards, at the head of the Brenner Pass, were cut and most of the sidings blocked in raids Friday and Saturday by Italy-based heavies.

Forts and Libs of the 15th Air Force Saturday also attacked synthetic-oil targets at Brux in Czechoslovakia.

Forts Batter Nazi Rail Points

In an effort to block choke-points on road and rail routes carrying supplies and reinforcements for counter-attacking German forces along the U.S. First Army front, more than 300 Fortresses of the Eighth Air Force attacked road and rail junctions in western Germany Tuesday.

FEB 17, 1945

FRANKFORT

Death Brings Fliers Top Awards

452ND BOMB GROUP, May 14—1/Lt. Donald J. Gott, 21-year-old Fortress pilot from Arnett, Okla., and 2/Lt. William E. Metzger, 22-year-old co-pilot from Lima, Ohio, who gave their lives in an unsuccessful attempt to save the life of a fellow-crewman, have been posthumously awarded the Congressional Medal of Honor, highest U.S. decoration.

Last Nov. 9 their Fortress Lady Jeannette was ripped by flak while over the target, a railroad yard at Saarbrucken, Germany. Two engines were set afire and disabled, a third damaged, and the plane's interphone and electrical systems destroyed.

Losing altitude rapidly and fully ablaze after being hit at low level by more German ack-ack, the Fort managed to get over friendly territory. With an emergency landing field in sight, Lady Jeannette slowly circled the clearing, but, when only whose sake they had remained with the bomber.

Fort Navigator Wins Congressional Medal

WASHINGTON, May 14 (ANS)—The Congressional Medal of Honor has been awarded posthumously to 2/Lt. Robert E. Femoyer, an 8th Air Force navigator of Huntington, W.Va., who, although mortally wounded, brought his Fortress safely back to its base, it was announced today.

Femoyer, assigned to the 447th Bomb Gp. (H), died last Nov. 2, shortly after his crippled B17 landed on its return from a raid near Merseburg, Germany. When three anti-aircraft shells struck the plane, wounding the navigator in the side and back, he refused morphine injections and remained for two and one-half hours

Note the ages of these two young officers who were trying to land and save the plane and the lives of wounded crew members.

MEDAL OF HONOR RECOMMENDATION

M ajor Daniel P. Mclean, Operations Officer of the 850th squadron prepared a recommendation for the Medal of Honor for Sgt. Dardo Garbiero who died on the April 5th Unterschlauersbach mission. However it was never approved.

In part, it read:

"Sgt. Dardo (Gabby) Garbiero, serial number 16072467, distinguished himself by valor and heroism beyond the call of duty while serving as a waist gunner on a bombardment mission April 5, 1945. On this day, the 490th Bombardment Group (H) was leading the Third Air Division, Eighth Air Force in an attack on Nuremburg, Germany. Assembly was planned over the continent, but weather conditions there were so poor that the low squadron,-----finally bombed with only eight planes ----- Lt. Martinson, pilot, followed the 'briefed' route from the assembly point to the initial point in an effort to join some formation with which he could bomb his objective. Failing to find any other formation he turned back to the base and climbed up through weather until he broke out into the clear at about 27,000 feet. He stayed close to the top of the cumulus cloud formations in order to have the protection of the clouds in the event of a fighter attack. This caused him to pass through some of the higher clouds for as long as two or three minutes -----.when the aircraft broke out of the clouds nose gunner , T/Sgt Daniel Lockstead, called out, " Formation of fighters at 12 o'clock level, let's get out of here." The pilot banked left 70 degrees and began a steep dive. The co-pilot felt the plane shudder and heard rendering noises that he had never heard before from the rear of the ship. Shortly thereafter the aircraft appeared to roll out to level off for a short period after which it began to spin sharply to the left. While in this spin, it evidently broke in two at the bulkhead at the forward end of the bomb-bay.

During the maneuvers and gyrations of the aircraft, the crew members were almost constantly planned against their seats or the sides of the plane by the centrifugal force created. ---------- The co-pilot and engineer escaped from the front of the aircraft after it had broken in two.

Sgt. Garbiero had all always been looked to by the plane commander and the members of his crew as the commander of the after section. He watched over the other crew members, made certain their oxygen was working, helped the ball turret gunner into and out of his turret and answered to the pilot for the readiness of action for his 'rear echelon.' Sgt. Gentzle, ball turret gunner, was standing at the left waist position when the aircraft first began its steep bank. When the full effect of the bank took hold, he was pinned against the side of the aircraft where he stood. He lost consciousness almost immediately but later came to enough to realize that he was lying on the floor. His head on an oxygen flask that had come off the side wall, his left hand injured so that he could not use it and blood running was into his eyes from a cut on the head. ------The plane was still airborne and seeing the door missing from the right side, Gentzle crawled to it with the idea of getting out. Sgt. Garbiero stopped him from crawling over the door sill, stood him up, hooked his parachute on for him and helped him to the door to jump.

Sgt. Garbiero, although ready to jump at a time would be reasonably expected to abandon his post to save himself ---- instead, he chose to remain in the plane to see that other crew members in the back section of the aircraft escaped. In spite of the wild gyrations of the aircraft, he succeeded in assisting the ball turret gunner, injured and only semiconscious, to bail out. Then, knowing the careening aircraft could not last much longer, Gabiero stayed to go help the radio operator. Within a very short time the bomb load exploded. He paid with his life for his sense of responsibility to his crew mates!

Lt. Jones, co-pilot, was last to be thrown clear of the wreckage from the forward part of the aircraft. He saw the parachutes of the tail gunner, ball turret gunner and the engineer below him as soon as his own parachute opened. Almost immediately after counting those parachutes, he saw a shower of small fragments of the aircraft falling about him. It seemed evident that the bomb load had exploded shortly after the aircraft had been torn apart.

This display of valor, involving self-denial, disregard of personal safety and heroism beyond all call of duty, is highly indicative of Sgt. Dardo Garbiero's ability and the highest credit is reflected on himself and the Armed Forces of the United States."

Daniel P. McLean, Major, AC

> *"My theory: the award was not approved because such acts of heroism and self-sacrifice were expected of the young airmen aboard the heavy bombers of the Mighty Eighth!"*

"Hutch"

Parchim – Fighter Attack

We were rousted out of the sack at 03:00 and went through the motions of dressing in our cold damp Nissen hut. The fire in our little stove was banked for the night and putting out very little heat. The other crew in Hut 54 was not flying today. They stayed snug and warm in their bunks while we headed for the Mess Hall and on to mission briefing. The "mission breakfast" of hot coffee, eggs and meat warmed us up and the news at our briefing cheered us up. It was April 7, 1945 and Germany was "on the ropes." American and British ground forces were closing in from the west, while Russian armies were attacking from the east. Ninth Air Corps tactical bombers and fighters not escorting bombers were strafing and bombing strategic targets while Mighty Eighth and RAF heavy bombers were blasting factories and major targets. Today we were going after an enemy airfield!

The Luftwaffe was growing weaker each day as they lost pilots and fighters they could no longer replace. The primary target was a German ME-262 airfield at Parchim! Our group was getting a chance to punish the Luftwaffe fighter pilots who were getting leaner and meaner as they faced defeat. There were reports that German pilots had agreed to use a semi-suicide tactic and formed "rammer squadrons". If they were attacking a bomber formation and ran out of gas or ammunition they were instructed to try to ram a bomber or try to clip off its tail or wing-tip before they bailed out. The Luftwaffe was so short of pilots that high ranking officers like Colonels and Generals were flying in a last desperate effort to defend Hitler's Third Reich.

Our mission was a matter of self-preservation; destroying jet fighters and fuel on the ground was a much better idea than meeting them at 25,000 feet. The German jet fighter, ME-262, needed a long runway to get airborne, this made their airfields easy to locate. Out take off was delayed until almost 09:00 due to fog. The 490th put up thirty aircraft with Major Clarence J. Adams leading the mission. Our Templeton crew was leading the high squadron. A large group of P-51 escort fighters joined us after we merged with the bomber stream and headed for revenge. We were also "fighter bait" and we knew it. When you hit a hornet's nest; there's going to be hornets!

Lt. Templeton gave the alert over the inter-com, just before the formation reached the IP to start our bomb run.

"Bandits at twelve o'clock high "

I looked out the top hatch and saw two ME-109's above us as they came diving down on our formation with machine guns blazing. (They also had a 20 mm cannon.) Our gunners were returning the fire with a hail of 50 caliber slugs and tracer bullets zoning in on the attackers. The enemy fighters shot down a bomber out of our high squadron (Lt. Druhot) on the first pass. I saw the B-17 to the left of us slide out of the formation with an engine on fire. The pilot held it level as the crew bailed out. I tried to count the white chutes as they popped out of the stricken plane. Our formation gunners concentrated on the two fighters as they circled and came in for another pass. Being in the lead bomber, our gunners had a good crack at them as swooped down on us. Bert Allinder left waist gunner, and Roddy in the top turret were sure they hit one as it burst into flames and dived into our squadron. The fuselage was burning off the fighter and its frame looked like a flaming orange crate. I saw the pilot's lifeless body in the cockpit as the plane missed us and rammed into another bomber in our right, (Lt. Cagels ship) bounced off and fell to the earth. The badly damaged Cagel plane dropped out of formation, but managed to stay aloft and make it to an airbase in France. The Group claimed credit for a downed fighter!

Sgt. Colby LeNeve, ball turret gunner on the Lt. Caroll Cagel bomber, tells of his narrow escape on that mission in an excerpt from The History of the 490th Bomb Group.

"Around mid-day the intercom rattled with the dreaded sound that bandits were in the area. Indeed there were, within seconds ME - 109s came blazing in, head-on. On the second wave, one of the enemy fighters tried to close in on our tight formation and was knocked out of control. It had no place to go but down, in between B-17s stacked wing-to-wing. We were in the wrong place and the inevitable was about to happen---we were going to be rammed. My eyes closed and words from the 23rd psalm parted my lips 'The Lord is my shepherd, I shall not want. He maketh me-----'at that instant our B-17 was rocked by the impact of the ME-109 as it hit and started a half-revolution around our ill-fated bomber-------- the fighter struck the rear of our left wing where it meets the fuselage; this is where the wing and bulkhead join. Luckily, that is the very backbone (strongest point) of a B-17. Had the impact been several inches behind this point, we surely would have been sliced in two."

The fighter continued to spin around and under the belly of our ship, badly damaging the ball turret which I occupied. The turret entry and escape hatch was sprung open and carried away by the slipstream --- leaving me with nothing but my safety belt to keep me in the turret. This turned out to be another lucky break because oil from the Vickers unit drive of my turret was leaking. (a definite fire hazard) My turret travel became jerky and I was only two thirds of the elevation on the way up so I could enter the plane when it stopped moving! However, with the escape hatch missing, several crew members were able to grab my parachute harness straps and pull me free of the turret and back into the bomber. (Sgt LeNeve had escaped with only a broken arm.) The impact of the fighter caused the right rear trunion of my 50 caliber machine gun to break loose and the machine gun casing slammed across my right arm, snapping it like a matchstick. The gun casing continued on to smash my Sperry gunsight just inches from my head!

The collision ripped off the number three engine supercharger and broke a prop blade on number four engine. A great deal of skin was stripped from beneath the right wing and a hole as large as a door was added to the radio room. At first we in the back where not sure if we were headed down out of control, but the ship was being skillfully maneuvered by our pilot, Lt.Carrol Cagel and co-pilot, Lt. Robert Barnard who were fighting the controls while salvoing the bombs at the same time. Again we were blessed, for the pilots found some cloud–bank cover to level off into as enemy fighters chased behind, trying to finish us off.

Our navigator, Tony Belzer, plotted a course to get us out of enemy territory as fast as possible, because no one knew the real extent of the damage we had sustained or how long the plane could remain airborne. The starboard engines were creating a great deal of drag and the port engines had to be boosted to maintain flight – the guys at the controls certainly had their hands full."

Note: A crew member gave LeNeve a morphine shot from the plane's First Aid pack to ease the pain and he slept until the bomber was preparing to land on an air strip at Merville in northern France. The gunners hunkered down in the radio room to prepare for a rough landing.

"Our pilot tried to assure us that the plane was under control and that it should hang together for one more landing. Old '058' had survived eighty-four missions and she settled down gracefully despite a partially deflated main landing gear wheel and an un-stowed ball turret dragging at least one gun barrel as we swallowed up the runway. A flare had been fired to alert the ground that an injured person was aboard and an ambulance was there to spirit me off to a small hospital. After the crew inspected the battle damage and scrounged a few souvenirs, they cleaned up and ate. Then they all came by to visit. The following day they said their goodbyes as orders had arrived for their return to England and the war."

Four days later, the wounded ball turret gunner began his tour by ambulance through the war-torn country-side of France. The trip ended at a U.S. full-field hospital field in San Quentin, France. Two weeks later, he was returned to a station hospital in England where he spent two and a half months before being returned to the States. He was homeward bound! Sgt. Colby LeNeve ends his story:

> *"While I was traveling down the Columbia Gorge by rail the great news was announced that Japan had surrendered. It was indeed a splendid day to arrive back home!"*

"The ME-109 was a swift and deadly fighter that caught the immediate attention of B-17 gunners. We were glad for the protection of our P-51 escort fighters in the final days of bombing raids over Germany"

Hutch

THE 490ᵀᴴ MONUMENT

The following inscription is in Czech and English:

We honor the sacrifice of these nine American airmen who were murdered while prisoners of war on April 19, 1945."

849 th Bsq
B-17 #43-38078
Lorenzo G. Smith, Jr. 1ˢᵗ Lt.
Leo L. Borden 2ⁿᵈ Lt
Carl B. Johnson, Jr. Sgt.
Gordon P. Lake Sgt.
Robert A. Johnson Sgt.
Peter Malires Sgt.
850 th Bsq
B-17G #43-38701
Joseph A. Trojanowski 2ⁿᵈ Lt.
Wilbur L. Lesh   Sgt.
Lyle E. Dole Sgt.

FREEDOM

"War loves to seek its victims among the young" Sophocles

OUR BLACK THURSDAY

The Templeton crew did not fly the Aussig mission, but it was very important to us because we lost four planes. Wilbur Lesh, our former ball turret gunner and a very good friend was on one those downed bombers. It would be years before I learned of Wilbur's fate. Our former tail-gunner, Ralph Moore flew and survived that mission.

The April 19, 1945 mission to Aussig, Czechoslovakia was the next to last mission of the 490th Bomb group. It was truly our Black Thursday, because of the loss of crewmen and bombers. It was reported that a major mistake was made when the group overshot the IP (initial point) to start the bombing run and flew too close to Prague. The formation then had to circle west and come back to the IP. The 490th formation was attacked by a group of Luftwaffe Me-262 twin-engine jet fighters before they got back to start the bomb run. Four of our B-17 bombers were shot out of the low formation in a very few minutes. The following stories are based on recollections as printed in the *"History of the 490th Bomb Group* and/or interviews with others who have provided information about that fateful mission to Aussig. Stories may vary, but the reader should remember that they are based on memories of those who were there in the heat of battle and/ or research on a tragic incident that happened more than sixty-three years ago.

Lt. Lawrence J. (Larry) Bellarts, pilot in the 849th squadron, was flying in the low squadron on his 35th and final combat mission to complete his tour of duty:

"I was flying lead of the third 'V' with Lt. Buford E. Stovall on my right wing and Lt. William E. Mc Allister on my left. Lt. Robert A. Norvell was leading a diamond element below and behind me. Near the target an Me-262 came in from two o'clock high and Stoval went down. Norvell brought up his diamond to fill the empty position on my right wing. The jet came in again from ten o'clock high and Mc Allister on my left wing was hit and went down. The enemy fighter made another attack from two o'clock and the Norvell plane fell out of the formation. He came after us once more from behind (six o'clock,) but was hit before he could pick me off. I had told the all the gunners to start firing, even before he was in range. I think that might have saved us. The doomed fighter passed under us; close enough for me to see the shattered cockpit with the black-suited pilot hanging lifeless out the left side."

Lt. Buford E. Stovall was the pilot of one of the bombers shot down. His graphic account illustrates the perils of bailing out and surviving against the odds:

"A swarm of ME-262 jets appeared without warning and swept through my low squadron formation. They missed our plane on the first two passes. The third time around we were hit between the two left engines and a quarter of the wing was blown off. That hit knocked us out of the formation. Flak began bursting all around us and the fighters made six or seven more passes. Our flight controls, automatic pilot radio and oxygen systems were all hit. The three of us around the cockpit-co-pilot, engineer and myself were not wounded, but everybody else in the crew had at least five holes in them from flak or bullets. One man was hit forty-three times. I gave the order to bail out and held the controls while everybody jumped. When I went out, the left wing broke off where it had been hit between the two engines"

Lt. Stovall landed in a pine forest and injured his legs, but managed to avoid SS troops in the area. He made contact with a Czech forest ranger who helped him hide for a few days until Russian troops liberated the area. On his trip back to England, he met his ball turret gunner in Paris and learned that the rest of his crew had been captured ,but were okay now. One crew member who had been wounded many times was left in a Czech hospital.

Sgt. Dennis M. Richardson a gunner on the Stovall bomber also gave an account of the mission:

"The mission was going fine until enemy fighters attacked us at about 11:30 a.m. that day. After a running battle that was pretty hot, we were shot up so badly that we had to bail out about half-way between Aussig and Prague. Every crew member was wounded to some degree, but we all lived through it except our radio operator, Frank Mateyka. He was killed some time after he reached the ground. I had about forty shrapnel wounds in me by the time I landed, but I kept moving until I came to the small town of Litten. A Czech doctor dressed my leg and side and then directed me to a hospital. About midnight, only twelve hours after bailing out, I was captured by the Germans and held there until April 22 nd. They took me to Rucine, just outside of Prague where I was held until the 6th of May when the Czechs and Russians moved in and chased them out. The Germans moved back towards the western front and took me with them. We reached the American lines on May 9th and I was free."

EPILOGUE

Maj. Joel R. Johnson (Ret) was 2/Lt. Johnson in those days and co-pilot on the Lt. Robert Tennenberg plane which was also flying in the low squadron on the Aussig mission. In 2010, Joel shared some of his memories of that fateful day so long ago::

"We were flying right wing in the lowest element of the low squadron An element is made up of three planes. Number one is the element leader, his left wing is number two and his right wing is number three. I remember two or three ME-262 fighters coming in from two o'clock high. They hit the lead squadron first with cannon fire and one plane on the left side blew. (Snyder) The next attack was on our low squadron and we lost three bombers in a matter of minutes. I really had a front row seat flying in the right seat on the bottom right of the low squadron. I had a clear view of the lead squadron. The first plane to go down was in the lead squadron, then I would say our low element leader was second, the airborne spare was the third and the right wing in the element above us was the fourth. So in the low squadron, that would have been Stovall, Norvell and Mc Allister. But, I am not sure of the names or the order they went down. Only one ME- 262 jet flew through our squadron with all of our gunners firing at him. He was trailing black smoke and John Gann, our nose gunner said he was going so fast that he could hardly get a bead on it. However, our crew got credit for a "probable" downed fighter. All this action transpired in a time frame of five minutes or less and we were busy trying to survive and deliver our bomb load. This was my last mission and the first time that the palms of my hands perspired. I believe that if there had been four or five German jets with enough fuel; they could have shot down the entire 490th Bomb Group that day!

Lt. Mc Allister's bomber was the second to fall out of the formation with the number two engine on fire. However, they were able to extinguish the fire, rejoin the group and bomb the target. Sadly, the plane exploded in mid-air shortly after leaving the target and there were few survivors. Co-pilot Lt. Glen Howard, on his thirty-third mission, bailed out just before the explosion and tail gunner, Sgt. Paul Webb was blown out of the plane by the explosion. This was Lt. Mc Allister's first mission and he carried it gallantly to the end. The fighter attack and loss of four bombers did not stop the 490th Bomb Group from completing their mission; they continued on to bomb the railroad yards at Aussig ! It was the next-to-last mission flown by Me-262 jet fighters and also for the 490th Bomb Group. The following story tells of the sad fate of eight airmen taken prisoner by the SS Troops.

" We salute the men who flew the Aussig mission"

GERMAN SS ATROCITY

The 157th mission of the 490th Bomb Group on April 19, 1945 sent thirty bombers to hit the railroad yards at Aussig, Czechoslovakia. The mission with a total of 500 bombers turned out to be the next-to-last raid our group would fly and one of the most disastrous. The 490th Bomb Group formation was attacked by ME-262 jet fighters as it made a 270 degree over Prague to get back to the IP (initial point) and start the bomb run. Four bombers in the low squadron were shot down or damaged minutes before they reached the target. Some crew members of the Lt. Buford E. Stovall, Lt Robert A. Norvell and Lt. Paul A. Snyder bailed out into enemy territory. A few escaped into the heavily forested countryside and were aided by sympathetic Czechs who realized the war was nearly over. Other men stayed with their plane, hoping they could stay airborne. Lt. McAllister managed to extinguish an engine fire and re-join the formation to bomb the target.

Much of the following information was pieced together through the research information of Andrew Grier Smith Brunson and Scot Lowry. Both have visited the site of the atrocity and the Memorial.

A garrison of German Waffen SS troops was stationed at Konopiste Castle near Benesov, Czechoslovakia. Ten of the downed parachuting airmen landed inside SS Training Grounds and the SS troopers had been waiting as they floated down. One man was instantly killed, one managed to escape into the forest and eight were taken prisoner and interrogated. The fact that the war was almost over did not deter the SS soldiers from murdering their eight prisoners of war. This all happened only eleven days before Germany surrendered and asked for a truce! The Americans were prisoners of war and should have been treated as such. Their murder was an atrocity that reveals the brutality of Hitler's fanatical thugs. Germans in the SS (Schutzstaffel) wore their black uniforms with pride. They were Hitler's elite guard, and had been empowered to enforce Nazi policy without fear of prosecution. In short, they had a license to murder !

S/SGT. WLIBUR LESH

Wilbur was a former member of our crew. He was eighteen and newly married when he joined us in Sioux City for aircrew training as our ball turret gunner. We flew together for three months in crew training, and on our first four combat missions. Then the Templeton crew was made "lead crew" and flew bombers with the PFF radar dome in the place of a ball turret. Wilbur and our tail gunner, Ralph Moore were transferred to the 490th gunnery pool to fly missions with crews needing replacements. They often came back to visit Hut 29 and share the "fish and chips" we ordered from the pub up the road. Wilbur flew with our crew again on the January 20th mission to Sterkade-Reine. He later trained to operate the ECM Jammer equipment, a device to "scramble" enemy radio and electrical signals. I believe he was flying that position on the Lt. Paul Snyder plane when it was shot down. Wilbur was a great friend and it was a shock to our crew when we heard that our buddy's plane had gone down. We could only hope that he bailed out and landed safely.

It was sixty years later before I learned the details of his murder. The information was first given me by Eric Swain of London, England, the 490th Bomb Group Historian and Archivist. I included it in my first book, Through These Eyes." I have since gained more detailed information on the tragedy from the research of Grier Smith Brunson and Scot Lowery who had relatives on the Aussig mission.

FIRST LT. LORENZO G. SMITH JR.

Lt. Smith was the co-pilot on the Norvell plane, "Little Red's Wagon" and they were flying their twenty-seventh mission. The number two engine caught on fire during the Me-262 attack and most of the crew bailed out. Andrew Grier Smith Brunson, the son of Lt. Smith, was one month old at the time of the atrocity. Mr. Brunson has done extensive research on the Aussig mission, visited Czechoslovakia and the site of the murder of his father and the other seven prisoners. The following information was provided by Mr. Brunson:

"The airmen were interrogated, robbed of their valuables and dog tags. (identification) Each man was executed by a pistol to the temple sometime after midnight, so there were no witnesses. The SS squad then placed the bodies in a wagon and drove to a field two miles away. They buried their victims in a common grave and covered it with a haystack. The unmarked grave was discovered a few months later by a Czech farmer. My father, Lt. Lorenzo G. Smith was identified by dental records and re-interred at Arlington National Cemetery in 1949.

The Commandant of the SS Garrison, General Otto Haupricht and the SS Commander, Albert Karasche were allegedly tried for war crimes at Nuremburg, but testified that the prisoners were shot while "trying to escape." They avoided punishment and survived in Germany for many years. Members of the execution squad were never tried for their crime. Mr. Andrew Grier Smith Brunson states: "My father was murdered at Konopiste castle and I have spent a great part of my life making sure this war crime is not forgotten."

Today, at Konopiste castle, near Benesov, Czech Republic, there is a monument honoring the memory of the nine U.S. bomber crew members who were captured and murdered by German SS troops eleven days before the end of the war. The Czech people suffered greatly during the Nazi occupation. They have always been grateful to the United States for freeing them from Germany. The mayor of Benesov sent a copy of the Memorial drawing to Mr. Brunson for suggestions regarding the design of a new memorial which was re-dedicated in 2005. Town officials and military personnel hold wreath-laying services at the site of the monument every April 19th to honor the 490th Bomb Group airmen who died to free their country.

Mr. Brunson continues: "My hat is off permanently to you magnificent airmen who fought so nobly for the freedom your children enjoy, and I wanted to add my voice to the thousands of Americans (and Europeans) who thank you for your courage and sacrifice. We shall not see the like of your generation again."

Sincerely, Andrew Grier Smith Brunson (adopted)

SGT. NEWTON PARKER

Newton Parker, tail-gunner on the Norvell plane, was the uncle of Scot Lowry. The stories Scot heard from his uncle as a young boy, encouraged him to do extensive research on the Aussig mission. I am indebted to Mr. Lowery for the information his research and interviews have provided for his story of the his uncle's escape..

"The Norvell plane had lost its number two engine, dropped out of the group formation and the crew was ordered to bail out. However, Lt. Norvell and the engineer stayed with plane, jettisoned the bombs and flew eighty miles before they were shot down and became prisoners of war. Ten men who bailed out of the downed Fortresses landed in an SS training ground. One was killed while trying to surrender, one escaped and eight were captured and became prisoners of war. The eight captives were taken to the SS headquarters at Konopiste castle for interrogation. Shortly before midnight on April 19, 1945 the SS troopers took their bodies away from the castle in a truck. These men were prisoners of war and should have been protected under the rules of the Geneva Convention, but they were murdered and buried in a mass grave."

The airman who avoided capture was Sgt. Newton Parker, tail-gunner on the Norvell crew. Years later, he told the story of his miraculous survival to his nephew, Scot Lowry:

"A strong wind caught his parachute when he landed and it dragged him towards the woods and away from the German soldiers who were firing at him as he fled into the trees. Sgt. Parker slipped out of his chute harness and ran for his life. He hid in heavy briars thickets and burrowed into snow banks while the Germans searched for him. He heard shots fired by troops searching for other American airmen. Although it was April, the Czech mountains still had snow and freezing temperatures. Parker had lost his boots when he was dragged by the parachute. However, he knew he must run or be captured. For seven days, he hid during the day and traveled by night, barefoot without food or water. The gritty tail gunner traveled many miles with the aid of his compass before he collapsed from exhaustion. A Czech railroad worker found him lying near the railroad tracks and took him to his home.The Czech family lived in the small village of Tochovice, in the middle of the Czech countryside. They helped my uncle recover, dressed him in farm clothes and passed him off as a deaf-mute son. The family heroically hid an American airman, knowing they would be executed if they were found out. He was very fortunate to be have been kept safely by this family until the war ended."

Sgt. Newton Parker had narrowly escaped from the murderous SS troopers, but he said he had nightmares about the Aussig mission for the rest of his life!

April Report of 490th BG

April 1945: After stand-downs on the first two days of the month, the 490th BG flew fifteen missions in the next eighteen days. Visual missions were carried out on thirteen missions as the weather over Germany and Czechoslovakia had improved. This was a factor that greatly improved our heavy bombers. The 490th took full advantage of the weather and bombing results were excellent. The first two missions were to the submarine pens at Kiel and the only ones using radar. The "Mickey operators" had a field day and reconnaissance photos proved that they did an excellent job on harbor installations.

The April 5th mission to an airfield at Unterschaulersbach, thirty-six aircraft, led by our commander Col. Frank Bostrom, flew through severe weather all the way across Belgium into southern Germany before breaking out into clear skies just before reaching the Initial Point to start their bomb run on their target. Lead bombardier, Captain Cleo Mace, dropped his bombs smack in the middle of the air-field which earned the 490th an excellent rating and definitely denied Germans the use of the air-field. Three aircraft were lost: the aircrews of Lt. Henry J. Martinson, Lt. Darril F. Roufs and Lt. Charles E. Bates did not return to base.

April 7: The group went to Parchim and bombed the air-field there with excellent results. Because of enemy fighter attacks, we bombed in group formation, but the squadrons tucked themselves in so tightly that a heavy pattern of bombs laid directly on the target. The hangers and flight buildings were completely destroyed. Major C. J. Adams led the group with Maj. Day and Lt. Devoucoux as squadron leaders. The credit for the bombing went to Captain Fogelberg's lead crew and his bombardier, Lt. Starkey. Two ME 109s hit the group out of the sun just before we reached the IP and Lt. Druhot's plane from the high squadron went down. Lt. Cagle's plane was damaged by one of the fighters when a German pilot, killed by our formation's gunners, crashed into the ball turret. Lt. Cagle successfully nursed his plane back to a friendly base. The group claimed credit for one enemy fighter.

Note: Our Lt. Bill Templeton crew flew lead position of the high squadron. I am not sure who was on board as Command Pilot, Bombardier and Mickey Operator. I seldom saw the Command officers flying with us because they usually at the last minute. They usually entered and exited the plane through the nose hatch in front of the bomb-bay. We were a skeleton crew of seven with three Command officers and a Mickey operator added for each mission. Now you know why the Lt. Bill Templeton lead-crew photo on the cover shows only seven airmen (actually four teenagers and three young men.)

April 9-10: Targets for these two raids were the airfields at Schleissheim and Neuruppin, which were bombed with good results. On the Neuruppin raid, Captain Caspari and his lead crew, with Lt. Little as bombardier, literally plastered the hangers and other buildings on the airfield an received rating of 'excellent' for the job.

April 14-15: The 490th bombed defense installations at Royan with very good results. These two missions helped French troops who were moving in on Nazi troops still holding out there.

April 19: During the mission to Aussig, Czechoslovakia the Group was attacked by six to eight enemy ME 262s while turning over Prague. The lightning attack came from out of the clouds and four B-17s were lost before many of the crews knew what was going on. Two jets were claimed by the Group gunners; were seen going down in smoke. The four aircraft lost were piloted by Lt. Snyder, Lt. McAlister, Lt. Stoval and Lt. Norvell.

April 20: The last combat mission of the 490th Bomb group was flown to bomb the rail junction at Nauen.

April 28- June 23: After Germany asked for a truce in late April, the Group flew five Mercy missions to drop food packages to the starving citizens of Holland. The 490th also flew two Revival Missions to return French Prisoners of War from Linz, Austria to their own country.

May 8: VE Day (Victory in Europe), Germany had surrendered and plans were made for the 490th BG to return to the USA and later join the war against Japan in the Pacific.

July 6: Thirty B-17 Flying Fortresses took off from Eye airfield for the final time. The 490th Bomb Group was flying the Northern Route to Wales, Iceland, Newfoundland to Bradley Field, Connecticut!

Statistics: The 490th Bomb Group (H) was assigned to the Eighth Army Air Force in April 26, 1944 as a B-24 Liberator group and flew their first mission on May 31 as a B- 24 unit. August 6 they were switched to the B-17 Flying Fortress. The group flew158 combat missions (40 in B-24s)

- 490th Squadrons: 848, 849, 850 and 851
- 22 Aircraft were MIA   (ten lost in April)
- Airmen Killed in Action (KIA) 58 ---
- Airmen Missing in Action (MIA) 196   plus 37 killed in line of duty

There was no report on the number of airmen wounded during missions.

Fortunately several airmen reported missing survived

The 400th claim to fame: Lowest MIA losses of any Eighth Air Force bomb group in combat for an extended period of time.

During the 158 combat missions a total of 13,613 tons of bombs were loaded and 459,139 rounds of 50 caliber ammunition were fired.

These missions were of all types, from 'recalls' and 'milk runs' to deep penetrations into enemy territory. Many had been to the roughest and most heavily protected targets in Germany.

Heavy bomber pilots and crew members agree to the following statement:

There was no such thing as an easy combat mission. Flying around a fully loaded B-24 or B-17 for six to eight hours in close formation 25,000 feet above the earth at 40 below zero was tough duty.

Note: Add the fact that every man was wearing heavy flying gear, oxygen mask, electric heated suit, flak helmet, flak vest and a parachute. The threat of mid-air collisions, fighter attacks and anti-aircraft fire put the fear of God in every crew member on every mission!

VE Day (Victory in Europe)

Germany asked for a truce in late April and signed the formal surrender on May 8, 1945. The Axis dictator, Adolph Hitler, knew by mid April that his Third Reich was defeated. His troops were surrendering in mass and some Generals were committing suicide. The Yanks were coming from the west and the Russians from the east. Hitler knew what happened to his partner, Mussolini. Thus the man who planned to rule the world turned the government over to his second-in-command, Admiral Karl Doenitz. The admiral was left to negotiate Germany's surrender and save what was left of his devastated country.

Russian troops had surrounded Berlin and capture was certain. Hitler feared the Russians most of all. He knew they were seeking revenge for German atrocities committed in their homeland. Now, the shoe was on the other foot! Hitler retreated to his luxurious underground bunker in Berlin and issued orders to his servants to prepare for the end. April 29th, he married his longtime mistress, Eva Braun, making an honest woman of her. The next day, they committed suicide, both took poison and then, Hitler shot his new wife and himself. As planned, their bodies were carried out by the servants, doused with gasoline and cremated. (No doubt this was one of the shortest honeymoons on record!)

Shortly before this incident, General Mark Clark's Fifth Army had conquered most of Italy. The men in his army had literally marched and fought their way across the length of Italy from the toe of the boot to the Alps mountains. Italian officials surrendered and brought an end to Mussolini's dictatorship. However, Benito Mussolini and his mistress tried to escape to safety in the neutral country of Switzerland. The attempt failed; they were caught and killed by Italian partisan forces. Their bodies were mutilated and they were hung by their heels in the town square of Milan for public viewing. The Italian partisans wanted to prove to the people that the dictator was really dead and they were free to re-build their war-torn country.

Adolph Hitler and Benito Mussolini, brought ruin and destruction to Europe and their own countries. Millions died and millions of lives were ruined because of these dictators. It would take years to restore the damages to their own country and those they had countries they plundered. El Duce (Benito Mussolini) died a horrible death at the hands of his own countrymen. Adolph Hitler feared the same treatment and chose to take the coward's way out. Many of his cohorts also chose suicide. Both dictators were examples of men who gained complete power over the citizens of their country and became madmen seeking to conquer the world. Each generation should see to it that their crimes against humanity will never be forgotten.

WAR CRIMES TRIALS

Nuremberg was the sight of Hitler's huge Nazi party rallies and Roman Empire type pageants. He had a special stadium to stage huge political extravaganzas, complete with hundreds of red banners with the black swastika. Hitler adapted much of his symbols and pageantry from the ancient Romans, right down to the salute. Germans were awed by the parade of "goose-stepping" troops and their straight arm "Heil Hitler" salutes. The majority of the people were sold on bringing Germany out the Depression and building the Third Reich into a world power.

Hitler's patriotic rallies at Nuremberg and his rise to power took less than six years. In that short time he became a dictator with complete power. His plans for Germany could not be questioned. Those who didn't support him soon had more troubles than they could handle and often became political prisoners in the concentration camps he built to exterminate German citizens--- the Jews!

The Allies used great psychology in choosing Nuremberg as the site for the International War Crimes Trials. The final accounting and punishment for the Nazi leaders was to end where it started. The city had been bombed from 200 to 400 times and was in ruins, but quick repairs were made in order to hold the trials there in the German Palace of Justice.

The War Crimes court was comprised of eight judges: two each from France, Britain, Russia and the U.S. This International Military Tribunal tried twenty -four major German criminals from November, 1945 to October, 1946. Several prisoners committed suicide, including the number two Nazi, Reichsmarshal Hermann Goering, former head of the Luftwaffe. Others were hanged or given life sentences and a few were acquitted. Nine of the most evil were sentenced to hang. The court agreed that these men had disgraced the military and did not deserve the dignity of a firing squad The Nuremberg Trials continued for those with lesser crimes until 1949. Eventually the court tried 199 Nazi leaders; thirty-six were sentenced to death, twenty-two were given life imprisonment, 103 received shorter sentences and thirty-eight were acquitted. (five committed suicide before the end of the trials.) Justice had come to Nuremberg!

The trials went on for some time, but for the Allied Forces it was two down and one to go. Now, all Allied Forces focused on the defeat of Japan in the Pacific. The 490th Bomb Group was notified that it would be the second group from the third Air

Division to return to the USA. We were soon attending classes to prepare us for combat in the Far East."Psychology of the Japanese," "Geography of the Pacific Ocean Area" and "Escape and Evasion" were a few of our classes. Meanwhile we were flying and testing equipment to be sure our war-weary bombers were fit to fly across the North Atlantic. However, we were hoping that we would be switched to the B-29 when we went to the Pacific.

The Grand Tour

The mechanics on our ground crews and all the support personnel from the parachute riggers, bomb-loaders etc to the cooks deserved to see what our bombing missions had accomplished. The hard work of the ground personnel had made it possible. The guys on bomber crews were also excited because we had never had a close look at the destruction caused by our bombing missions. You don't see much from 25,000 feet when you are dodging flak and fighters!. Boy, it was really great to cruise along at low altitude without oxygen and all

the bulky clothing. I never saw a flak jacket or helmet again until I visited the Eighth Air Force Museum at Savannah, Gain 2007. It was hard to believe the destruction of the German cities we had bombed. Large urban areas had been completely obliterated; bridges and railroads were torn up. Germany had really taken a beating. We also enjoyed a low level tour of Paris; the Eiffel Tower and Notre Dame were especially impressive.

2/Lt. Joel Johnson, (Major, Ret) writes: "I took a "cook's tour" in a B-17 E with the squadron commander, Lt. Col. C. J. Adams as pilot and I was co-pilot. We took thirty ground personnel on a low level flight over the Ruhr Valley to survey the damage and see the results of all their hard work that kept the 490th in the air. We also circled the heavily bombed city of Cologne where the cathedral was the only building standing."

A toast:

"To the arms of war, may they 'rust' in peace"

Operation Home Run

The 490th Bomb Group was notified in late May that they would be the second group from the Third Air Division to return to the States. Many practice flights were made to check out planes and equipment to be sure the war-weary bombers were fit to fly the North Atlantic route home. Each B-17 would carry twenty men and their duffle bags. The wait stretched from days to weeks, but finally on July 6th thirty aircraft and their crews waved goodbye to England flew to Prestwick, Scotland. The next day they took-off for Iceland, the first leg of their journey home.

July 8th ,The rest of the B-17 Flying Fortresses lifted off from Eye and the "Bromedome" for the final time. We landed in Valley, Wales to spend one night, before flying northwest to Iceland. Planes carried twenty men and their duffel bags. Our crew rode in their regular flying positions and the waist area served as the lounge area for the passengers on the long flight across the Atlantic. Pilot Bill Templeton's crew of Dale Rector, Bruno Conterato, Ewing Roddy, Lee Hutchinson, Bert Allinder and Dwight Parrish was joined by navigator Chet Deptula and bombardier Jim Cambell, both had flown missions with us at various times. Our passengers were Richard Fleck, Foster Wisdom, Bill King, Martin Orsan, John Piwkiewicz, Stan Raimey, John Robinson, Dan Quattrocchi, Claude Dowling, John Sedor and Bill Buchannan. They all signed my "short-snorter" during the flight.

The mess hall at the Iceland airbase had a treat for us, they served milk and hamburgers, the first we had since before boarding the Queen Mary nine months earlier. We laid over a day because one of the war-weary bombers had an engine problem. That gave some of us a chance to hike down a road through the stark boulder strewn landscape surrounding the airbase. There was no vegetation, just the bare countryside. Five of us intended to visit a small fishing village crowded against the sea, but didn't get half way there before we realized it was too far. The majority voted in favor of going back to the airfield for supper and more milk and hamburgers. That was without a doubt a wise decision, because we hadn't been told that many of the Icelanders were German sympathizers!

The temperature in Iceland was pleasant, but I wouldn't want to be found there in January. We continued our trip on July 12th and flew out over an ocean full of icebergs and past the southern tip of Greenland. It was near dark when we touched down on the runway at Gander, Newfoundland. It was a welcome sight after flying all day across the North Atlantic. Early dawn the next the morning we began the last leg of our journey to the USA! Our destination was Bradley Field, Connecticut, but first we flew to Hartford and "buzzed" the home of our pilot, Lt.

Bill Templeton. He had called ahead and his entire family and neighbors were out in the yard waving gleefully as our bomber circled the house a few times before heading on to Bradley Field. It was a great feeling to be welcomed home in our B-17 by a group of thankful Americans. I knew my folks at home would never see me in one of those magnificent planes that had carried us safely through twenty missions.

Note: Our war-weary planes made the long flight with only one mechanical problem which caused a day layover in Iceland. However, sixty –three years later, Michael Fuenfer, son of Albert Fuenfer, a radar technician, shared a story about his Dad's experience on that trip. I was happy to include it as, "The Final Flight of Little Miss Dottie" in my second book, "Bombs Away. Albert was riding in the B-17 which got lost, ran short of gas and had to make an emergency landing on a very short grass airstrip in rural Connecticut. The bomber used up all the strip and ended up with its nose about ten feet from a stone fence. There no injuries, but the guys who had survived a war and flown the North Atlantic had to hitch a bus ride on to Bradley Field. "Little Miss Dottie" was later dismantled and hauled away, but her last mission was a great success!

We turned in our plane and flying equipment (they even took our sunglasses and watches) at Bradley Field and were suddenly no longer airmen. They sent us down to Camp Miles Standish, Massachusetts by train. It would be sixty years before I flew in another B-17 Flying Fortress (the Liberty Belle). We were back in the USA and everyone was sent to an army camp near his home (I went to Camp Atterbury, Indiana) and received a 30 day furlough to return home and see their families before crews met again at Drew Field, Florida to wait and prepare to go to the Pacific. The Army gave us lots of "rest and relaxation" time in Tampa and on the Treasure Island beaches. Sadly, our crew was separated. Sixty two years later, after I published "Through These Eyes," I was able to contact our waist gunner Bert Allinder and engineer Ewing Roddy and we were able to meet again and share memories of our WW II adventures in the Mighty Eighth.

I was sent to a B-29 bomber airbase at Gulfport, Mississippi, but never got on a plane. Instead, they assigned me as radioman on a boat in Air

Sea Rescue in the Gulf of Mexico! However, before I ever got on a boat, I was shipped out to the same job at the Lake Charles, Louisiana airfield. The war in the Pacific was boiling over and everything concerning Eighth Air Force airmen was put on hold. Once again, I never got on a boat in the Gulf. Things I remember about Lake Charles: -- hundreds of German prisoners of war were being held on the airbase --- we were free to drive our jeep all over town while wearing Navy fatigues --- the golf course greens were sand --- I saw one of the new Fords with a price tag of only $900 --- best of all, they gave me a twenty day furlough and told me to go home and report back to Gulfport. Thus, I was home August 6th and 9th when the atomic bombs were dropped on Hiroshima and Nagasaki. Japanese Emperor Hirohito surrendered on the 14th and I celebrated V J Day (Victory in Japan) in my hometown with family and friends! Thousands of American troops had been poised to invade Japan when President Harry Truman gave the OK to use the atomic bombs. His decision meant millions of American and Japanese lives had been saved. I hurried back to report at Gulfport Air Base five days early and the barracks were empty. Everybody had been shipped out to a separation center near their home.

World War II was over and with my 20 missions and over 300 hours of combat flying time I had more than enough "service points" to be discharged early. They sent me to Baer Field, at Ft. Wayne, Indiana and before I knew it I was an honorably discharged veteran.

Suddenly, I was a civilian owned nothing but a uniform and duffel bag full of GI clothing. I had an honorable discharge in my hand, three hundred dollars in my pocket and a Greyhound Bus ticket to Bedford, Indiana. It was November 15, 1945. I was five months beyond the age of twenty and I had just joined the ranks of unemployed veterans!

War- time factories were closing and the only job I could find in my home town paid a dollar an hour. It was the GI Bill that saved my bacon. It paid my tuition at Indiana University and a stipend of ninety dollars a month for living expenses! This government program for veterans allowed me earn my first degree in education and a teaching license which I used for the next thirty-seven years.

Surviving members of the 490th Bombardment Group (H) keep in touch through a quarterly newsletter, "Bombs Away." The group also holds annual reunions and many of the veterans gather to meet old buddies, recall WW II days and honor all the men (boys) who served our country so valiantly at Eye, England.

Four hundred thousand young Americans died and thousands more suffered life-altering wounds to defeat the Axis powers and protect our nation's Freedoms.

> *Four freedoms: the first is freedom of speech and expression---everywhere in the world. The second is freedom of every person to worship his God in his own way, --- everywhere in the world. The third is freedom from want---everywhere in the world. The fourth is freedom from fear---anywhere in the world.*

> *Franklin D. Roosevelt*

CHAPTER NINE

GENOCIDE - THE HOLOCAUST

The Nazi government built hundreds of death and slave labor camps in Germany and conquered countries to eliminate Jews undesirables and political prisoners. These extermination camps were different from the prisoner of war concentration camps built to hold enemy soldiers.

Early in his climb to power, Hitler blamed the Jews for all of Germany's depression and financial problems after World War I. German Jews became the scapegoat and the persecution began as early as 1933. Hitler became Chancellor and German citizens bought the idea that his government could end the depression and bring prosperity back to Germany. They voted the Nazis (National Socialist Workers Party) into power. Hitler became "Der Fuehrer" and eventually dictator. He planned for his Third Reich to rule Europe and signed the Pact of Steel Treaty with Benito Mussolini (Il Duce) of Italy and later Hirohito, (Emperor of Japan.) Millions died in countries around the world during the next twelve years and three Axis countries were destroyed in World War II.

It's impossible to talk about World War II without including a story about the murder of six million Jews in the Holocaust (death by fire). The attempt to destroy the Jewish population in Germany and occupied countries was one of the most horrendous deeds of Hitler's government. The Axis powers of Germany, Italy and Japan ruled by terror, ruled their own people with an iron fist and eliminated all who resisted including any high military or government official who questioned orders of the Emperor or dictator in charge. They created terror by bombing and mass killings of civilians in war against others. Germany 'annexed' or attacked its neighbors, Italian armies marched across North Africa and Japanese troops killed or enslaved millions in China and the Pacific islands. The sneak attack on Pearl Harbor, the Bataan Death March and concentration camps were examples of Japanese warfare against the United States.

Germany's plan to enslave and/or kill every Jew in Europe was a cruel and sadistic attempt at genocide: the destruction of a human race! Hitler's Eiensatzgruppen (a mobile killing unit) was formed with five killer squads (Einstazkomandos.) The men in these special killer squads (most were criminals) followed regular troops through conquered countries. These men were given permission to murder Jews and political prisoners without fear of punishment. The mass graves of victims were found across Poland, Russia and other conquered countries. The largest atrocity was at Babi Yar near Kiev, Russia where 33,000 Jews, men women and children, were murdered in two days and buried in a mass grave. Allied troops later recovered hundreds of photos taken by German soldiers to document the atrocities committed against the Jews. Many of these photos were later used in the Nuremberg Trials to prosecute Nazi Leaders. I have seen photos of unbelievable torture and death of men women and children committed by those depraved, and power- mad 'killing units.'

One member of an Einsatzkommando mobile killing squad took a photo of the mass killing at Vinnitza, Ukraine in September 16, 1941 where the goons shot 2,800 Jews and political prisoners. Again, officers often took photos to show the results of their "work" to commanding officers. This photo shows twenty-five or so German soldiers at the edge of a large pit full of the dead. One victim is crouched on the edge of the pit full of bodies, while a soldier with a pistol shoots him in the back of the head. On the back of that photo was written, "The Last Jew of Vinnitza."

THE FINAL SOLUTION

Jewish persecution became even more organized and deadly as the war progressed. Killing and disposing of the bodies of so many victims became a problem. Heinrich Himmler, head of the SS (Schutzstaffle) secret police, and Adolph Eichmann, in charge of the Jewish problem, decided they needed a faster and more efficient plan to speed up their "extermination" program. Nazi leaders met in 1942 to plan a more efficient and systematic extermination of a human race.

The Holocaust (destruction by fire) was developed to speed-up murder. Gas chambers and furnaces for the cremation of bodies were installed in Death Camps. Commandants could now bury ashes rather than bodies. They called it "The Final Solution" to the Jewish problem. It was an inhuman plan to use the newly invented poison gas pellets (Zyklon B) to murder Jewish children and adults unsuitable for slave labor and burn the bodies in gas furnaces.

The Nazi government began persecuting Jews when they came to power in the early 1930s. Later, all Jews were ordered to wear the yellow 'Star of David' on their clothing. Starting in 1942, entire Jewish families were arrested, rounded up, loaded into railroad cattle cars. They often traveled for days with little food or water and were taken to the death camps. In Poland the railroad tracks ran directly into the Auschwitz death camp and the sign over the entrance read "Work Will Set You Free!" However, the majority of Jews entering that gate were doomed, the able-bodied men and women would serve in slave labor camp until they died from starvation; the children and those too sick or old were immediately sent to the gas chambers. Auschwitz was built in 1939 after Poland was conquered. It was one of the worst death camps and the first remodeled to carry out the 'Holocaust.' It is estimated that 2,500,000 died at Auschwitz. The Holocaust was quickly expanded as crematoriums were installed at near-by Birkenau and later at Buchenwald, Dachau, and Treblinka and other death camps. Special railroad tracks allowed the trains with cattle cars of Jews to pull directly into the death camps like Auschwitz and Birkenau in Poland. The families were unloaded from the cattle cars and SS troops sorted them into two groups there on the station platform. They were stripped of jewelry and other possessions. Healthy men and women strong enough to work at slave labor were marched away, tattooed and put to work to help the German war effort! Hitler used slave labor from Jews and men of defeated countries because most all able-bodied German men were in his armed forces. Thousands of these slaves died from malnutrition and abuse. The children, the weak and old people unable to work were taken to the 'showers' where they were told to take off their clothing and clean up after riding in the cattle cars. The unsuspecting victims were crowded into a large shower room. The guards closed the sealed doors and turned on the poison gas 'showers' (Zyklon B) pellets. The 'innocents' suffocated in a few minutes. The doors were unlocked and Jewish slaves entered to carry out and stack the bodies near large gas-fired ovens for cremation. Eichmann bragged that they could dispose of 2000 bodies a day. Allied soldiers over-running these camps in 1945 found thousands of bodies stacked beside the furnaces. The victims German guards had not had time to burn.

American armies discovered death camps, slave labor camps and POW (prisoner of war camps) as they advanced farther into Nazi territory. Many camps were located in Poland and other conquered countries. The camps were placed near places where slaves were needed to build German military operations. Slave labor was used to strengthen the military power of those who had made them slaves. By war's end, many prisoners were living skeletons, so starved that they were too weak to crawl out of their bunks. They were literally living skeletons needing medical attention. Allied troops liberated many more concentration camps as they advanced.

General Patton was with his troops when they liberated the death camp at Ohrdruff-North Stalag. The Nazi prison guards shot all the prisoners and ran away before Allied soldiers reached the camp. The General vomited when he saw the dead prisoners and the hundreds of bodies stacked near the crematoriums and the condition of the starving men who had survived. The mayor and citizens of the nearby town swore they were unaware of the terrible condition at the camp, however the mayor and his wife hanged themselves that night!

The Holocaust is unbelievable for many in today's generation. Some say it never happened, but photographs, eye-witness reports by U.S. soldiers, and the Nuremburg Trials prove that it did. The Holocaust was indeed genocide and a crime against humanity. Auschwitz has been preserved by the government of Poland as a memorial to those who died there! It is also a reminder to the world of Nazi Germany's inhumanity to man. German citizens dared not complain about government policy during Hitler's rise to power. Those who did so, found themselves on a cattle car with a one-way ticket to a concentration camp. Hitler's Nazi government continued to purge Poland, Germany and all conquered countries of Jews until the end of World War II.

Martin Niemoller, a German protestant pastor and student of religion spoke out against genocide. He was arrested and survived eight years (1937-1945) in a concentration camp, and he later wrote:

> *"In Germany, they came first for the communists,*
> *and I didn't speak up because I wasn't a communist*
> *and then they came for the trade unionists*
> *and I didn't speak up because I wasn't a trade unionist*
> *and then they came for the Jews*
> *and I didn't speak up because I wasn't a Jew*
> *and then --- they came for me*
> *and there was no one left to speak up!"*

Women and children on the Birkenau arrival platform known as the "ramp."

There will never be victims more pure and innocent as the children and the old or sick adults who were unloaded from cattle cars and sent directly to the poison gas showers at camps like Auschwitz and Birkenau! An estimated 6 million Jews were murdered in the concentration camps of the Holocaust.

THE AUSCHWITZ ALBUM

The above photo is only one of the 193 contained in the Auschwitz Album. The only surviving Auschwitz

Album exists because a young Hungarian Jewish woman who had survived as a prisoner was very cold when the camp was liberated by Russian troops on January 27, 1945. She found a camp guard's coat which she took to keep after she was liberated. In the coat pocket she found a photo album. It contained pictures of what went on in the extermination camp. Imagine her reaction when she saw a photo of herself coming off the train as well her family who were already murdered.

Note - It is estimated that almost a half million Hungarian Jews were loaded into cattle cars and transported across Europe to the Auschwitz extermination camp in Poland!

Album Introduction: "The Auschwitz Album is the only surviving visual evidence of the process of mass murder at Auschwitz-Birkenau. It is a unique document and was donated to Yad Vashem by Lilly Jacob-Zelmanovic Meier.

The photos were taken at the end of May or beginning of June 1944, either by Ernst Hofmann or by Bernhard Walter, two SS men whose task was to take ID photos and fingerprints of the inmates (not of the Jews who were sent directly to the gas chambers). The photos show the arrival of Hungarian Jews from Carpatho-Ruthenia. Many of them came from the Berehovo Ghetto, which itself was a collecting point for Jews from several other small towns.

Early summer 1944 was the apex of the deportation of Hungarian Jewry. For this purpose a special rail line was extended from the railway station outside the camp to a ramp inside Auschwitz. Many of the photos in the album were taken on the ramp. The Jews then went through a selection process, carried out by SS doctors and wardens. Those considered fit for work were sent into the camp, where they were registered, deloused and distributed to the barracks. The rest were sent to the gas chambers. They were gassed under the guise of a harmless shower, their bodies were cremated and the ashes were strewn in a nearby swamp. The Nazis not only ruthlessly exploited the labor of those they did not kill immediately, they also looted the belongings the Jews brought with them. Even gold fillings were extracted from the mouths of the dead by a special detachment of inmates. The personal effects the Jews brought with them were sorted by inmates and stored in an area referred to by the inmates as "Canada": the ultimate land of plenty.

The photos in the album show the entire process except for the killing itself.

The purpose of the album is unclear. It was not intended for propaganda purposes, nor does it have any obvious personal use. One assumes that it was prepared as an official reference for a higher authority, as were photo albums from other concentration camps.

Lilly never hid the album and news of its existence was published many times. She was even called to present it as testimony at the Auschwitz trials in Frankfurt during the 1960s. She kept it all the years until the famous Nazi-hunter Serge Klarsfeld visited her in 1980, and convinced her to donate the album to Yad Vashem.

In 1994 the album was restored in Yad Vashem's conservation laboratory and information on each one of the photos was typed into the computerized databank of the archive. The staff of the archive was able to compare and match the pictures with aerial photos taken by the US Army Air Force on several occasions in 1944-45. In 1999 the entire album was scanned with the highest quality digital equipment.

There are 56 pages and 193 photos in the album. Some of the original pictures, presumably those given by Lilly to survivors who had identified relatives in the photographs, are missing. One of these pictures was recently donated to Yad Vashem."

Story of the Auschwitz Album by courtesy of Yad Vashem

Chowhound Missions

Combat bombing missions ended after the April 30th truce, but our Third Division B-17 and RAF Lancaster bombers were switched to flying "Mercy Missions" on May 1st. Holland was by-passed by the Allied invasion and was still occupied by German troops. The land had been flooded by the Germans to

prevent an invasion, but this created a serious food shortage. It became so bad that the Dutch people had been eating onions and tulip bulbs and hundreds had died of starvation. Allied and

German commanders arranged for an air corridor and a cease-fire for this humanitarian operation. The bomb-bays of our bombers were altered to carry loads of ninety-two water-proof (10 and 1) boxes or of food. We dubbed them "chow-hound" missions. Five of the low level missions were flown by Third Division bombers of the Mighty Eighth to drop food to the starving people in Holland.

Our planes flew in at 500 feet and lower, to drop the family size food boxes dubbed 10-in-1, at designated areas marked by large white crosses. Hundred of bombers flew these mercy missions and dropped almost 4,000 tons of food. It was estimated that the Mighty Eighth delivered five million meals while the RAF dropped another seven million.

The Templeton crew flew two of these flights and it was a wonderful feeling to be dropping food instead of bombs. We saw the cheering people waving flags, sheets and table cloths from roads and rooftops to thank us for the food. We were so low we could see people's faces. Many ran to get the boxes as soon as they hit the ground; others waded into the water. They toted the heavy cartons away or loaded them on bicycles or pushcarts. The German soldiers, (the first I had seen,) were standing guard, in full uniform. They didn't wave, but I'm sure they were also hungry. Our crew's first food drop was at the Schipol airbase, used by German fighters. We were anxious about the mission. The German fighters were still there and so were the anti-aircraft guns to worry about. Everyone kept their fingers crossed, hoping that the Luftwaffe would observe the truce

On the second mission, in a field near the dropping area at Alkmaar, the Dutch laid out a large white sign saying: "Thank You Boys." Today, a large monument stands at the main site where the food was dropped.

The people of the Netherlands celebrate the 'food drop' each year on their May 4th Celebration Day. In many areas, food packages are dropped from small planes to commemorate the event and remember the airmen in the bombers who delivered groceries instead of bombs!

Flying those 'mercy' missions gave me a wonderful feeling- the war was over and we were saving people instead of killing them!

Hutch

The group also flew three "revival missions" to pick up and re-patriate thousands of American, French, and British prisoners-of-war. It was important that these men who had been freed from German POW camps be evacuated to their homeland. Fifteen 490th bombers with skeleton crews flew to Linz, Austria on May15th and each plane picked up thirty French soldiers to transport to Chartres, France. The four hundred and fifty men had been Nazi slave laborers for four years and became very emotional when the planes flew into France.

GERMANY ASKS FOR TRUCE – MAY 1ST !!!

VE Day (Victory in Europe) May 8, 1945
Mercy Missions

German leaders asked for a truce on May 1, 1945 and Eighth Air Force Third Division bombers took off on "mercy missions" or "Chowhound Missions" for the starving people in Holland. Bomb-bays were loaded with water-proof boxes of "10- in- on" concentrated meals. They were joined by RAF bombers loaded with British "compo rations" of meals for several days. The flooded country had been occupied by Germany for five years and many Dutch people had died of starvation, others were eating onions and tulip bulbs to survive. A large white cross in a field near the Schipol Airport was our target. We were dropping tons of food near the same airport formerly used by Luftwaffe fighters that came up to attack us on bombing missions.

Our 490th Bomb Group flew down to 300 feet and I could see the happy faces of thousands of grateful people waving and cheering to thank us for the food. I flew two mercy missions and it was a wonderful feeling to know we were saving people instead of killing them!

The war was over, Mussolini had been killed by his own people, Hitler had committed suicide and Germany was in ruins. April 30, 1945 German leaders asked for a truce. The shooting had stopped and feeding the starving people in Holland was a top priority. The country had been occupied for five years. German troops had looted this rich country, broken its dikes and flooded rich farming areas. It was estimated that 16,000 people had died of malnutrition and starvation in the winter of 1944-45. People were eating sugar beets and tulip bulbs to survive.

The Allied High Command had worked out a "Mercy Missions" project with urgent "chowhound or food-drop" missions.)

On the morning of May1, 1945 Hundreds of B-17 Fortresses and RAF Lancaster bombers took off on the first of many Mercy Missions. Every plane's bomb-bay had been fitted with special flooring to carry a load of food in water-proof boxes or burlap bags. We crossed the North Sea at a very low altitude and dropped down to 300 feet when we crossed the Holland coastline flying single file; no bombing formations today. I had a clear view of the country-side, windmills, builds. Thousand of grateful people lined the streets, waving and cheering to thanks us for bringing food! We were so low I could see their happy faces. I also saw armed German guards at various checkpoints in the country side below. It was the first time I had seen German soldiers in uniform. At last, after all this, I had finally seen the enemy! We were a little nervous, wondering if they would honor the truce, but their fighters were grounded and there were no soldiers around the anti-aircraft guns! I guess they were as hungry as their prisoners!

A large white cross in a mile square field near the Schipol Airport was our target. It was ironic, because our bombers were dropping tons of food near the same airport where Luftwaffe fighters once came up to attack us on bombing missions. We were approaching the target and it was "bags away." We made a wide circle of the area as other planes "bombed" the field with food. The crowd scrambled for the packages. Some people dived into the water after floating boxes. They toted boxes away or loaded them on bicycles, pushcarts or baby buggies. The Chowhound missions continued for several days. It was later reported that a total of 11,410,200 meals were delivered to the starving Dutch people by US and RAF planes. The people of the Netherlands still celebrate the event on their May 4th Liberation Day. In some areas they fly light planes and drop food packages to commemorate the event.

I flew on two 'Mercy Missions' and it was a wonderful feeling —the war was over and we were saving people instead of killing them!

Hutch

THE T/SGT "PICK" PICKENS STORY

Note --- Parts of this story are repeated from my second book to present amazing new information discovered by Pick's daughter and descendents of the other crew members..

My books, "Through These Eyes", A World War II Eighth Air Force Combat Diary" and "Bombs Away" have brought informational and complimentary phone calls, e-mails and letters from readers. Many were from veterans of the 490th Bomb Group or their children. Some of the most interesting have been from children whose fathers have passed away or men who died fighting for their country. Mrs. Carolyn Reilly of Louisville, KY was one of those people with a sincere desire to learn more about the father she never knew:

Dear Mr. Hutchinson, --- my father was a radio operator on a B-17 that was shot down over the Netherlands on April 5, 1945. His name was Lilbert D. "Pick" Pickens, T/Sgt in squadron 851 of the 490th Bomb Group at Eye Air Base. ------- In reading your book and re-reading his letters to his mother, I realized that he was stationed at the Sioux Falls radio school, Yuma gunnery school and Sioux City combat crew training bases at the same times you were. ----- It was such a wonderful coincidence to know that you were there when he was. My mother, who died in 2002 rarely talked about the circumstances surrounding his death---I was born on June 19, 1945, so she was a new widow and mother at the same time. In the early 1990's, I began my own investigation of my father's death --- A report I received from a member of the Dutch military stated:

"Thursday April 5, 1945 at around 1325 hours, several aircraft coming from the east overflew the villages of Middelharnis and Sommelsdijk, flying in a westerly direction. One of the aircraft was hit so heavily by the flak coming from German naval vessels in the harbor of Middelharnis, that it caught fire and crashed in a field in the Westplaat-polder in Sommelsdijk. The aircraft, which was nearly totally burned, was a so-called flying fortress, #338131 and of American origin. The nine crew members were partially burned and maimed and thrown from the wreck. Members of the Red Cross----recovered the bodies and brought them to the morgue of the general cemetery in Sommelsdijk, where they were buried on Saturday April 7, 1945."

That was my father's plane. The planes' name was the "Mary Kay" and the pilot was Lt. Darrel Roufs. Four members of the crew, including my father, were later buried at the Ardennes American Military Cemetery near Liege, Belgium."

I responded to Mrs. Reilly that I did not remember meeting "Pick" in those long-ago days, but I'm sure our paths crossed many times in training classes, the PX or the Mess Hall in the ten months we spent at those airbases. I found a photo of the bomber, "Mary Kay" on the internet and later, while searching through my old Air Force records, I discovered more information:

The "Orders from Headquarters" for squadron 848 replacement crews were issued on November 15, 1944 at Eye Airbase in Suffolk, England. Three newly arrived crews were assigned for combat. My yellowed sixty-six year old copy of those General Orders listed the names of the enlisted men of the Lt. William Templeton, Lt. Robert Tennenberg and Lt. Darrel Roufs crews. The Radio Operators on those crews were; James Lee Hutchinson, Edward L. Miller and Lilbert D. Pickens!

The first mission for these three new crews was to Berlin on December 5, 1944. We flew several missions together that winter. By April of 1945, the Allies realized that Germany was near defeat. The Eighth Air Force was flying 'maximum effort' missions to destroy Hitler's military forces and end the war. The 490th flew fifteen missions in eighteen days. The group lost ten planes in that period and the first big loss was the fifth of April!

Col. Frank P. Bostrom, Commander of the 490th Bomb Group (H) was the mission leader of the group's 146th mission. Thirty- six B-17s with red tipped tails and red bands around the wings took off from Eye airbase the morning of April 5, 1945. The Lt. Darrel Roufs crew was flying in the lead squadron. The target was a hornet's nest; a Luftwaffe airfield at Unterschlauerbach. The 490th flew through severe weather across the North Sea, Holland and into southern Germany. The weather cleared over the target and the bombing results were excellent. Three aircraft piloted by Lt. Henry J. Martinson, Lt. Charles E. Bates and Lt. Darrel Roufs were lost.

The Roufs bomber was flying very low before it crashed in Holland while returning from the mission. There were no survivors. The radio operator on the Roufs bomber was T/Sgt Lilbert 'Pick' Pickens.

1945 Crash Report from Holland

Recently, Mr. Dennis Notenboom of the Netherlands sent a WW II crash report to Mrs. Reilly. It tells of the work of the Dutch Red Cross at time of the crash and provides detailed information on fate of the Lt. Darrel Roufs crew and 'Pick' Pickens. The report adds a new dimension to my research. I saw several planes go down during my missions, but this is the first report I have seen from enemy territory.

The Lt. Roufs aircraft, crashed and nine crewmen perished about three weeks before the Germans asked for a truce. Mrs. Reilly never lost the desire to learn as much as possible about her Dad's service in the Mighty Eighth. Sixty-five years after the Lt. Darrel Roufs bomber went down she received new information from Netherlands officials working to preserve their WW II history. It was a copy of an April 8, 1945 report completed by Mr. H. Boomsma, the Red Cross Director at Middleharnis at the time of the crash.

The report stated: "On the 5th of April, about 1250 hours, while at the home of a friend, I heard an airplane overhead. I went outside and saw a four motored airplane type Fortress, which came from the east and going northeast. The plane was burning and apparently trying to make a crash landing in a field northeast of Sommelsdijk. Later I found this plane had been hit by German anti-aircraft located in patrol boats in the harbours near here.

The plane crashed about 500 yards north of Sommelsdijk, Holland and I immediately went to the scene of the crash. When I arrived, the plane was still burning, but we were able to rescue 5 bodies from the planes and to recover 3 from the ground near the plane, but were forced to wait until heat had died down before we could rescue the last body from the front of the plane.

These nine bodies were laid out in a row near the plane. In the meantime, the Germans arrived and would not let us attempt to identify the bodies. The Germans took the identification tags, wrist watches, rings etc. from the bodies, then trucks took the bodies to Municipal Cemetery in Sommelsdijk, Holland, where they were buried 7th of April 1945. I believe the Germans found six identification tags these were put in an envelope and buried with the men. The Germans did not attempt to record the identity of each man, but only recorded them as a group, thus all identity of each body has been lost. The burial record of Hartkoff, Paul---grave number one, is not necessarily true, it cannot be depended upon, as it is quite likely that someone else is in grave one, while Hartkoff is in some other grave, etc. Of the nine men, six names were found, the other three were never identified. The Germans with the assistance of the Cemetery Caretaker buried the bodies, and no Dutch were allowed to interfere. I obtained the information as per above in the performance of my duties as Director of Red Cross, Overflakkee Island, Holland, other people were not allowed near.

I further believe that there is no one who can assist you to obtain identity, for no other than myself and the Caretaker were allowed near."

Signed, H. Boomsma, Director of Red Cross Voorstraat 234, Middelharnis, Holland.

S/Sgt. Carl Hultquist

Sixty-six years later our 490th Bomb Group historian, Eric Swain of London, England, made an interesting discovery. One man on the Roufs crew had survived the war! By a twist of fate, S/Sgt Carl Hultquist, ball turret gunner on the crew, did not fly that mission because of a severe cold. He had managed to make the two missions to the heavily protected harbors at Kiel on April 3rd and 4th, but was too sick to fly this third mission in a row and was "grounded" by the Medical Officer. His pilot and crew probably realized Carl was "sick as a dog" and urged him to stay in the sack. Cramped up in a ball- turret on oxygen at 24,000 feet and 40 below zero was no place for a sick teenager. Flying at high altitude with a head cold causes extreme pain in the ears because of air pressure. I know because I did it a time or two and I would not recommend it to my worst enemy. I'm sure Carl hated to miss the mission because they were near to finishing their tour of duty. Every airman wanted to complete his tour of duty with his own crew, however another ball-turret gunner from the "gunners' pool" was assigned to the Lt. Roufs crew for that fatal mission.

By a simple twist of fate, a substitute gunner died and Hultquist survived. The war ended three weeks later and S/Sgt. Carl Hultquist, ball turret gunner, later made the return flight home to live a full life. He passed away in 2006. *Courtesy of the Hultquist family*

The Netherlands Honors Airmen

Holland was over-run and occupied by Germany troops in 1940. The Dutch people suffered greatly and respected the Allied airmen fighting to free their country. During the war, members of the Dutch Underground risked their lives to hide downed airmen and/or help them escape to safety. Every year during the month of May the people of the Netherlands honor the memory of the airmen who helped liberate their country and those who flew 'food drop' missions to feed the people who were free but starving!

Mr. Dennis Notenboom is President of the WO2GO Foundation (

Dutch abbreviation for "Second World War on Goeree-Overflakkee.) The Foundation plans to collect, restore and display local historical objects from the WW II war years of 1940-45. Mr. Notenboom plans to co-author a book about the air war over his island, Goeree-Overflakkee. The Foundation has two goals. They want the book to remind today's citizens of the sufferings their ancestors endured in those dark days of World War II. They plan to erect permanent panels to honor the young airmen who died for their freedom.

Mr. Notenboom says:

"We want to show the people and especially the younger generation that these young men were just like them, full of plans and dreams for the future. They left all of this behind for a higher cause and many of them paid with their lives. We in the Netherlands are still aware of all that fact and will never forget their sacrifices made for the freedom we enjoy today!"

Mr. Notenboom also told of the WO2GO Foundation's role in the annual celebration of the Allied 'food drop' missions in May and Netherland's liberation in WW II.

May 4th is National Remembrance Day in the Netherlands and in some communities, small planes re-enact bomber 'food drop' missions by flying overhead to drop food packages. May 5th, the people of the Netherlands celebrate the 65th anniversary of their Freedom. Toward the end of May, the Foundation held a Liberation Festival and 3,000 attended. This year the Foundation unveiled four memorial panels in honor of the air- crews of U.S. and British aircraft that crashed on their island. They plan to do four panels each year. A memorial for the Lt. Darrel Roufs crew is scheduled for completion. Mr. Nottenboom has visited the Ardennes Cemetery to decorate the grave of T/ Sgt. Pickens and other airmen with tulips and flags of the Netherlands and United States.

"Isn't it great that people we liberated in WW II
continue to honor the airmen
who died for their Freedom?"

ODDS AND ENDS

HAUNTING MEMORIES

Ed Charles and I played a lot of golf together a few years after the war and sometimes traded stories about our WW II days in the Mighty Eighth. Ed was a true blue Eighth Air Force man. He finished his 25 missions as a navigator in the 336th squadron and volunteered to stay with his group to fly as a lead navigator. Ed rose in the rank with his extended service with the 95th Bomb Group, stayed in the Air Force Reserves after the war and retired as Lt. Colonel William (Ed) Charles.

Of course, Ed had many more stories because he had arrived early in the war and stayed until it was over. One day I told him about an unusual experience I had while visiting a radio school buddy at the 486th Bomb Group in Sudbury. I stayed overnight, but the only bed available was that of a radio operator whose bomber had been shot down on his first mission that day. I got very little sleep that night while lying in that poor guy's bunk, surrounded by pictures of his family. It was an eerie and unforgettable experience.

Ed then told me a similar story from his outfit:

"The action was really heavy by February of 1944, and we were flying missions every day the weather was clear. One night everyone in our barracks was sound asleep when the CQ (charge of quarters) came through our door and started searching the room with his flashlight.

He asked, "Is there an empty bunk in here? I gotta a new officer out here. He just flew in and I gotta find him a place to roost"

I told him the bunk next to me was vacant and they came on in. The CQ introduced the new officer, Lt. Jones. I got up and offered to help him unpack his B-4 bag, but he said he was tired and needed some sleep. We shook hands, but I didn't really get a good look at his face. He said he had been assigned to our group as a replacement navigator. We all went back to sleep, but about two in the morning the CQ and his flashlight woke us up again. He stepped inside the barracks and said, "Sorry Lieutenant

Jones, but they are short a navigator for today's mission and you're on the list to fly."

The new navigator dressed for his first mission with the 95th BG and left the barracks for breakfast and early morning briefing. We all went back to sleep through what was left of the night. That afternoon, when it was about time for our bombers to return, I went over on the flight-line to join the airmen and the ground crews. Everyone had a buddy or a bomber they hoped to see touch down safely on the runway. I was especially interested in seeing what our new roommate thought about his first mission. Our group returned and I could see that this one had been a rough mission. Several bombers with wounded aboard fired red flares and peeled off to land first. I counted five planes missing and several others were coming in with feathered props on one or two engines. A little later I learned that Lt. Jones's bomber was one of the five shot down that day! It hit me kind of hard, because not only did he die on his first mission but he didn't even have time to unpack! I went back to the barracks where his B-4 bag was still sitting on the floor where he left it and his brand new A-2 flight jacket was lying on the bunk. I picked it up before the clean-up crew arrived to collect his belongings. That jacket is now on display at the Memorial Air Museum at Framingham, the 95th Bomb Group's first airfield in England.

Lt. Jones had spent less than a day as a member of the 95th Bomb Group at Horham airfield, but his story spread and the young navigator was remembered as The Man Who Came for Breakfast."

THE LIBERTY BELLE RADIO ROOM

June 12, 2009 (my 84th birthday) the B-17, Liberty Belle flew into the Mt. Comfort Airport and I took my third flight since WW II. My son-in-law, Mike Alexander, and I made the trip to Mt. Comfort Airport east of Indianapolis for the media flight. Four other Air Force WW II veterans were also there to fly in a B-17 again. Mike's dad, Ralph Alexander had been a mechanic with the 95th Bomb Group in WW II. The other passengers were TV and newspaper reporters taking a guest ride and looking for a stories and photos about the Liberty Belle and veterans of the Mighty Eighth.

During our flight, Mike roamed through the plane to experience test flights his father might have made after repairing a bomber. The flight did wonders to refresh memories of my 400 hours on a B-17 Flying Fortress 65 years ago

So there I was, sitting at my desk in a B-17 radio room sixty-six years after my World War II combat missions in 1944-45. The Liberty Belle was soaring over Indianapolis and memories of my teenage days returned to those missions in the deadly skies over Germany. The roar the four 1200 horsepower engines and the vibrations of the plane seemed very familiar. Once again, outside my window over the left wing, I could see the whirling propellers and search the sky for flak and enemy fighters. The BC-348-Q radio receiver and Morse code key were on my desk in front of me and the big BC-375-E transmitter hung on the bulkhead behind my swivel chair. The rheostat for my electric suit and the oxygen connection were there on the wall to my left. The "bail-out bell" was still mounted on the wall above my head near the bomb bay entrance. That's one bell I never wanted to hear! The flat storage space over the bomb-bay was empty, but it once contained a large inflatable life raft in case our B-17 was so shot up we couldn't make it back to England and had to ditch in the North Sea. Landing a 55,000 pound bomber in the sea took great skill and if successful, the plane would stay afloat less the three minutes! The emergency life raft was another thing on my "I never want to use" list.

The bomb bay was loaded with several five hundred "dummy" bombs and all 50 caliber machine guns were in place, but lacking the long belts of bullets used in combat. We were prepared for any "bandits" we might encounter!

Memories rushed back to England 1944-45 and I recalled the boys of our air crew on our first mission. It was BERLIN! Our Bomb Group had left the 490th air base at Eye at 0730, assembled with our group and joined the bomber stream. We were soon over the North Sea and climbing to 25,000 feet before reaching enemy air space over Holland. Our pilot, Bill Templeton gave the order over the intercom:

"Pilot to crew, Pilot to crew --- man the guns, keep checking your oxygen mask for icing and be alert for flak or fighters. 'Call out' the location of anything you see!"

Bert Allinder and Orville Robinson were behind me at the waist guns; Ralph Moore crawled back past the tail wheel to his small space behind the tail guns and I saw Wilbur Lesh slide down into the ball turret under his twin .50 caliber machine guns. My radio room in the middle of the plane gave me a good spot to see the four guys behind me, but I had no idea of what the guys up ahead of the bomb- bay were doing. Everyman wore his flak jacket, steel flak helmet and snapped on his chest-pack parachute. We were flying the last position at the rear of the low squadron often called: Tail-end Charlie, Coffin Corner or the Purple Heart position. New pilots were given that position until they proved they could fly in a tight formation. It was one of the more dangerous positions in the formation, because Tail-end Charlie did not have the full protection of gunners in the formation and enemy fighters often hit 'Charlie' first.

However, I wasn't worried on this mission. The historic Liberty Belle was the only B-17 Flying Fortress in the sky. We were flying at 5000 feet and there was no report of flak or enemy fighters over Indianapolis!

Since becoming an author I have been given several free flights in a B-17 Flying Fortress. I have gone on three "media" flights in the Liberty Belle and once flew as the 'honored guest' in the Aluminum Overcast. Several non-profit foundations and museums exist to preserve the history of the fighters and bombers that helped win victory in World War II. A small number of WW II planes are still in good flying condition and tour the nation to allow the public to view and purchase rides on one of the last historic planes from the Greatest Generation.

LIBERTY BELLE LOST

My 86th birthday on June 12, 2011 was a dandy with a family reunion, cards and presents from family and friends. June 13th, I was looking forward to another flight on the Liberty Belle B-17 Flying Fortress, with my son-in-law Mike Alexander. We arrived at the Mt Comfort Airport east of Indianapolis at noon eager to be in the air in less than an hour.

The Liberty Belle was not there, but a pilot of the company's P-40 Flying Tiger fighter pilot was waiting to give us the sad news. The historic WW II bomber had been destroyed by fire that morning. It had taken off from the Aurora, Illinois airfield when the pilot of a T-6 Texan plane flying beside them saw flames under the number two engine on the left wing (out of the sight of the B-17 pilot). A five page report issued by Ray Fowler, Chief Pilot of The Liberty Belle Foundation provided clear information on the event.

" The T-6 pilot radioed the Liberty Belle pilots, who quickly shutdown and feathered the prop on the number two engine, activated the fire suppression system, lowered the landing gear and performed an on-speed landing in an Illinois cornfield. The crew and passengers quickly and safely exited the aircraft."

Four miles away, the Aurora airfield dispatched firefighting equipment to the forced landing site. The Belle was undamaged by the landing and the wing fire damage was relatively small. The crew actually unloaded bags and waited, hoping the fire trucks would arrive in time to put out the fire and save the plane. The firemen arrived but decided the field was too wet to cross!

The report continues: ------"So while standing by our burning B-17 and watching the fire trucks parked at the field's edge. They sadly watched the wing fire spread to the aircraft's fuel cells and of course, you all have seen the end result. There is no doubt that had the fire equipment been able to reach our aircraft, the fire would have been quickly extinguished and our Liberty Belle would have been repaired to continue her worthwhile mission"

I consider the loss of the historic B-17 bomber a tragedy. The Liberty Belle was an educational flying museum. It had carried more than 20,000 passengers who wanted to experience the thrill of flying in a four motored bomber from the WW II era. Eighth Air Force veterans like me loved to fly and relive their days in England. I sincerely appreciate my two flights. The Liberty Belle flew to tell the story of the young airmen who served in those deadly skies so many years ago. Another piece of WW II history has been lost, perhaps it is fitting that she was destroye by flames like so many B-17 flying Fortresses in World War II.

TIME AND THE TEMPLETON CREW

Today, September 11, 2011 the Lt. Bill Templelton crew has been reduced from ten to two. My recovery time from open-heart surgery in January 2000 (six by-passes) gave me time to reflect on my blessings. My prayers and those of my family brought me through this second event when my life was again on the line. God had spared me in combat in World War II at nineteen and again as a seventy-four year old Senior Citizen. I began to wonder about the men of the Templeton crew of 1944-45 and where they were after 55 years. I had heard that our pilot, Bill Templeton married and had three young children, but died in an auto accident years ago. There was information that co-pilot, Dale Rector was a doctor in El Paso, Texas and someone in Texas signed for a registered letter for our waist gunner, Orville Robinson. I only learned the details of the murder of S/Sgt. Wilbur Lesh, our former ball turret gunner, in time to include it in the second book, " *Bombs Away!*" He had been transferred to another crew, shot down, captured and murdered by German SS troops eleven days before the end of the war.

I also learned of the Air Force career of Ralph Moore, our former tail-gunner. Ralph's wife, Doris and his son Chip and I exchanged e-mails. I later met his wife Doris and his daughters at the 490th BG reunion in Washington DC. S/Sgt. Ralph Moore had completed thirty combat missions .(he flew the first four with us) and five "food drop" (mercy missions) to Holland. Chip provided a list of Ralph's combat missions and I discovered that we had flown on several of the same bombing raids after he left our crew. There was another coincidence; he was on the Aussig mission when Wilber Lesh went down. Ralph and I were on the 490th Group's final mission to Nauen the following day.

Ralph's family said he didn't talk much about his WW II combat days. However, he told one story when he thought God had intervened.

He became sick after the April 7, 1945 mission to Parchim. (ou crew flew lead position that mission. Our formation was hit by ME-109 fighters and we lost two bombers) Ralph said that sickness "grounded" him for almost a week and caused him to miss three missions in a row. *The gunner who replaced him on each of those missions was either wounded or killed!*

Ralph remained in the Air Force and served during Korea and Vietnam. He trained in electronics and served at various USAF radar installations. Ralph Moore retired after thirty years service with the rank of Chief Master Sergeant and was one of the last WW II combat crewmen in the Air Force. He passed away a few years after his retirement. It was a pleasure to meet his wife, Doris and daughters at the Washington D.C. 490th Bomb Group Reunion in September, 2006. It was great to learn that the youngest kid on our crew had a long and successful life serving our country.

My search also located Bert Allinder, armorer/waist gunner and Ewing Roddy, flight engineer/top turret gunner. We exchanged letters and phone calls for almost two years. Dr. Bert Allinder had a successful dental practice in Independence, Missouri before he retired to his farm. He once informed me, "I didn't practice, I always knew what I was doing!" Like me, he had also had heart surgery. My wife, June and I arranged to meet Bert and his wife, Jo Ann, at the 490th 2002 Reunion in Branson, MO. Our daughter, Susie, came up from Memphis and our other daughter Sherri and husband Mike joined us later. What a great experience to meet an old buddy after fifty-seven years. Bert flew as toggleer on our first four missions and then as one of the waist gunners for the next sixteen as a lead crew. When we met, I reminded him that he had defended our bomber against two fighter attacks over Germany. I told him that he had saved my life and gave him a baseball cap with the WW II Eighth Air Force Emblem. He promptly dubbed it his "hero cap" and wore it proudly. I realized that he really hadn't changed that much since those long-ago days in England. Bert had an excellent memory and we had a ball recalling the war and the men, (boys) who flew with us on our twenty missions. We discussed a lot of events which helped provide stories and information for my book. My wife and I met them again in Branson the following spring. The next year Bert and Jo Ann visited our farm in Indiana. Several times during our visits, Bert expressed his regret that we had not gotten together sooner. Perhaps it was an omen because shortly after his visit, he had an auto accident which eventually resulted in his death. Roddy and I sent a red, white and blue wreath in memory of our days on the Templeton crew.

I am so thankful that we old Eighth Air Force buddies found each other after all the years. I give both Bert and Roddy credit for saving my life on the two fighter attacks on our bombing missions. They had truly protected me many other times during the 400 hours we spent in a B-17 through training and combat.

Ewing Roddy, Bert and I had talks on the phone many times. Now Bert is gone and Roddy is 600 miles away in New Jersey. Rod and I had parted company at Drew Field, Tampa, Florida in September of 1945. We decided that we would not pass up the opportunity to meet at the 490th Reunion in Washington D.C. in. September of 2006.

And so, the last two members of the Templeton crew met face-to-face again in another September after 61 years! Rod and his wife, Dolores, drove up with their daughter, Erin and son in-law George. My family rented a van and all five of us headed east to another reunion. (Son-in-law Mike, daughters, Sherri and Susie, my wife June and I) We all wanted to visit my crew's engineer, the man who manned the top turret and saved my life sixty-one years ago! It was an emotional meeting and we had lots to talk about in the days we spent together! Rod had also contributed information for my book, "*Through These Eyes.*" It was hot off the press and he was eager to see what I had written about our days in the deadly skies over Germany. I know he was pleased, because he ordered twenty copies and has since sold several copies of both my books. I call him my East Coast agent. We keep in touch and he's a good source to confirm my memories of our days in the Mighty Eighth. I'm sure he saved my life several times when we were teenagers in combat missions over Germany so many years ago!

Today at age eighty-six I reflect on the many twists and in my life and I am thankful to God for seeing that my travel through time has been steered and protected by family and friends who helped push me up and over the hill. I hope my short stories give readers a glimpse of history and the boys who sacrificed so much to win victory in WW II.

"Time marches on and history fades away, but
some memories should never die!" Hutch

*L to R "Hutch" and "Rod" visit the WW II Memorial During
the 490ᵗʰ Bomb Group reunion in September, 2006*

Missions Of The Templeton Crew

1.	December 5, 1944	Berlin	Chemicals
2.	Dec. 15ᵗʰ, 1944	Hanover	Rails
3.	Dec. 16, 1944	Stuttgart	Railyards
4.	Dec. 24, 1944	Frankfurt	Airfield
5.	Jan. 2, 1945	Bad Kreuznach	Trains
6.	Jan. 3, 1945	Aschaffenburg	
7.	Jan. 14, 1945	Derben	Oil
8.	Jan. 15, 1945	Augsburg	Rails
9.	Jan. 20, 1945	Sterkade	Rails
10.	Jan. 28, 1945	Hoenbudburg	Rails
11.	Feb. 17, 1945	Frankfurt	Rails
12.	Feb. 22, 1945	Ansbach	Railyards

13.	March 1, 1945	Ulm	
14.	March 21, 1945	Plauen	Airfield
15.	March 28, 1945	Hanover	Rails
16.	April 7, 1945	Parchim	Airfield
17.	April 17, 1945	Roudnice, Czech	Oil Depot
18.	April 20	Nauen	Railyards
19.	May 1,1945	Schipol Airfield, Holland,	Food Drop
20.	May 3, 1945	Schipol Airfield, Holland	Food Drop

The 490th missions Hutch completed during Air Force service from August 4, 1943 through November 16, 1945. Overseas time was from November 10, 1944 until July 14, 1945.

B-17 Specifications

Wing Span	103 ft
Length	74 ft.
Height	19 ft.
Engines	Four 1,200 HP Wright Cyclone R-1820 radial - turbo chargers
Weight	36,000 lbs.
Weight fully loaded	55,000 lbs
Top Speed	170 mph
Mission Speed	135 to150 mph at 25,000 feet
Landing Speed	75 mph
Combat Range	1,850 miles
Gasoline (wings tanks)	2,789 gallons
Oil	148 gallons
Armament	Thirteen .50 caliber machine guns Rate of fire 400-450 rounds per minute
Bomb Load	2,600 to 12,000lbs
Cost	$276,000

EIGHTH AIR FORCE HEAVY BOMBER BASES IN ENGLAND

Group	Station	Missions	Losses
34th	Mendelsham B-17	170	34
44th	Shipham B-24	343	153
91st	Bassingbourn B-17	340	197
92nd	Padington B-17	308	154
93rd	Hardwick B-24	396	100
94th	Bury St. Edmonds B-17	324	153
95th	Horham B-17	320	157
96th	Snetterton HeathB-17	321	189
100t	Thorpe Abbots B-17	306	177
303rd	Molesworth B-17	364	165
305th	Cheveston B-17	337	154
306th	Thurleigh B-17	342	171
351st	Polebrook B-17	311	124
379th	Kimbolton B-17	330	141
381st	Ridgewell B-17	296	131
384th	Grafton Underwood B-17	314	159
385th	Great Ashfield B-17	296	129
388th	Knettishall **B**-17	306	142
389th	Hethel B-24	321	116
390th	Framingham B-17	300	144
392nd	Wendling B-24	285	127
398th	Nuthampstead B-17	195	58
401st	Deenethorpe B-17	256	95
445th	Tibenham B-24	382	95
446th	Bungay B-24	273	58
447th	Rattlesden B-17	257	97
448th	Seething B-24	262	101
452nd	Deopham Green B-17	250	110
453rd	Old Buckenham B-24	259	58
457th	Glatton B-17	237	83
458th	Horsham St. Faith B-24	240	47
466th	Attlebridge B-24	232	47
467th	Rackheath B-24	212	29
486th	Sudbury B-17	188	33
487th	Lavenham B-17	185	48
489th	Halesworth B-24	106	29

490th	** Eye 134 B-17	158	40
491st	Metfield B-24	187	47
492	North Pickenkham B-24	64	12
493	Debach B-17	158	41

TOTAL BOMBERS LOST

B-17s - 4,754   B-24s - 2,112

FIGHTERS LOST

P-47s - 1,043   P-38s – 451 P- 2,201

DATES AND DATA

Various sources of information give slightly different information on the WW II Strategic Bombing campaign in the European Theater of operations.

The U S European Strategic Bombing Survey of 1946 reported data on all Air Groups:

Bombing missions -1,440,000 ---Tons of bombs dropped - 2,700,000

Maximum number of planes of planes available - 28,000

Fighter missions - 2,680,000 ----- Men in combat - 1,300,000

Men lost - 79,265 --- Planes lost beyond repair - 18,000

British airmen lost - 79,281--- British planes lost beyond repair, 22,000

In a single 376 plane raid in August 1943, 60 B-17s were shot down. That was a 16 percent loss rate and meant 600 empty bunks in England . In 1942-43 it was statistically impossible for bomber crews to complete a 25-mission tour in Europe .

However, our enemies took massive losses. Through much of 1944, the Luftwaffe sustained uncontrolled hemorrhaging, losing 25 percent of aircrews and 40 planes a month. And in late 1944 into 1945, nearly half the pilots in Japanese squadrons had flown fewer than 200 hours. The disparity of two years before had been completely reversed.

As new aircraft, many combat units transitioned in combat. The attitude was, "They all have a stick and a throttle - go fly 'em." When the famed 4th Fighter Group converted from P-47s to P-51s in February 1944, there was no time to stand down for an orderly transition. History says that the Group Commander, told his pilots, "You can learn to fly your new P-51 Mustangs on the way to the target."

There will never be another air war like World War II. Present battles are fought with million dollar fighters, bombers, helicopters and remote controlled drones over Afghanistan and Iran. Computer guided aircraft and missiles have replaced the "Boys in the B-17."

However, within living memory, men left the earth in 1,000 plane formations and fought major battles five miles high, leaving a legacy that should never be forgotten!

READER'S GUIDE AND GLOSSARY

1. B-17 Flying Fortress – four motored heavy bomber – cost $276,000 ten man crew – no heat 50 zero below at 25,000 feet – not pressurized for high altitude – oxygen masks required

2. B-24 Liberator – four motored heavy much the same.

3. Box formation - three squadrons flying staggered at high, middle and low levels to maximize fire power of their gunners against enemy fighters

4. 43 American B-17 and B-24 bomb groups in Eighth Air Corps

5. Lancaster and Halifax - RAF heavy bombers

6. Fighter groups --- RAF Spitfire, Mosquito and Hurricane --- U.S. - P-51Mustang, P-47 Thunderbird and P-38 Lightning

7. Squadron - 12 to 14 bombers each with a crew of ten

8. Combat formation – thirty-six bombers

9. Bomb Group - consisted of four squadrons

10. Wing – three to four Bomb Groups

11. Division – three or more wings –

12. Royal Air Force (RAF)

13. Flak – shrapnel from bursting shells

14. Flak happy - mental problems from combat

15. Chaff – aluminum coated paper tossed out to foul up flak gun radar

16. Gestapo- Geheime Staats Polizei (German state secret police.)

17. Happy Valley or Flak Alley- heavily protected targets in the industrial Ruhr valley

18. Hardstand --- parking space for a bomber

19. Electrical Jammers- equipment to distort enemy's radio and radar

20. Ditching – emergency of a landing of a damaged bomber in the sea.

21. Electric suit – gloves and socks worn under heavy clothing and boots – plugged into outlet at each crew-member's position

22. Mae West – inflatable life preserver vest worn under the parachute harness.

23. Parachute –chest pack hooked to a harness – seat pack type for pilots

24. Flak vest – Apron of sheets of steel covered with canvas to protect the torso front and back- weighed 45 pounds

25. Flak helmet - regular steel helmet - with flaps to cover headsets

26. Mess Hall – food (chow) for the base – we lined up cafeteria style with metal trays - officers mess was a separate section

27. Chowhound – a hungry GI

28. GI –government issue- slang for soldier, we were all GIs

29. Latrine – toilet and shower room

30. Lucky Bastards – men who completed the required missions to go home

31. Turret – rotating machine gun position on bomber

32. Mission Alert – notice to fly a mission next morning

33. Red Alert - air raid ---- enemy bombers or buzz bombs

34. Red-lined – mechanical problems - plane cannot fly

35. Milk Run – easy mission – not much flak

36. MACR – missing air crew report

37. POW Prisoner of War

38. Kriegie German term for POW

39. Purple Heart – medal awarded to wounded or killed

40. Purple Heart Corner, Coffin Corner or Tail-end Charlie – last plane in each bombing squadron of the formation– easy target for fighters

41. PX- post exchange (store) on the base

42. Air Medal awarded for every six missions

43. Prop Wash – air disturbance from propellers of planes flying ahead of you

44. Sack – cot or bunk bed

45. Sack time- sleep or rest - a good place to keep warm.

46. The hut was usually cold – very little heat from the little hut stove – coke rationed

47. Sad Sack – a 'goof off 'or poor soldier

48. Ground Pounders – non-flying personnel in support units. They kept bombers ready to fly. Mechanics – radio- radar, bomb, ammunition, and gun technicians plus cooks, firemen, medics and don't forget the parachute packers! Every airbase was a small town of specialists to keep bombers flying.

49. Crew Chief – head mechanic of ground crew assigned to maintain the plane

50. Bogey or Bandit – enemy fighter or unidentified aircraft

51. Scuttlebutt – rumor or gossip

52. AWOL – absent without leave

53. Piccadilly Commando - London prostitute

54. SS German national secret police (Shutzstaffle)

55. SNAFU "situation normal, all fouled up"

BIBLIOGRAPHY

1. Gerald Astor, *The Mighty Eighth*

2. Time Editors, *The Time –Life History of WW II*

3. Lightner and Holland, *Historical Record of the 490th Bomb Group*

4. Martin W. Bowman *Echoes of England*

5. *U.S. European Strategic Bombing Survey Summary Report 9/30/1945*

6. Eighth Air Force Historical Society

7. United States Air Force Museum

8. Robin Neillands, *The Bomber War*

9. Noble Frankland, *Bomber Offensive-the devastation of Europe*

10. Robert Kelly, *Broken Wings*

11. Donald Summerville, *World War II Day by Day*

12. Corbin Willis Collection (AFC/2001/001/2220 Veterans History Project, American Folklife Center Library of Congress

13. Michael P. Faley, *High Noon Over Haseluenne*

14. Leonard Streitfeld, *Hell From Heaven*

15. Don Mc Combs and Fred Worth, *World War II, Strange and Fascinating Facts*

16. Ian Hawkins, *B-17s Over Berlin –Stories from the 95th Bomb Group*

17. Roger Freeman, *The Mighty Eighth*

18. Stars and Stripes, (News Items) 1944 -45

19. John C. Walter, *My War*

20. Robert Morgan, *The Man Who Flew The Memphis Belle*

21. James L. Hutchinson, *Through These Eyes, and Bombs Away*

FILMS AND VIDEOS

1. Warbirds of WW II (www.timeless-video.com)

2. Twelve O'Clock High 1949

3. The Memphis Belle 1998

4. Hart's War 2002

5. Stalag 13 19536. The Great Escape

6. The Longest Day 1962

7. The Best Years of Our Lives 1946

8. Hope and Glory UK film

9. Hutch's DVD and Smithville Phone video at: http://video.smithville.net/?p=17

Lightning Source UK Ltd.
Milton Keynes UK
UKOW01f1226230817
307784UK00002B/119/P